THE SECRET FOOTBALLER: WHAT GOES ON TOUR

www.penguin.co.uk

The Secret Footballer is the author of:

I Am The Secret Footballer
Tales from The Secret Footballer
The Secret Footballer's Guide to the Modern Game
The Secret Footballer: Access All Areas
The Secret Footballer: How to Win

Follow The Secret Footballer on Twitter @TSF

THE SECRET FOOTBALLER

WHAT GOES ON TOUR

BANTAM PRESS

LONDON • TORONTO • SYDNEY • AUCKLAND • JOHANNESBURG

TRANSWORLD PUBLISHERS
61–63 Uxbridge Road, London W5 5SA
www.penguin.co.uk

Transworld is part of the Penguin Random House group of companies
whose addresses can be found at global.penguinrandomhouse.com

First published in Great Britain in 2017 by Bantam Press
an imprint of Transworld Publishers

A CIP catalogue record for this book
is available from the British Library.

ISBN 9780593078792

Typeset in 11.5/15pt Minion by Falcon Oast Graphic Art Ltd.
Printed and bound by Clays Ltd, Bungay, Suffolk.

Penguin Random House is committed to a sustainable
future for our business, our readers and our planet. This book
is made from Forest Stewardship Council® certified paper.

1 3 5 7 9 10 8 6 4 2

To all those who looked the other way.

We owe you our shame and there is nothing left to repay you with. You see, the road of excess leads to the palace of wisdom, which, frankly, is overpriced for what you get.

Contents

Foreword by Mrs TSF

I really didn't want to write a foreword for this book.

The pay is poor and I already know what rich young guys get up to in places like Ibiza and Las Vegas. Even what they hoped to get up to in Marbella in the early days. I don't need the gory details to be dredged up and examined all over again, if I'm being honest. I don't need him wondering what I was doing when he was away.

I've read all his books. He sulks if I don't. I don't really want to read this one. But if your husband pulls off the feat of actually writing a book and then he gets it published, you have to read it really, don't you? Like when one of the kids does a painting in school. It has to go on the fridge door.

Anyway, it encourages him. When he gets around to writing the book about how it feels to be a footballer's wife, we'll have more in-depth discussions. Meanwhile I know that somewhere along the line, you are always going to have your nose rubbed in something unpleasant by some force that you just can't control. Often, for instance, you just can't control the strength of other

1

people's jealousy or their belief that they know exactly how you should run your life.

As Hillary Clinton said many years ago, 'You know, I'm not sitting here, some little woman standing by my man like Tammy Wynette. I'm sitting here because I love him, and I respect him, and I honour what he's been through and what we've been through together. And you know, if that's not enough for people, then heck . . .'

Whatever happened to her, by the way?

When I think of football, I like to remind myself of all the good times. The funny times. The times when nobody knew who you were and what you were up to. Those were the best of times. On the threshold of the big adventure.

I didn't really know what it meant to be a footballer's wife when he signed for his first club. But I reminded him recently about what he had said to me at the time. Very subtly (not!) he told me that it was now important for me to look stylish.

I wasn't stylish before? It sounded like I was going to be put on the free transfer list.

So he set about buying me all these clothes to wear. He was going to liberate me from my frumpiness. He's not allowed to buy me clothing any more, because as his shopping spree went on, the garments had less and less fabric with which one could cover oneself. They were so skimpy that I thought he must have been expecting to get a transfer to a Spanish club.

Surprise! Many of the clothes he bought me were nothing like I would wear. They were footballers' wives' clothes. Stuff he'd seen on telly. But he did strike lucky with a fairly cool

2

pair of white Diesel high heels; we both agreed that they were a beautiful pair of shoes. In fact we agreed again and again and again.

'Do you like them?'

'Yeah. Really nice.'

'They are, aren't they?'

'Yeah.'

'They were a good choice, weren't they?'

'Yep. Still a good choice.'

'I have an eye for stuff, I think.'

'That can be changed.'

(Hopefully he never donates a vital organ to somebody. Do you like the kidney? It was my best one . . .)

Anyway, having hit the fashion jackpot, he made me wear the white shoes all the time. He said it was important that we always looked good. I think he felt that we were being stalked in the aisles of Lidl by *Hello!* magazine.

It turns out that you can't look the part all the time. Not if you're shopping for lino at Carpetright. As we left the store and walked into the car park I got my heel stuck in a metal drain cover. You can buy clothes but you can't buy elegance.

We were less than a mile from the stadium in an industrial park and nobody knew who the fuck we were. And that's the point. The reality is lino at Carpetright and laughing about it later. The fantasy is a handful of moments when we got to live in somebody else's world. We weren't always comfortable there, but it was a hell of a trip to go on together.

TSF has always chosen our houses. He hasn't screwed up yet. I mean, if you can trust a man with buying a pair of shoes . . .

So far I've liked all the houses I've lived in with him – and there have been a lot of them.

The house we lived in when we moved to the catchment area of his first professional club was bigger than we needed and right on the edge of what we could afford. It wasn't a home, it was a house. We couldn't afford to furnish it too well – hence the lino. Two of the four bedrooms in the house didn't have a bed. Or carpets. Or curtains. We regularly missed mortgage payments, which were £800 a month. We still miss mortgage payments. Just today they're bigger.

I remember the day his team-mate came round to the house and knocked on the door. The pair of them shared a Ford Fiesta that they'd bought together for £500; they'd nicknamed it 'the love bubble'. I didn't want to know why. How they felt about each other was their own business.

I answered the door and the team-mate asked me, 'Have you spoken to TSF?'

I told him that as far as I knew, TSF was supposed to be with him.

That's when I found out that football works a little differently to other jobs. My boyfriend, as he was then, was on the other side of the country signing a contract with a Championship club. Not so much as a phone call or a text about a career move. Life for footballers is the ultimate male game. A game in which women will always be in second place. A distant second.

I enjoyed living in that first city. We both did. It's a beautiful city and we don't travel back there enough. Despite the books, my husband isn't a big one for nostalgia, as he feels that looking back all the time prevents him moving forward. Which is a shame, because there were happy times, despite the bread-line finances. Just simple things, like a cup of coffee on a crisp morning sat outside Starbucks in the town square. All wrapped up and carefree. Or lunch with no kids to have to worry about, no clock-watching. And nobody bothering us. Later it became impossible for us to walk into a coffee shop and sit down. It became a stealth operation. We would watch the queue from outside before running in and ordering, then running back out again to drink the coffee on the go. No magazines any more, no newspapers. Always moving like sharks. Like angry, starving, unhappy, well-paid sharks.

In this book are stories from the wild side. Some of them I have heard before. Some have come to me in heavily edited versions.

After a life in football, I can say that maybe the best times were when we had the lino on the floor and one foot stuck in the drain.

But you don't know that till you've tried out all the other stuff.

Introduction

You don't know me. You may have heard of me. You may have seen me at work. You may even have read a book I wrote. It was called *I Am The Secret Footballer*. I've written another four since. But even if you have heard of me, seen me or read me, you don't know me.

For fifteen years, I played professional football. Sometimes in front of 500 people on a cold Tuesday night against Carlisle United, sometimes in front of 75,000 people on a Saturday afternoon at Old Trafford against Manchester United. Sometimes the 75,000 made more noise. I played with and against the best players in the world. I played against Steven Gerrard, Wayne Rooney, Paul Scholes, Xabi Alonso, Fernando Torres and even Ronaldo. I also played against Robbie Savage. But, whatever . . .

Football is the greatest game in the world. It allows you to express yourself in ways that make it impossible for others to judge you. They can't do what you can do. End of debate.

Football is the best game in the world because it offers you freedom and possibility; opportunities abound. You meet people from all over the globe, and if you're lucky, really lucky, you'll get to be a hero to some of them, and to sleep with several of the others.

It's the greatest game. I'm not talking about what happens on the pitch. You see, the thing about playing football is that you only watch us once or twice a week for ninety minutes. Matches are the tip of the iceberg of our existence. And in the summer you don't see us at all. We melt away, out of sight. But it is what lies beneath the surface of the football ocean that is the real reason why it's the greatest game in the world. If you happen to be a footballer, of course . . .

Leisure. Recreation. Experiences. Opportunities for personal growth.

In 1960/61, when Jimmy Hill and the PFA were fighting to abolish the maximum wage for footballers, the Stoke City chairman, Albert Henshall, commented: 'The players' demands are unreasonable. To even expect £30 a week, a rise of fifty per cent, is unheard of.'

The PFA won. In 1960, Liverpool's total wage bill was £517 a week. Never again. Today the average Premier League player makes roughly £2.5 million a year. That's 60 per cent more than the next best-paid league on the planet, the Bundesliga.

Now there are some things I can explain.

The Premier League signed a record-breaking domestic TV rights deal for 2016–19 which will bring in £5 billion just from UK rights; total income from domestic and foreign rights for the next three-year period might reach £8.5 billion, which is almost double the previous TV rights deal.

And there are some things I can't explain.

8

For instance, Gordon Taylor, the chief executive of the PFA, was paid a total package including benefits of £3,368,653 in 2014.

Anyway . . .

In November 1992, when the Premier League had only been open for business a few months, Manchester United bought Eric Cantona from Leeds for £1 million and paid him a colossal £10,000-a-week wage. We called it a 'mega deal'. The party had begun, and it was followed by a series of landmarks.

Three years later, Dennis Bergkamp was getting £19,000 a week at Arsenal. In 1996, Alan Shearer signed for Newcastle United from Blackburn for a world record £15 million. His wage was £34,000 a week. How quaint.

Roy Keane was on £50K a week at United, Patrick Vieira £70K a week at Arsenal, Gerrard £100K a week at Liverpool.

In the summer of 2016, Paul Pogba, whom Manchester United had sold for £1.5 million four years earlier, re-signed for the club for a world record £87 million. His wage? £220,000 a week. After tax, that is.

My entire career took place between the Cantona mega deal and the Pogba return.

You probably want to know where the money went.

PART ONE

Pre-boarding for Peasants

1

When a footballer retires, people always say 'he'll never have to work again, the lucky bastard'.

Yes, that's because our afternoons at the London School of Economics told us all there is to know about the necessity of prudence in financial matters. We get the best advice, we make the best investments; when we get given shedloads of money, we are mature enough and shrewd enough to protect ourselves from sharks and from ourselves.

Actually, here's a thing that will make you weep. In my first job, I earned slightly less than £11,000 a year and I lived very much hand to mouth. Now, after a lifetime in football, I have a mortgage of £11,000 a month. There are months in the year when I can't pay it. So I have a mortgage that my agent got me into during the good times, and a bank who just loved me to death during the good times, but now that bank can't give me a new mortgage because I am an ex-footballer and don't have a recognizable permanent pensionable job for them to enter into their £19.99 calculators.

I don't want sympathy, but there is a real family living under that heavily mortgaged roof. Real little people. The pressures for me today are the same as for everybody else. It sometimes feels as if football never happened. I sometimes feel like Steve Martin in *The Jerk* when he realizes that after accidentally getting very rich, he has now accidentally gone very broke. He sweeps all the 'stuff' off his desk. 'I don't need any of this,' he says. 'I don't need this stuff. I don't need anything. Except this. This ashtray. That's the only thing I need. Is this. Just this ashtray. And this paddle game. The ashtray and the paddle game, this is all I need. And this remote control . . . and these matches . . . and this lamp . . .' And he shuffles off in his dressing gown with his trousers bunched around his ankles.

I have a snooker table that I bought. I love it. It is the one thing that takes my mind away from the struggles of life. And I do have struggles. But I'm fucked if I'm selling my snooker table. That's all I need. That snooker table . . .

I signed my first professional football contract for £550 a week, but as I'd had a job outside football I was still wired in to thinking of earnings in per annum terms. £550 a week is £28,600 a year. I thought I'd hit the jackpot. So did my friends. They envied me for not being broke in the fourth week of every month. I was still thinking that way too and I was pretty pleased with my lot. Until I realized that as a footballer I needed things that I couldn't afford. I was still broke by the fourth week of every month.

The truth is, I would have signed for £200 a week to be a footballer. The game is poor at negotiating. Money cures everything. Rub some money on that gunshot wound, you'll feel better, son. Need more? It's in a bucket in the corner.

14

I always think of the Beatles in this regard. After Brian Epstein died, the boys needed a new manager. Three of the band members recommended Allen Klein, the American business guru who was already manager of the Rolling Stones. Paul McCartney was the one to hold out. The boys visited McCartney to put the screws on him. They told him that Klein would do it, but he wanted 20 per cent and the contract had to be signed immediately. (It didn't.)

McCartney said: 'Tell him he can have fifteen per cent.' They said: 'You're stalling.' He replied: 'No, I'm working for us; we're a big act.' I can recall the exact words: 'We're a big act – the Beatles. He'll take fifteen per cent.' But for some strange reason (I think they were intoxicated with the American) the others said: 'No, he's got to have twenty per cent, and he's got to report to his board. You've got to sign, now or never.'

Sadly they overruled McCartney and signed Klein, and, like the Rolling Stones, wound up in years of litigation (the Stones' $1.25 million advance from Decca back in 1965 was deposited into a company Klein had set up and the fine print of the contract didn't require him to release it for twenty years. Even in football that would be a sharp stroke.) But I've always remembered that McCartney quote. I'd have it over the door of any school of economics. I'd nail it over the door of the FA too, if I could find a proper fucking door instead of the revolving one they have for all the staff who come in and leave again soon after.

I thought of McCartney when watching Roy Hodgson at the 2016 Euros. Why make him the highest-paid manager? Offer him half! The man is over sixty, the job is the culmination of

15

his life's work. You really think he'll turn it down? Just like I wouldn't have turned down £200 a week for the chance to play football.

You think the amount of money footballers make is indecent? Listen, different laws apply. Gravity doesn't work on football money. It just goes up and up, with no relation to market forces. And so the guys who do the work or play the game get the lion's share of what people are happy to pay for.

At my first professional club, when I had moved into what I regarded as the big leagues, I thought that certain things were expected of me. Not just expected of me by the club, but by my friends and by the general public, who talked about little else but my life and lifestyle.

Mrs TSF was now the wife of a professional footballer. Forget all that stuff about having a degree and a life of substance in the real world. She was going to have to make a step up too. She has discussed this a little in her intro at the beginning of the book. No need to look back if you skipped it. I don't come out smelling of roses.

You know when couples say that they stay together for the kids? Years ago the basketball player Dennis Rodman wrote a book called *Bad As I Wanna Be*. A year later his wife brought out a book called *Worse Than He Says He Is*. Well, Mrs TSF could bring the game of football to its very knees if she decided to write a book. So let's just agree that her foreword is to literature what Gaudí was to architecture and Einstein was to science.

We've had a lot of interesting times together since I signed for my first professional club. And whereas most players' wives spend a fair amount of their time looking sideways out of the window as the juggernaut hurtles down the outside lane of the Premier League highway, Mrs TSF always looked dead ahead.

At first we were both rabbits in the headlights, Mrs TSF and I. Christ knows what we'd have been like if I'd been signed by Manchester United instead of a League One struggler. As I say, I had blind faith that somebody would spot me doing something interesting with a football one day, but until it happens it's just a warm feeling inside that tempers the reality of working in a warehouse with a sadistic arsehole that calls himself your boss and who hates you more than his own life.

Football was going to change things. Not quickly enough in reality. But in an alternate universe that was built on half-truths, plain bullshit and wishful thinking on our part, it would change our lives immediately. For we had decreed it in our living room at home on the day I'd signed.

I'm afraid that we fell for the lure of what people thought the trappings of football ought to entail. And our friends assumed that we now had it all. They didn't hear 'League One' when they found out I was a footballer, they heard the word 'footballer', and every stereotype that came into their brains thereafter was from what they'd read about the private lives of David and Victoria Beckham.

And I suppose it was intoxicating to play up to that. Even though we couldn't. We also, I feel, believed it. We were part of the footballing fraternity now and we wanted to act like it. We too didn't see the £550 a week, we saw the word 'footballer' when I wrote it down under 'occupation' as I applied for a mortgage. That word 'footballer' does something to people.

When I was changing addresses for the utilities as we moved into our first house, the man on the end of the phone line at Sky stopped in his tracks when I said I played football. And then proceeded to ask me everything he'd ever wanted to ask about football, and tell me everything he'd ever wanted to say.

I was suckered in. I was. I don't deny it. So was Mrs TSF. There is a saying in football reserved for youth team players that get too big for their boots: 'they think they've fucking made it'. For a little while I thought I had too.

My only comeback to Mrs TSF's intro is that she went along with most of the madness. We thought that we had made it and therefore we had to live like footballers. The professional footballer followed a lifestyle we'd only read about in the papers. But I was now a professional footballer. The lifestyle was obligatory. We'd just have to demonstrate champagne taste while living on a cider budget.

Jesus. The shit you do. When I became a professional footballer, I thought that Louis Vuitton washbags were pretty much mandatory. If I was seen padding around the dressing room with anything else, my credibility would never recover. So I bought one. Not a fake. It cost me half a week's wages. I used it for a while even though they were so common in the dressing room that it was hard to tell sometimes which Louis Vuitton washbag was my one.

One day, when I had been playing for a while, a fan came up to me. He had a little boy tugging at his sleeve. The man was more nervous than the kid was. 'Excuse me,' he said, 'my son has a question that he's always wanted to ask.'

I played the role of the benign Santa Claus. I put them at

18

their ease. I can talk to ordinary people. It is refreshing. Why, of course.

So I bent down, ready to give the little fella the enduring gift of a really wise and thoughtful answer to his question. In fifty years' time he would be telling people: 'I met him once. He said something to me that I will never forget.' And people would lean in: 'What did TSF say?'

'Yes?' I said, beaming at the little fella.

'Erm, you know those bags that you all have? Do you all get given those when you become footballers?'

I never used the Louis Vuitton washbag again. Still have it though. I'm not a total idiot. Half a week's wages. Some day it will either be sold on eBay or become an exhibit in the TSF museum.

Of course holidays were another problem. I was a professional footballer now so Skegness was out of the question. People would say: 'Skegness? With his money? What a fucking cheapskate!'

So I took my £2,000 signing-on fee, and we borrowed another £2,000 from an uncle of mine, and Mrs TSF and I headed off to a destination where we thought we might well run into Becks and Posh. Mauritius. The fun we would all have. They'd call their first-born Brooklyn, we'd call ours Mauritius. I still think Tom Cruise would find that funny if we all got together now.

We had paid for a really swanky resort, and a swanky resort was what we got. Sadly, we stood out like two teenage backpackers from poor backgrounds trying to make it around the world on a gap year they couldn't afford. We couldn't buy any of the food available at the hotel, so every day we had to head off on a rickshaw into the dodgiest town since Dodge City cleaned up its act. There we'd stuff our faces with creole food for about a dollar a day and live off the heartburn till bedtime.

We'd thought we could suddenly afford to go to places like Mauritius. We actually couldn't. But two and two always equalled five in those early days. Living beyond our means? No way. Football would catch up and it would improve our means. That's how the world seemed to work.

Not that Mauritius wasn't perfect. We have our happy memories of that time. Every night, for instance, there was a dramatically beautiful sunset over the perfect white sands of the beach. Our hotel kept a stable of former racehorses that people could hire just so they could gallop down the beach and create perfect moments. Of course we didn't have enough money to hire one to carry us up and down the beach. We couldn't have afforded a donkey with a straw hat. So we'd sit and watch, and convey the impression that we were so bored with riding racehorses that it actually gave us more pleasure to see other people experience the novelty.

The sun setting, the scent of the sea in your nostrils, the wind in your hair . . . it was widescreen cinematic perfection. One night, as we sat on the beach with the sun slowly sinking and the waves lapping soothingly, a couple came past riding two beautiful horses at full speed. As we turned to look at them, the sun silhouetted them perfectly so you could just make out that it was a couple on horseback.

Mrs TSF grabbed her camera and took a quick snap. The picture was something beautiful. It would have made a nice gift for the couple who were riding the horses, but it struck

Mrs TSF and me that in silhouette, they looked exactly like us.

For years afterwards this framed picture of a couple of strangers hung prominently in our house. Two people we didn't know from Adam or Eve. We told everybody that, yes, it was us riding our handsome steeds on the white sands of Mauritius. When in Mauritius, do like the Mauritians . . .

People would look at the photograph and shake their heads. You guys are so lucky. You are living the dream right now.

'Yeah, well . . . footballers now!' we'd say.

Mauritius wasn't my only holiday that summer. After a year of grafting in the coalmine of lower-league football, I was now a two-holidays-a-year man. One holiday with my main squeeze. Another with the lads.

That summer I had a week in Malia. My chance to enjoy the cultural side of things that Mrs TSF wouldn't really appreciate. I don't know if you've been to Malia, on Crete, but if you've been to Ayia Napa, Faliraki, San Antonio, Magaluf or Hell then you've been to Malia.

My group of mates were slightly different to everybody else's mates but they were the best that I could afford. I guess we were all shy of women, but we told each other that we actually liked to talk about the things in life that really mattered. We talked about music especially. We all loved good music. The Beatles. We could talk about the Beatles all night. But we were clubbers too. Nothing if not versatile. We'd talk about the big tracks, the transition from house to big beat and back again. We all followed big beat.

Malia is a shithole but once upon a time it was a beautiful fishing village. And then some time in the 1990s the English

21

rocked up and conquered the place. Not at all within our national character, as any of the colonies will tell you. We brought with us the Sunday roast, factor 30 sun cream, and *Only Fools and Horses* playing on a non-stop loop in twenty-four-hour pubs called The George. We sent geezers who knew how to set up commercial businesses to cater for the masses.

Lucky Malia.

We were different, but not that different. The locals never approached and said, 'Oh thank God, you guys are here at last. Have you seen what they've done to our lovely fishing village?'

Our accommodation was awful. I don't know if you've been on those holidays where after you land you get on a bus with a load of other pale retards before heading off on a tour of the region's worst hotels, but I have.

You pull up to the first hotel and pray: 'Oh for fuck's sake, please God, not me. I've got children. Well, I haven't, but I hope to one day. I want to survive!' And some other poor suckers get off the bus and you bang as loudly as you can on the windows. 'Haha! Byeeee and fuck you, wanker!'

On it goes until you pull up outside your own reeking shit-hole. Is this a building or a local ruin they are showing us? That's when you realize that the phrase 'five star' has lost something in translation. Three and a half stars is what it has lost. Could we go back to the first place? That actually looked inhabitable. Can somebody escort me from the kerb to the front door? It looks dangerous. Aw shit, should have got the full range of injections. Is it just me or are there no lights on?

Inside, all is charming. The manager behind the desk has a mouth entirely hidden by a moustache. She gives you the keys with the disgusted look of a bordello owner dealing with somebody who brought along an STD the last time he was here. The carpet in the room is daringly undersized and has a worrying sticky texture when you walk on it. Air con comes separately in the shape of a fan that can be rented for about £100 a week. The fridge to keep the beers warm is a bathtub with lukewarm water. The plug doesn't quite fit, so the water gradually seeps away, leaving cans of warm beer marooned in the dirt-ringed valley of the bath.

It was really as if the locals weren't grateful for everything we had done for them. Still . . .

Those were the days when it was cool to wear your matchday shorts in public – just to show the world that you were a footballer. I say cool. I mean chic. Back then the club shop didn't sell numbered shorts, even in the Premier League. So you could spot a professional footballer by the fact that he was wearing numbered shorts while on holiday. It was a unique and respected sign of our profession. Grenadier Guards wouldn't wear their bearskin hats when away on holiday. Strippers wouldn't sashay into the hotel dining room wearing stars and tassels on their tits. But we footballers wore our matchday shorts.

We thought we were a beloved sight for the general public. Sometimes you'd see great bunches of us walking around together in the very shorts we had sweated our bollocks in for months on end. It beat any sight you might see on an African safari.

Youth team players really loved their shorts. Youth team players seemed to know that they had to make hay while the sun was shining. They made hay through the non-traditional

23

medium of sleeping with women. They could have tried harder in training, but it was almost as if they knew they weren't good enough.

Seven or eight of the young lads would wander around on their pre-season tour with their numbered shorts on. An open invitation to women everywhere. I've heard George Clooney once offered to pay a large amount of money for a numbered pair of nylon Scunthorpe shorts. No dice. You've either got it or you ain't got it, George.

These days you can buy shorts with any number you like on them, but back then the expert wearing of numbered shorts was the privilege and duty of the elite professional. The marketing director had yet to cotton on (pardon the pun) and spoil it all. If you walked down a street, any street but particularly one abroad, with numbered shorts on your arse then everyone knew that you were a professional footballer. You could walk down Sniper Alley in Sarajevo and the guns would fall silent out of respect. You could walk towards the sea and the waters would part. You could walk towards a woman and hope for the same effect with her legs.

I'm not ashamed to say that I wore my shorts. Yes, it is a little cringe-making when I think back now, but I was actually proud. I really was. I'd worked so hard to get to that point. I wanted everyone to know that I was a footballer. Why wouldn't I? I see lads doing it now and I think, 'Ah, seriously mate, don't do that.' Unless you're planning to write a book one day. But back then it was different.

So the first proper thing we did upon landing in Crete was have a good cry about the state of our hotel room. We considered calling our mums and dads and asking them to come and rescue us from the prospect of living for a week in a microwave with a cheap bed in it. Then we manned up and walked down the main drag to hire a moped each, with no thought as to how we were going to get the vehicles back until after the money had been taken.

Like all groups of lads, we drove the mopeds as if Ayrton Senna had decided that the real thrill lay in 50cc Vespas rather than Formula One cars. We had never known a thrill like having one of those whiney hairdryer contraptions between our legs as we raced each other, the locals timing us using an old sundial.

Malia has a main drag that winds down to the beach from the top of a hill, where it is crossed by a busy road that bends like a boomerang as its apex joins the party road. Turning on to the drag off the busy road is dodgy. Going around the apex is also dodgy because it is very easy to misjudge how sharp the turn is.

See where this is going? Not everybody did at the time.

I'm not a beach man really. Generally, people hate me for being beautiful, and on the beach in my numbered shorts, the resentment becomes unbearable. Still, going to the beach did mean that I could look at women without actually having to talk to them.

And, if nobody was looking, I could read a book. Maybe sneak in a chapter before somebody would realize what I was up to and kick sand in my face and call me a perv. I would be systematically abused until I put the book away and borrowed a copy of *Nuts* magazine to keep up appearances.

25

Anyway, after drinking heavily through the first night we made our way to the beach the following morning on our Vespas. We approached the bend more or less in a line, because visually that made us look like the Red Arrows on heavy sedation. There were six of us. Craig was at the front. We were going pretty fast, but we were young and cocksure. The odds of anything bad happening to us were as remote as me talking to a girl.

The road looked clear. Craig turned left on to the main drag. He turned just as a lorry came around the corner. It clipped his back wheel and spun him back in towards the wheels, where the last of the lorry's twelve massive tyres ripped Craig's arm straight out of its socket and crushed it. He woke up in a local hospital long after we'd gone home. Craig was scarred across his face, he was missing some teeth and had lost his left arm. He had been due for a trial with Coventry City two weeks after we got back. He was an amazing footballer.

When I had signed for my first professional club, it was Craig who interrupted the end-of-season presentations at our non-league club to tell the room that he was so proud of me. He wanted me to spend my career making all the players from our area proud. All the guys who had never made it.

I have tried to do that. I hope I did.

Years later I got the chance to help Craig a little more than any of us could in Malia. I took him to see our club physio, a very highly regarded man in his field. Craig had broken his leg skiing.

Lucky Craig we call him.

26

2

Craig and I were just two of thousands of kids who thought they could make the grade. Now, every kid thinks that he is good at something. Even if he isn't that good at anything, he should think that he is. That's part of being young, and nobody should take it away from you.

When I was young, I thought I was good at football. In fact, I knew I was good. I had proof. The teams I played on always won. People always picked me first. Football was my thing. I had friends who were good at music, or good at school, or smooth with girls. I was a footballer.

If I could see that, I thought everybody else could.

It took a long while for me to realize that just because I believed in me, not everybody else did. There were times when my confidence got badly bruised. When you are young and your confidence takes a kicking, it takes a long while to heal.

I was twelve years old when I had a trial with Watford. At the time they were a pretty big deal. I could remember Watford in the old First Division when they were decent enough that the first sentence commentators would utter about them didn't always have the words 'Elton' and 'John' in it. They were Second Division when I went on trial there. I felt that they needed me.

I was crap. There is more to trials when you are a kid than just playing football. You have to front it up a bit. I played crap, but I could change that. Sadly I was also crap at all the other stuff. I was a shy and nervous kid who didn't make friends easily and who didn't like talking to people. All the other kids seemed to be full of chat and confidence. Or full of shit, as I would think of it later in life.

The scout who had got me the trial came up to me afterwards as I was walking back to the car with my dad. 'You weren't yourself today,' he said. I was twelve and smart enough to know that he was telling me that I had been crap. Cheers. I really needed that.

I thought for a while that Watford's loss would be some other club's gain. The phone never rang though and my shoulder never got tapped by some old scout in an anorak. There I was, playing well week in, week out at a level where kids should have been getting plucked by the dozen, but it felt like I was invisible.

I carried on playing though. Because I loved football. When I was fourteen, I recall a kid called Matt Spring being taken on by a local team. Matt Spring could not lace my boots – as we say in the trade when we're looking to deride a fellow professional. I can remember his team, Broxbourne Saints, watching my team from the sidelines in a tournament and not being too impressed. In the next game we battered them 4–0. I remember that game better than I remember the game in which a team I played for beat Arsenal 3–1. (And I had to google that score, because at first I thought it was 2–1.) Matt Spring cried after that 4–0 defeat. And at that point I knew I was good.

When I was seventeen, the youth team I was playing for was forced to disband because the idiot groundsman scorched the grass off the pitch with a cocktail of three parts fertilizer to one part water; it should have been the other way around. The saddest thing though was that I had been scorching the place for a few seasons and nobody had batted an eyelid.

So much talent was wasted when that team broke up. Most lads lost interest and surrendered to the vices of the day: weed, alcohol and girls. I stuck with the idea of football, if not the practice of it. I knew I was better at football than I would ever be at weed, alcohol or girls.

There was so much talent in our area. The north London overspill had produced an abundance of footballing prospects in those years, but the old clubs were still doing things the old ways and looking in the same old places.

Locally, I was the best of a very talented bunch. But I was also the youngest. It was almost as if the occasional scout passing through felt that the furrow had already been ploughed. So they overlooked me. I will never forgive them for that, because I was the last snapper in the net. Then again, they missed so many talented players. It was a disgrace. I have seen talent come and go over the years, but never have I seen such a waste of talent as there was in our little patch of the country.

How bad was the scouting in our area? Well, at one stage I ended up having a trial with a club that would reject me on a free transfer when I was nineteen and not too committed about playing with anybody.

In the trial they asked me to play at centre-half. I agreed, because that's what you do. I asked the coach if I should play left or right centre-half. The coach and the other trial players, who were keen to be seen to be licking the coach's balls, all fell about laughing, like it was the funniest thing they had ever heard. 'Left or right?' came the reply. 'You're a centre-half. You play in the middle!'

So I played as a centre-half, even though I had told the coach I was a midfielder. And the coach carried on shaking his head and laughing to himself.

Funny. Today that guy is hailed in some quarters as one of the FA's great technical brains, laying down the template for the entire nation in terms of how we play football. His fingerprints are over everything. He even has a say in deciding who the next England manager will be. But he can't spot a player in League One.

He didn't foresee my career path any more than I foresaw his. In fairness he remains blind and he makes a living leading the blind. Or should that be, in fairness he remains bland and he makes a living leading the bland?

I see roundy forward Wayne Rooney stuffed into a little square hole in England's midfield at Euro 2016 and I think of my trial as a centre-half. You could end up in the back four yet, Wayne.

At the ripe old age of twenty I had a trial with Millwall. I spent a week with them. I did really well, but they still didn't sign me. I had my real job by then and I came away feeling that the whole thing had been a big fat waste of my time. I couldn't see what Millwall got out of it either. You take somebody on trial for a week. He clearly does well. You usher him out the door again. I came to understand what it was all about later though.

The odd thing was that some of the hardcore Millwall fans had seen me or heard that I had done well. Fans can be funny about players that have slipped through their net. The footballers who almost played for their team always stick in their minds. Of course clubs like to bullshit their fans too. It sugarcoats reality. The reality here was that both Watford and Millwall rejected me. If I had rejected them, I would be the first to say it. Yet later, whenever I went back to play at those two stadiums, especially The Den, I would be roundly booed by the fans. They felt that I had rejected the idea of playing for them, not the other way round. Why would I have done that? Twelve-year-old me telling Elton John, 'Look, take your club and stick it where the sun don't shine, Rocket Man'? Right.

Why would they even have the impression that I had rejected them? Well, some clubs placate their fans by constantly linking themselves to players they have no intention of signing. Sometimes they are big names for whom they put in unrealistic bids. Arsenal are market leaders in this regard. They'd be going for La Decima in Champions League trophies themselves if they had signed half the big-name players they've been 'linked' with. Luis Suárez must still chuckle to himself in his sun-bleached Catalan villa when he thinks of Arsène Wenger's £40 million-plus-£1 bid for him.

For smaller clubs it's even easier. Some schmuck like me comes on trial for a week. They have no intention of signing anybody, but a year or two later the same schmuck turns up

31

playing for somebody else and making something of a name for himself. So the club puts it about: 'Oh yeah, he could have come here. We spotted him, had him for a week, offered him terms, but he thought he was Billy Big Bollocks, didn't he? Ooooh, wouldn't come here. No thanks.'

The fact is, I just wanted to be a footballer. I would have played for anyone. I would have walked barefoot across hot coals and broken glass and junkies' syringes for the chance to play. Yes, even for Millwall.

Then one day there was a phone call. Not for me. For the manager of my non-league club. I was enjoying it there. After my youth team had disbanded I had given up playing football and it was only when I was twenty that two friends I worked with encouraged me to go for a trial at the local club. They were season ticket holders. I went. I signed. I played for £10 a week. I worked weekdays doing something else entirely.

It was a tough dressing room. It was full of older players who had genuine claims to a life in professional football. There was a guy who had once been on trial at Southend. I assumed he meant at the club, not the courts. Another guy had actually played for Leyton Orient. For half a season. Two other players had been affiliated with Stevenage Borough. And there was a veteran right-back who had been in Arsenal's youth team in the 1980s. The manager had had a very decent non-league playing career too, winning the Conference, as it was then, a number of times.

Most of the others had played a good five hundred games of non-league football. That's a bloody effort, to keep going through five hundred games at that level. The tackles come so late that they arrive when you are back at work the next day. The fans don't just know where you live, they probably live next door. People say it's tough at the top, and it is, but life is no bowl of cherries when you are at the bottom.

They were all very capable players. As individuals they could have been contenders. I was the youngest. The shyest. The most naive. It was a steep learning curve. Much of the time I had absolutely no idea what anybody was talking about in terms of their everyday conversation. I felt that they were all street-wise and I was still about twelve years old. I always felt like an outsider in football, even back then. That feeling stayed with me.

That non-league team was very good and I was helped by having great players around me. I made up for my mistakes with energy and effort – the two prerequisites for a career in English football. Energy. Effort.

You don't escape non-league football by playing like Andrés Iniesta. You work like a carthorse and put yourself about like a man who doesn't care whether he keeps his teeth or not.

So one day my manager told me about this phone call he'd had with the manager of a League One side. I waited for the catch. There was none. This was different. They didn't want to take me on trial. They didn't want to hold me up to the light and examine my credentials from all angles. They just wanted to sign me. For real money.

The funny thing was, they were the same club that had asked me to come for a trial as a midfielder two years earlier and then played me at centre-half and told me to go away. They could have had me for free then. I forgave them though. Like I said,

33

I'd have played for anybody. So I became our non-league club's first ever transfer to a league side.

I went home and told Mrs TSF the good news. She ran out on to the street, did three backflips and ended up needing a skin graft after performing a Klinsmann dive down the median line of our busy road.

Well, no. In fact she had no clue as to what it all meant. She had a degree and a great job, and the idea of somebody actually earning a living through playing football seemed dubious to her.

Still, £550 a week was a good contract back then. I signed, and soon after we bought our first house for £90,000. Millwall were right. I was Mr Billy Big Bollocks.

Everything about my new working life was perfect. Except the job.

I hated it.

I hated everything about the game apart from the ninety minutes on a Saturday.

I just couldn't get to grips with 'the banter'. People talked shit non-stop. There was a hierarchy of shit in the dressing room. Every time I tried to talk, one of the players would just say 'shh'. He'd say it over and over again until I gave up. He and his personal audience found this hilarious.

The older professionals would try to make me remove my cap when I sat down to eat lunch. It wasn't like I was wearing a trilby, but the cap became a battle zone. We'd be in the canteen and my headgear was the only topic of conversation.

34

'Take your cap off. You eat with your cap on at home? It's disrespectful. Shit by you.' And so on.

I fucking hated them. I'd seen enough prison movies to know the solution. I'd perform some act of violence on one of the ringleaders. They'd respect me then.

But just as I was auditioning potential victims I was stopped in my tracks. By myself. I began to start matches. I got my revenge by playing well.

Did they respect me now?

You bet they didn't. They fucking hated me more.

But whenever I won a man-of-the-match award and the bottle of champagne that came with it, I'd stick them both up on the windowsill of the changing room and leave them there till they had company. Then I'd make a big show of trying to get four or five awards and champagne bottles into my kit bag to take home. I didn't even know why I'd won them. Running a bit further maybe. Trying a bit harder perhaps. Energy. Effort.

In those early days I was still a bit of a rogue in terms of doing things that I wanted to do when I wanted to do them. I've always been like that, and at this stage of my life it's unlikely that I'll ever change. So if I woke up one morning and decided that I didn't feel like playing football that day, I would just phone in sick. Just as I had done in my previous job.

I'd go through the whole Peter Kay routine. 'Shh, I'm phoning in sick! Don't make me laugh. Please! Stop it.' Then, in a half-croak, half-whisper, 'Hello? Hello? I won't be in today . . . dying, mate . . . yeah, really, really bad . . . hopefully it's just a twenty-four-hour thing . . . OK, tell the gaffer . . .'

Or sometimes Mrs TSF was sick. Or perhaps yet another

35

relative who had been poorly had now died and I had a funeral to go to.

One day the manager called me and asked where I was. I told him there was a cow on the line so all the trains had been cancelled. It probably occurred to him that for this to happen, the cow would have had to superglue itself to the tracks and then kill itself. He may have sensed that I was actually in London shopping with Mrs TSF. He just said to me, 'You've got one hour to get here.' He put the fear of God into me and I bolted for the train station.

When I arrived there was nobody else about. He sat me down in his office and told me that there were certain hard facts young non-league players didn't understand about being a professional footballer. My level of understanding was different, however, he added. I was just taking the piss. And then, rather awkwardly, he said, 'I know you're . . . different. But you can go on to play for England or you can fuck off back to the shithole that you came from. See you tomorrow at nine a.m.'

Well, seeing as how he put it like that . . .

The gaffer was right. I didn't have any idea that football worked differently. Why would I? The level of seriousness that goes into making a life in professional football only begins with the fact that we can't take days off whenever we can't be arsed to show up. You can't just miss matches because you've made other arrangements ages ago. Football is not like a proper job in that sense.

I hated authority though. I just hated it. Couldn't deal with it. I blame my father. I get it from him. He was brought up in a strict Catholic school where getting beaten was the most palatable of the abuse options on offer. My father came to interpret the Bible in a different way entirely: he decided that it was all bullshit. I agreed. Still do. So from my father's influence sprang a very different footballer.

Dad's career had been cut short when a couple of blokes slashed his side with a broken bottle. They left him with the scars of sixty stitches trailing across his midriff. He told us it was a footballing injury he'd suffered playing for The Two Anchors – a make-believe pub he had invented to fit the yarn. In fact he had been protecting my mum on the streets of Tottenham when two fellas had come up alongside him and raked the glass through his flesh. When I found out the truth I became a little more rigid, less trusting. An incident like that was enough to make a pub hero of a father figure in the place where we were brought up. He never traded on the story though, and what I took from it was respect for Dad and a burning desire to get out of there and rake my name across the footballing landscape, whether football liked it or not.

I didn't succeed. Not right away. But when I did get out, I learned my lessons about being a professional fairly quickly for a latecomer.

I had cost the club £15,000. They were a club that took punts on a lot of players like me. As it turned out, I was the only success. The rest all went back to non-league football. For every Jamie Vardy, there are hundreds of players plucked from non-league clubs who simply never cut it professionally.

Why did I make it? Or Jamie Vardy? Leave football and technique aside. I wasn't driven by the sunny positive motivations you read about in how-to-be-better-than-you-

37

really-are manuals. I wanted to prove the bastards wrong. I loved the game, but was I a professional because I loved the game? No. I knew the real world, and I wanted to prove the bastards wrong, and I wanted to get to the big money as quickly as possible.

So I did what I had to do.

Just turning up was the first lesson. *Always* turning up, I mean.

Along the way I missed my sister's wedding, the births of so many kids (not all mine), so many christenings and so many funerals. Some people never forgave me. They were like I used to be, though. They didn't understand how football really worked.

When I have my perfunctory interview at the gates of hell and they note, approvingly, that I hardly ever went to the funerals of friends or loved ones, I will have to explain about being a professional footballer. Then they'll just direct me to the express line. Just behind Robbie Savage probably. It is hell after all.

So that was the first lesson in professional football. Turn up! The reason I grew up reading about games in the Sunday papers was because games are played on Saturday. If you are a footballer, that is the sacred time in your week. It is the most important occasion in your life. Every week, the same. Nothing comes close to it.

Football is full of flash young guys trying to look like individuals. In its soul, though, football is a game of the team. The ultimate team game. It starts with the premise that we all make the same commitment. We all believe in the sacred nature of Saturday. Can you imagine just saying to your team-mates 'Sorry lads, I've got to attend a christening this weekend'?

Fuck off. Go back to non-league, you piss-taker.

That stays with you all the way to the top. Lots of players miss the births of their own kids. It's football. Not the real world. Nobody gives you a medal for making the sacrifices. The sacrifices are taken as read when you sign up.

The wages are another good reason to comply. They don't pay you £100,000 a week to attend funerals and christenings. One of the reasons they pay you £100,000 a week is so that you don't even think about it. The hand that feeds is very generous. You never bite it.

I got that. I was headstrong and I liked to do whatever I wanted, but I actually grasped the basics pretty quickly. As the gaffer said, I could do the job or I could fuck off back to my shithole. Lots of outsiders don't get that code.

Every day at that first club we had to meet at the stadium and then drive to the training ground on the other side of town. I didn't know anyone. I didn't know how to talk to people. I'd had an ordinary job. They were footballers. Even if I mastered the art of conversation, there seemed to be no common ground.

A black guy who had signed at the same time as me took me under his wing. He just told me to follow him. So I roomed with him for a time and watched and learned.

Like me, he didn't have a car. That's unimaginable today for professionals at any level in the game, not to have wheels, but that was us. Through our friendship I became what was known as 'an honorary brother'. That meant that the black guys looked out for me. They were mostly older players, north of thirty;

they'd been around the game a long time. They knew where all sorts of bodies were buried. I learned a lot from that gang about the game and what came with it.

Women!

These guys lived to sleep with women. They had a barber shop that they ran early in the morning before training. One of the guys would clip the hair of all the other black players and then we'd set off for training, apparently 'feeling fresh'. I called it Desmond's. And I took the piss out of them every morning until one day they jumped me and pinned me down and shaved all my hair off. The day before the team photo shoot. Bastards.

This was the routine. The hair would be clipped. We'd pile into two cars and drive to training. We'd get stuck in traffic. The guys would look in the cars around them until they saw an attractive woman and then they'd get out, walk over, knock on her door and just ask for her number.

I often wondered what the women thought not just of the routine but of the sight of a skinny white guy sitting between two black guys in the back of a black Saab with his nose pressed to the window. I should have made a card for myself to hold up against the window: Get Help!

I had never seen anything like these lads. It was so brazen. It was a lesson for me with regard to how footballers generally deal with women. No shame. If you believe that you can have a particular woman, then you probably can. And the odds get better the further up the leagues you go.

I liked those guys. They were good for me. In terms of just observing and learning, they were great. They taught me a lot about football and gave me one particular truth that helped with my naivety: be brazen in everything you do. You have one shot. Be bold. There is no room for being timid. The meek don't inherit the earth. That's a lie that the bold and the brazen circulated. The meek don't even get second-year contracts.

I learned that from them and decided to be that way on the pitch. I am still terrible at talking to women, but after my first year at the club, my wage jumped from £550 a week to £1,000 a week.

Unbelievable, Jeff.

3

I saw a lot of things at that first football club, and learned a lot. The place sanded the innocence off me. Not in a gentle way.

I saw my first fight between two players on the training pitch. I was shocked. Black v. Foreign was how the fight might have been billed. I'd call it a draw.

Fights could come out of nowhere, just bursting into life like gorse fires. Usually they were brought on by somebody having a bad day. Choose the wrong player to punish with a sulky tackle and it goes off. Fists flying. Men shouting. People step in to stop it but in our hearts we don't want it stopped too soon. It's diversion. Entertainment. Something different. Let them vent. They'll be fined either way.

In football, especially as you move up the leagues, money becomes part of the solution to everything. Not happy? Here, try some money. Wife isn't settling? Would more money help? Discipline? Look, we're going to take back some of the money.

Lower down, however, where clubs count every penny, they like to make sure that anybody on a salary is in some way always doing something for the club.

Early on, I was told that I had to do the commentary for a match on the local BBC radio station. I liked doing the commentary. I felt I had a natural ability for it. I couldn't see who I was talking to, so my shyness vanished. I just explained what was happening and it seemed to flow naturally. So I did more commentaries while I was waiting for my chance to get on the bench, and then the pitch. One day I got a little too cocksure of my radio skills and I questioned a substitution the manager had made. He took some of the money back: he fined me a week's wages. More lessons. Never question the manager publicly. Football giveth the money and football taketh the money away.

Football is a jungle and the big fat snake lurking in the undergrowth is ego. When you walk into a dressing room for the first time, it's like attending somebody else's family dinner. Everybody has a place where they sit, you just don't know where *you* are supposed to sit. So I just got changed into my kit and went about my business. The Scandinavian player whose space I had accidentally used, for about three minutes, threw my clothes all over the floor. He could have just said, 'Sorry, that's where I normally sit. There's a space over there that nobody uses.' But he was so full of ego and testosterone that he thought throwing my clothes all over the place was a reasonable response.

Or perhaps I am wrong to judge. I didn't know him in his life before football. He may always have been a prick.

Nothing you could do would ever satisfy the older professionals. Ego had calcified for a lot of them as they grew older. They felt that the inevitable could be fended off if they stuck

43

to a regular diet of bullying and booze. They drank their way through the dwindling weeks and days till they got the call to go to the manager's office and were put out to pasture.

They talked a good game though. They were never going to go easily. They'd bleed the fuckers for every penny they had. If you want to get rid of me, son, it will cost you. Just watch.

One of those players told me years later, when he'd swallowed his bitterness and become a decent person again, that he had gone into the manager's office to talk about a pay-off. Actually, not to talk. He went in to play hardball. Which when you are playing professional football is officially known as Fucking Hardball.

The manager asked him how much he wanted to leave the club. So he hit the manager hard. £25,000. Ha! Howdya like them apples, gaffer? 25K.

The manager sifted absent-mindedly through his desk drawer and found the cheque he'd pre-written in the sum of £25,000. He apparently had a small sheaf of them in the same drawer written out with amounts all the way up to £50,000. The manager had played so much hardball there was nothing left in the game to surprise him.

It was that easy. The player got what he came in for and left wishing he'd looked for more. There were 50K cheques in there. That easy. His career was over. He could count his regrets in more detail now that he had nothing to do. He was 25K down on what he might have had. Fucking football. It gives you so much and still leaves you feeling short-changed.

I was shocked by a lot of things that first year but I was especially shocked by how bad the football was. Technically some of the players were poor. So many passes never arrived at their destination that I thought Network SouthEast were interfering with our plans.

Bad decisions were more of a threat to us than any opposition. Bad decisions are what you really pay for in football. Decision-making is the standout distinction between top players and the rest. It's a bad decision when a player complicates what he is doing with the ball. If he is poor technically, most things are complicated anyway. So instead of the five-yard pass, he will try a fifty-yard pass. The ball goes out of play. Fools mutter to each other, 'Look, he's ahead of everyone. Somebody really should have seen that pass coming and run into the space.'

No. He's a useless twat, but now the crowd applauds the twat's effort, while the other team moves the ball up the field.

My captain was thirty and very well respected. I was twenty-one and not so well respected. I was generally incensed every time he failed to give me the ball. I didn't understand that it was poor form on the pitch to shout at an older pro, to tell him what he should have done. For a start, our ground was so quiet, everybody could hear me. Even people in the car park. The old guys hated me for that, as well as for just being young.

I wasn't always right. Sometimes they gave me the ball and I lost it when I should never have asked for it in the first place. That was their revenge. It cheered them up.

I wish that dressing room had been lucky enough to have a couple of wise and generous old salts sitting in corners, men who would have taken the time to give a few pointers to a young, wet-behind-the-ears guy like me. When I got older, I always tried to be that guy in the dressing room. I gave advice and I felt protective of young players.

I did that partly because I didn't want to turn out like the old guys I had started out with. There was probably little to learn from those old pros about the game, but even if there was something, they didn't want to teach me anyway.

In fairness to those players, they weren't millionaires. They'd had fifteen- or twenty-year careers some of them, and they were worried about the future. And they looked tired. Their legs were usually knackered and they had no savings and no plans. They had the weight of the world on their shoulders, wondering where their careers had gone and what they were going to do next. I can understand why they hated me, and why they came into the dressing room stinking of booze some mornings. I promised myself not to let it end like that when my time came.

In my first full pre-season, we went to an army barracks. Of course we did. Cheap and not cheerful has a strange appeal for lower-league clubs. Now, I am prone to depression, but this was worse than any bout with the black dog. A week locked up in barracks with a load of people who hated footballers. They detested us and everything we stood for. Or everything that we couldn't be arsed to stand for. I couldn't blame them. They had a real job to do, and it was tough, and they knew that the only time a crowd would turn out for them was if they came home from some war in a body bag.

They saw footballers as just the stereotype and nothing more. The lesson I took away with me was that no matter what I did for the remaining years of my career, I'd be trapped inside that stereotype. No matter what I said, what I did or how I acted, I was always going to be a footballer. Stupid. Overpaid. Soft. Mollycoddled.

Some time down the road, when we are deep into the grim aftermath of Brexit, television will realize that shows featuring professional cooks preparing incredible food have become inappropriate. They'll come up with programmes instead trying to convince us that bleakness, suffering and austerity are good things. Fun too. Here's a house we made out of sticky-back plastic . . . That's when I next expect to see the barracks we were sent to. If they did awards for sheer shittiness, it was the equivalent of a three-Michelin-star establishment. Some places are just natural shitholes. Other places put a lot of imagination and energy into making themselves world-class shitholes.

At five a.m., there was running. We actually don't play football games at that hour, you know, but here was Sir Lance Corporal General Lieutenant Captain Wilberforce-Wankface OBE (one of the Eton Wilberforce-Wankfaces; that's right, Winston's boy), who had breezed into work at three a.m. He instructed us to run down the road and leap straight into a lake in the pitch dark. Then we were to turn around, run back, strip off and nip into bed again.

It helped my first touch no end.

I often thought afterwards of Wilberforce-Wankface enjoying a nice port in the officers' mess and telling his chums that he had literally woken those infernal football chappies up and ordered them to take a run and jump. What larks!

I just wanted a football at my feet. In fairness, the way we played didn't require a football. It required mental toughness.

47

So we spent an hour instead sitting shivering in a pitch-black room listening to tape recordings of a little girl crying.

I had to assume that all this madness was just how it was. At every level. I can remember playing one of the worst matches of my career at Colchester United and the manager absolutely hammering me afterwards. Rebuilding my shattered confidence was not a priority. He just wanted to indulge himself. He was so angry that he threw a metal platter of sandwiches at me from across the room. The platter narrowly missed the head of our midfielder – he would have needed at least a dozen stitches. Then the manager grabbed me by the scruff of the neck and butted me. It wasn't a full-on headbutt but I think in a game you'd be looking at a straight red card.

I thought that all of this was normal. Players came up to me afterwards on the bus to say that I had taken it really well. I hadn't reacted and I had a good temperament. That's when it dawned on me that I was a naive mug. I never let anybody lay a hand on me again.

The pitch was where all the bullshit went away. We played horrible football under that first manager but I was just grateful to be a part of it. I didn't complain. Not publicly anyway. I had an idea of what good football should look like and I talked to my father and to my friends about it. That was my release from the banality of our game. Most weeks our fans didn't even boo us; they were conditioned to our grinding mediocrity. If we got a goalless draw, for them it was like Wilberforce-Wankface forgetting to wake us before dawn for a quick run and jump into the lake – a small reprieve from their lives of misery.

So I fell back on myself. I became self-absorbed and focused

48

on improving my own lot. I was hungry to succeed. I mentally separated all the stupid, soul-destroying parts of the game from the little encouraging things. A rating of '8' in the match report on Monday morning. A decent line or two in a national newspaper. A friendly word from somebody whom I respected and who had actually seen the game. Crumbs that could keep me nourished.

I survived. We got relegated and that cost our manager his job. I felt for him, but I was able to see that it was important to keep moving in football. My manager had come back into the game after five seasons away. Football had evolved. He hadn't.

Football changes season on season. Month to month even. People who pay to watch and people who get paid to watch often don't notice. But compare a pair of matches between the same two clubs three years ago and now. Not just the faces will have changed. The pattern, the rhythm, the tactics; all these things will be different.

And even if the two line-ups are exactly the same, the people wearing the jersey are different inside. Every game, every training ground row, every dopey motivational plan, everything adds a little layer of experience. Some players will have peaked. Others will be fading away. More will be just going through the motions, taking the money and not running.

I'd be lying if I said I didn't learn things in that first year, though. I had a manager who recognized that one of his £15,000 signings might actually be going to pay off. He encouraged me, in his own ruthless way.

Of course once I'd learned something, the manager was

fired. The only advice the older professionals gave me was to go to his office, shake his hand and thank him for the chance. Which I did. I walked in as he was packing up his belongings into a box. He told me to sit down. 'Keep working hard,' he said. 'You don't realize how good you can be. Cut the lip out. Stop thinking for yourself and listen and learn. And you will go on to play for England.'

He was close to being spot on.

That manager had taught me the importance of being ruthless. He handed down to me the belief that football was the most important thing in the world. The future of mankind lay in my ability. I swallowed it. I'm not bigging myself up here, but I have always believed that I am the future of mankind. I improved. In their sodden notebooks, scouts who watched me wrote things like 'Works hard', 'Very fit', 'Leader' and 'Rough diamond'.

After ten years in the game, most professionals would find those words insulting. They would consider themselves to be more evolved creatures. They would accept tributes along the lines of 'Technically superior', 'Been there and done it', 'Handsome – very' and 'Great lad'.

Sure. But when you start off in football, graft and dedication and ruthlessness are what sells.

And I got an insight into how the game works. We weren't a happy dressing room. The only happy dressing rooms are winning ones. When you are losing in football there is no such thing as 'women and children to the lifeboats first, gentlemen'. It's every fucker for himself. Top to bottom.

*

50

Managers at that level are always looked after by agents who bring non-league players into the professional ranks. It's like smuggling poor immigrants into a wealthy country.

The rewards are small, £5,000 or £10,000 usually, but if that player moves on to the Championship, it all starts to add up. The system works to that extent. Non-league players are given a chance. The right people earn an envelope for making it happen. Nobody is watching and nobody really cares, to be honest. The FA could clamp down tomorrow if it wanted to, but you'd never see another Jamie Vardy.

My manager and my agent knew each other. They knew how the system worked. I didn't. My non-league manager later told me that he was owed a £2,000 'drink' from my transfer into league football, but he had never got a penny. My agent 'fucked him'. Allegedly.

So today, even though he took me into the professional leagues, I don't feel too bad about having told that agent to fuck off. True story. I rang him once. He brushed me off. He couldn't talk; he was in the San Siro dealing with a passport problem for Sylvinho. First rule of being an agent: the client you are talking to at any given moment is the most important person in the world.

I had another agent for about eight months. He spent most of that time trying to persuade me to move to Northampton Town. When I sacked him over the phone, he cried. I had to tell him to grow up. I was twenty-one.

I finally got an agent who answered my calls 24/7, and it was the best decision I ever made. I stayed with him for thirteen years. As far as I know, I'm still with him.

Trust me, there is no such thing as a selfless footballer, on or off the pitch, but I had survived my first year as a pro. I was happy and becoming selfish and tough. There was better to come. Better days. Better money. I knew it.

There had to be.

And I was right.

PART TWO

Marbella With Love

4

In the beginning was the football. And the footballers.

For many years the footballers were the wretched of the earth. Their knees were knobbly, their shins were scarred and their teeth were often missing. The football chairmen were the fat and wealthy of the earth. Nobody, however, ever paid good money to watch a chairman eat his dinner.

But lo, it came to pass that the footballers rose up against the very nature of their world. The maximum wage became a sin and an abomination. The chairmen were still fat, just not quite as fat. And then the allied forces of television came over the brow of the hill, as magnificently as the US cavalry, and everybody cheered and bought satellite dishes and footballers were suddenly among the wealthy and exalted of the earth.

So for their holidays, footballers went to Marbella . . .

. . . and as an independent-minded young pro, I followed suit.

Marbella has several museums and innovative performance spaces, and a busy cultural calendar with events ranging from reggae concerts to opera performances. There are places of great historical importance such as the vaulted Roman baths of Las Bovedas, and the city can boast a significant archaeological heritage. Traces of Phoenician habitation date back to the early seventh century BC.

Yes, BC.

Interested?

Nah. Neither were we.

Marbella is on the Costa del Sol. Apparently that's the Coast of the Sun. Done deal, mate.

A few thousand years from now, archaeologists will look back at Marbella's civilization of blue swimming pools and warehouse-sized nightclubs. They will appreciate the cultural significance of the Golden Mile, which runs for four hedonistic miles and ends up at the yacht heaven of Puerto Banus, where the smell of money is as bracing as the sea air. They will find bits of chunky bling and shards of glass that were once part of obscenely expensive bottles of champagne. They will see that footballers enjoyed Marbella.

They fucking loved it.

For a while. Marbella had a good run back when I was starting out, but it's all over now, baby blue. The only footballers who are in Marbella now are the ones who can't afford to be in Las Vegas or Dubai or Miami. It's one of humanity's modern tragedies: the plight of the non-Premier League player. What is Red Nose Day doing for those guys with actual red noses and sunburned backs? Fuck all.

Marbella has lost out too, of course. Not just financially, but culturally. There was no drama more interesting than what unfolded whenever a group of, let's say, League Two players were gathered around a pool and bigging themselves up for the benefit of slack-jawed girls in bikinis.

Usually the League Two lads would be wearing bits and pieces of their playing kit. Not because they couldn't afford to go into Primark for something just as classy, but because they needed to tell the world. Look, we're footballers. Shorts were still the favourite accessory. Any prat could buy a replica shirt. Shorts were Marbella couture. I'm a footballer. Look, I've got the shorts.

Standing out matters to these players. It mattered to me. We were desperately keen to be recognized as footballers.

In my defence, I wasn't as keen as some others. They would wear their full kit to a pool party, the same scummy shorts they'd been playing in all season. They even walked around in them too, down to the beach, out to lunch, nights at the opera. I've even seen players wearing them at night in the bars and nightclubs.

They're my nylon shorts and I'm sticking to them.

Anyway, the lower leaguers might be having a pretty good time beside this pool in their shorts and loudly dropping heavy football references in case any of the girls don't get the picture. And then . . . a small herd of Premier League players might show up. It would be like Oasis arriving in your pub just when you were showing off on the karaoke machine.

I'm old now and I've been on both sides of this tension. As a League Two player, the confidence just drains out of your club shorts and on to the floor of the pool. Your gut feels slacker, your dick feels smaller, your bank account seems puny. The champagne you've been buying – it's the fucking cheap piss, isn't it. Your stories: fattened with exaggerations till some of them were pure fiction.

You recognize the Premier League bastards. Of course they don't recognize you. Even if they did, they wouldn't let on.

Before you can drown her humanely, some blonde on a lilo will shout out, 'Hey, these guys are footballers too, you must know each other!'

Of course we don't know each other.

She's now paddling as if her life depends on it towards the cabana the Prem guys have rented for themselves over the other side of the pool. Ten grand a day. Women want to see the inside of that cabana as passionately as some people want to see the ceiling of the Sistine Chapel. In fact, women want to see the ceiling of that cabana . . .

The Premier League guys are the jackpot for certain types of women. Bagging a centre-half from Rochdale and getting inside his mouldy kecks might be a good morning-after story for your mates. Bagging a Prem player might be a good morning-after story for the tabloids. Or maybe he will love you for your personality and you will never have to work again and you will bear his children and name them after the places where they were conceived. Costa and his brothers Del and Sol. Little Puerto Banus on the way.

League Two players feel very silly around Premier League players. Their sudden presence is an attitude adjuster. One moment you are the Adonis of the poolside. Next moment you are a dickhead. At first you are awed, then you are resentful. A pathetic part of you hopes one of the Prem guys will notice your mate who won an England Under-16 cap back in 2005

58

and you'll pile into the cabana and be their mates for ever . . .

When you're the Premier League player, well, forget about cock of the walk, you feel like a fucking king. Really, people should be corralled behind purple velvet ropes to watch you strut past. People who approach you should bend the knee and kiss your ring. You are untouchable, bulletproof, the bionic dog's bionic bollocks. Gold-plated and indestructible.

You have to remember very few things. People will do your remembering for you. Only one thing you really have to remember, and that's privacy. Who are you now? When you make a dick of yourself, when you fight with your mate with the handicap of being blind drunk, when you inhale laughing gas or suck the shisha pipe or lick the stripper's tits, somebody will be watching you and looking for a story to sell. You can trust the proprietors of the bars and nightclubs to help you with this one thing you need to remember. Privacy is expensive and they want to sell you expensive shit. Otherwise do it all in the cabana.

When you are in League Two, you know nothing of these First World problems. Your worst misdemeanour – if you debauched a nun on the high street, say – might just make page two of the *Billericay Bugle*. Mainly because she was a nun.

When you are a Premier League royal, when your world smells of fresh paint and easy money, you feel no real compassion for the League Two guy you once were. Footballers are competitive people. It's dog eat dog. Peacock eat peacock.

I've had girls turn their backs on the League Two players they were engaging with and just walk over to me. Obviously I have the body of a classical Greek statue and the looks of a younger Clooney, but still . . .

59

I feel the lads' pain. Well, a momentary twinge of it, and then I ask the girls what they would like to drink. They tell me, and I smile in a charming way and say, 'Listen, that cheap stuff could give you wrinkles and varicose veins. Why don't you try this?'

You're only in your twenties once, testosterone surging through your body, money like a torrent in your bank account. League Two can look down on non-league. I've been there too. When you get to the Premier League, you can look down on everybody. And you can back it up.

Even within the Premier League there's a hierarchy. The dressing rooms at places like Manchester United or Arsenal – especially Arsenal – make you look around with your jaw on the spotlessly clean floor. When you go there, your club is Marbella and the Emirates is, unsurprisingly, Dubai.

We have one genetic link. All footballers want to be winners, no matter what league they happen to play in. So when we run into each other poolside in Marbella, we Premier Leaguers front up and watch our backs.

At first, the lower-league sappers will go all silent and a little panicky, like warthogs when a pride of lions ramble past their watering hole. Then they'll regroup. They'll make their way back into the pool and strategically float towards our cabana. The girls are now sunbathing between the cabana and the pool. The food chain is clear. The girls are trying to attract our attention. The League Two guys in the water are trying to attract the girls' attention.

As the Premier League player, you must never ask the creatures in the water what exactly they think they are doing. It's tempting, of course, to emerge from the cabana wearing a deer stalker and brandishing a shotgun just to shout at them. Peasants, get off my land! That will just undermine your position though. It will make it obvious that you have actually noticed them hovering like horseflies. And it's needless. These particular girls may stay in the shallow end of the pool when it comes to thinking, but they have worked out where the money is.

So you keep your counsel and you check your Rolex. This is a tribal skill. If it's early morning, you can kick off your five-grand pair of Tod's Gommino croc moccasins (I'll have them in blue and not python skin. Crocodile, please. And make it snappy) and relax. The lads won't have had time to get too drunk. They will move on to pastures cheaper.

If you use your Prem witchcraft to lure away the love interest, you can guarantee that the women are 70 per cent drunk and the League Two players who made them that way are too. Some disgruntled little midfield general is going to make a stand. That's OK too. If you are nimble on your toes, it represents an opportunity.

Teaching Example:

Three tanned and beautiful-looking girls glide around the pool. They are heading in my direction. They are heading away from a group of heavily tattooed and uniformly dressed League Two players. The girls look like they are escaping the ghetto. I prepare myself to welcome them to the neighbourhood. I push my Maybach Diplomat shades up into my hair, and move distractedly just to show that my gut isn't sucked in League Two style. (It was like this anyway. Taut as a golden frying pan.)

We fall into conversation. Above-your-head stuff, so I'll say no more. Before long, because it's afternoon and he is drunk, out of pocket and out of love, one of the League Two guys decides to make his move. He's clearly hung up on one of these girls and the only way this little prince is going to regain his Cinderella is if he goes through me.

He approaches, paddling through the pool like a drowning mongrel. He tries to catch my eye as he nears the edge. It's tactically important for me to fail to register this at first. I keep chatting, smiling and nodding wisely. When he leans on the edge of the pool a few yards from our group and starts talking to the girl who flips his heart or strains his nylon shorts, I have to take notice.

'Eh, all right mate?' he says.

He plays the salt-of-the-earth card. He wants to know exactly how serious my little squad is about these girls. Not that he admits that he is serious about one of them, but he just doesn't want to see them messed around. He knows that we'll all be out tonight and the same thing might happen again in a nightclub. We might walk in, dragging our golden balls along the floor, and spoil it for everybody. Although he doesn't phrase it quite like that.

I push the shades back down on to the bridge of my nose so he doesn't know if we have eye contact or not.

I want to say to him that he should just enjoy this moment because unless his little club draws somebody big in the FA Cup, this exchange outside the cabana is as close as he is going to get to football royalty. If he wants to take a selfie, him and me, I'm happy to oblige.

But he wants that. He's salt of the earth. He wants me to make myself look like a Premier League arsehole. So from this moment on, every single answer I give has to gently undermine him without him or the girls noticing. Even when I get to the punchline they will suspect that maybe, just maybe, I was trying to be nice.

'So what are you lot doing here?' I ask him, as if I'm pleased by the coincidence. In fact I'm asking him if he can really afford to be here, or did he have to sell the Mondeo?

He realizes now that he should have got out of the pool and walked around. I am looking down on him from just outside my cabana. Premier League looking down on League Two. He doesn't want to clamber out of the pool. Nobody looks elegant doing that when half-drunk.

'The chairman sent us away for a week,' he says. This sounds mighty fine in his head. To me and the girls it screams 'Freebie!' How awful.

'Your chairman sent you away, did he? What, did you get relegated or something?' My voice is dripping with sincerity. The question sounds like a condolence. You poor, poor man. If I had known of your tragic circumstances I would have contributed too, but it was most charitable of your chairman.

The answer also says, 'Look mate, I actually don't know who the fuck you are. I really don't follow the lower leagues, I'm afraid.'

Now it seems as if everybody around the pool is listening. That poor man in the pool got relegated or widowed or something, and his boss bought him a holiday. How sad.

'Do you want a drink?' I ask charitably.

He looks at me with surprise. I've thrown him a lifebuoy. Everyone looks at me with surprise, apart from my team-mates in the cabana.

He turns around to look at his team-mates. They begin sidling up to the edge of the pool, now sensing an opportunity to go down in footballing post-season folklore.

'Yeah, OK, cheers,' he says.

'Great,' I say. 'Just do us a favour, mate, you get this one in. I'll get the next.' And I sit down on the lounger.

'OK, what do you want?'

And as he begins to swim off towards the bar, eager as a beaver, I call the order after him: 'We're drinking the Dom Perignon, mate . . . the Methuselah.'

'Cool,' he calls back doubtfully.

I'll let him find out when he gets to the bar that here at the Ocean Club pool party in Marbella a Methuselah of Dom Perignon will cost him a minimum of €10,000.

You see, this is theatre. Culture. Drama.

He looks around, hoping his team-mates will join him for a brief conference to discuss this crisis. There is no help to be found. They have decided it will be time for them to join the proceedings when the Premier League guys start paying.

He panics, and in desperation he gets out of the pool and waddles over to check his phone as if it has been ringing urgently. He checks it and rechecks it. He stares at it with an expression on his face that suggests his agent has texted him that he must choose quickly between Barça and Real Madrid, both of whom are clamouring for his services. He checks it for so long that Facebook becomes obsolete.

Then, still looking thoughtful and distracted, he pretends to dry himself down. By now he has been joined by some of those team-mates of his. They have the runs with fear that he has dragged them all into something costly and humiliating. They can't trust themselves to be in the pool any longer, not when they are shitting yellow. They all look as if they have just remembered an urgent appointment.

Then they shuffle off, stage left, hoping that enough time has elapsed for the audience to have forgotten the main plot.

We haven't forgotten. The point has been made.

They don't say goodbye, don't even look back as they scurry out.

'Are the lads gone?' I ask the girls after a while.

I'm an arsehole, of course, but the girls will never know that. If the lads had clubbed together and bought a €10,000 bottle of champagne between them, I would have bought them one back. It's a sign of respect. But I'm not buying the first bottle only for them to guzzle it and go back to Backwater Athletic bragging about how they got free champagne off that Premier League prat TSF and then did a runner. Legend!

Not on my watch, lads.

And I know they would have done just that. Once I was that soldier.

Marbella in its heyday was the place where the Premier League haves lorded it over the lower-league have-nots.

I once saw a Sunderland player order a bottle of champagne at a beach party. The bottle was so big it had to be delivered to him on a special trolley by three members of staff.

You see, for a lot of footballers it isn't the actual object that's important, it's the process of spending the sort of money most people earn in a year on something that you're just going to drink casually. It ain't what you do, it's the money that you

65

spend doing it. And the audience that you attract. It's about the process. The optics. The image. It's the whole grand ceremony of three immaculately dressed staff wheeling the bottle out with the reverence and respect of pallbearers. Then opening the thing as people take pictures and cheer. The story of you and your unfeasibly large bottle of champagne wires around the grapevine like an electric shock. It gets burned into folklore and legend. So what if you never won the Golden Boot? Your peers will remember you.

That's what it's all about.

That's what the media and the fans could never understand. All we were doing was entertaining and one-upping ourselves to spread our reputations. Great, lads.

Of course you need to think things out beforehand. The Sunderland player found that out. He had his moment of glory as the giant bottle was wheeled out and the staff uncorked the thing with the usual ceremony and geyser of spray. But once that was done he just sat there drinking the champagne glass by glass. And every time he wanted a top-up, he needed to summon the three staff members to operate the lever system on the trolley and lower the bottle down and back up again. He looked like a cock.

If he'd given a glass to everybody gathered around and the bottle had quickly emptied, he could have been golden. Instead he became his own punchline.

Football is small and insular. Players move around every season, they play against each other every season, they sleep with the same girls. Stories get out to players at other clubs with exaggerations and embellishments. Each club has its own changing room, but we're pretty much all undressing in the same room.

One false move and you're fucked for ever. That Sunderland player went down in history as a cock.

When I first began playing professional football, trips abroad at the end of the season were a big part of the culture. If you avoided relegation, it was generally expected that your chairman would pay for the lads to go to Marbella. If he was a tight bastard or you got relegated, you would be flown to Ayia Napa. You might boast about Marbella. You'd all agree never to speak of Ayia Napa.

Once upon a time it was all a novelty.

As I scrambled my way up the ladder, I realized that I hated the post-season trip abroad. It meant being with people I didn't overly like. Just like an office party. Work has thrown you all together. That doesn't mean it's a good idea to socialize and drink together.

At that time I was fully focused on playing football and getting to the Premier League as quickly as possible. In achieving that I was at the mercy, to a certain extent, of players who put more effort into a week staying in a microwave of a hotel room banging as many girls as possible than they ever put into football. Many of them didn't give a hoot about their own careers, let alone mine. A big part of what drove me to leave them behind was their attitude to the sport. What happened in Marbella was of considerably more interest to them than what happened on the training pitch.

Marbella was a place that was just about affordable for

footballers. Not flights and rooms. Just spending money. Guys would grab their best mate and the pair of them would pass the week as if they were Siamese twins.

It's cheaper to buy each other drinks than it is to buy the whole squad a drink. You get into a round system with the squad and the tightwads sit on their wallets until everybody is too drunk to remember who has bought and who hasn't. Anyway, what is a player going to do with thirty drinks if everybody buys a round? We're not fans. We're athletes!

It was best to partner up, and for you and your wingman to leave the bar where the team had gathered as soon as possible. I learned a valuable lesson one night when I offered a midfielder who hated me a drink. I was trying to get into his good books.

'TSF is at the bar, lads!' he roared. 'What's everyone want?'

I splashed most of my spending money on that one fucking round. Nobody bought me a drink in return. Every time the same midfielder tries to follow me on Instagram now it gives me enormous pleasure to press the red cross. Sorry, mate.

I look back at those days now as relics from another time. It was all such small potatoes compared to where us lucky ones ended up. Ultimately the holidays we took represent the story of professional football's journey from the forest to the golden beach.

It's a story full of lessons. Sometimes allowing people to show their true colours is all the instruction you'll ever need to learn about those people.

From Marbella to Miami, via Ibiza, Vegas and Dubai, we showed our true colours.

(We were never in Ayia Napa. I swear.)

5

'Oi, Shit Tits!'

The evening sun was beating down. The alcohol was flowing as if it were a natural resource.

Marbella. We were out to play.

It had been a long day. The low-rollers and the League One and Two types had been weeded out. This party was down to the elite. Natural selection, mate.

The women were strutting by the pool, heads held high despite the weight of their Balenciaga sunglasses. Waxed in all the right places and tits out and proud, despite the unsteadiness of the nine-inch Christian Louboutin high heels and the burning metal of the Chanel clutch bag straps slowly melting through their bony shoulders.

It takes plenty of money and a lot of pain to get on to this poolside catwalk, pretending that you are taking a casual stroll by the water but scoping the place out for discerning admirers as you go.

The effect was being ruined for this particular lady by the voice coming from deep inside our cabana.

69

'Oi, where you going, Shit Tits?'

She knows that it is her being referred to. She glances at our cabana from behind her shades. Of course I am lounging outside as if I am the ambassador of the cabana and have the ability to hurl insults at her without moving my lips. Her gaze falls on me and I feel mortified. Totally and utterly scarlet. This adds to the hilarity for the lads inside the cabana.

From behind my own shades, I try to express my disapproval. I try to give the impression that I am of the cabana but not part of this. It's hard to communicate that stuff visually when you are drunk and drowsy, but I do my best.

All for nothing. The voice comes again.

'Something the matter, Shit Tits?'

And a wave of laughter follows from within the cabana.

Fess up. You have a fixed idea about footballers. Overpaid, oversexed and overhyped. And that's just the good stuff. Soft. Spoiled. And mostly you've seen better players in pub teams. You'll pay to watch us play, but your tried and trusted, 'everything that's wrong with the modern game' routine always goes down well in the pub afterwards.

Get over it.

Stop for a second and imagine this.

You live in a little village. For generations the villagers have made a decent living from growing potatoes. Hard work, but it's a living.

One cold and drizzly day, a horny-handed son of the soil pulls up some spuds and says to his three-legged dog, 'Ya know, Lucky, the soil in these parts is unusually dark.'

70

A week or so later, the potato farmer rents a drill and a geologist, and lo and behold, the entire village is sitting on an underground sea of oil. Black gold. Everybody in the village is rich. They rename the place Gusher-en-Mer because it sounds posh.

Soon the village is swarming with design consultants, financial consultants, investment consultants, guys selling jewellery that costs more than a top sports car and guys selling sports cars that cost more than a large house. Grifters invade like a plague of vermin. There are high-class hookers on the high street and top-of-the-line rent boys on the village green. There are Class A drugs and three-Michelin-star restaurants that do takeaways for bona fide villagers. There are tailors who will sew suits from silk harvested by blind peasants from rare Peruvian worms. Cobblers who make shoes out of animals that the world believes to be extinct. There are women who just hope to be asked by *Heat* magazine what first attracted them to the multi-millionaire midfielder with the bad attitude and the shocking mullet.

Every gimlet-eyed stranger seems to want to syphon rivers of cash out of Gusher-en-Mer. The locals enjoy spending their money, but sometimes they feel overwhelmed by the world.

What everybody knows, but nobody talks about, is the fact that there is only ten or fifteen years' worth of oil. Then it's back to potatoes, unless you have enough to live on until you grow old.

It's a worry, but shit, there's so much good stuff out there to buy and to enjoy. There are more opportunities to spend money than your imagination can come up with. You figure

71

that if you can just avoid being hustled, then you'll be OK in the long run.

As time passes, the villagers develop a system. They trust only each other. They protect each other. They share information.

I dealt with him, he's a grade A bandit. This other guy is decent enough. That guy is a low-level grifter; he's shaking your hand and his other hand is in your pocket. She's a top-of-the-line gold digger. Run!

Being a top footballer is like living in that village.

You have plenty of everything, but everybody wants a piece of it. Every fucking bastard you meet seems to be on the make. You make new friends and your heart is heavy with waiting for them to tell you the idea they can cut you in on, the surefire investment opportunity they have just heard of, the desperate situation they are in. You watch them for months just to see what angle they are working.

When you were signed to a football club at the age of nine, ten or eleven and started making £20,000 a week before bonuses at eighteen, there was never really the time for anybody to equip you for dealing with all this shit. So you trust the other villagers. You ask advice in the dressing room. One guy gets a customized sports car from a dealer who delivers instantly and only marks the vehicle up 20 per cent? Everybody in the dressing room buys from that guy.

We are that village. Our village is contained in a bubble that only we can see.

All we really know is that people want to come in and take our shit, and a huge number of them succeed.

*

72

'Got a problem, Shit Tits?'

I have to give credit here to this lady who at that stage was known to me only as Shit Tits. First, she wasn't too shitty of titty. Second, apart from the quick glance in my direction, she didn't let the insults break her elegant stride or diminish her hauteur. I felt embarrassed for her and for myself, so I hissed loudly in the direction of the cabana comedians to shut the fuck up. This was too much.

'Leave it out, you melt,' came the reply. 'Do you know who that is?'

I didn't. But I was about to find out.

Another voice from inside the cabana took up the story. Shit Tits was an old flame of the player who had been flinging the abuse at her. Actually, she was more than an old flame. She was an entire case of arson. She had had a major bearing on the player's life and career. In fact it was no stretch to say that if it wasn't for this woman, then our friend wouldn't have been with us that evening. Not in this cabana. Not at our football club. Not in our company.

That doesn't sound so bad, I hissed in the direction of the cabana, tell me more . . .

The cabana cleared its throat.

Two years earlier, our man in the cabana had begun an affair with this woman, who was, it transpired, a former beauty queen. In the real world, people would have said that he was punching above his weight, but for footballers those weight divisions don't really exist. You can be a warty homunculus from the Championship and still end up with somebody many times more beautiful than yourself.

73

That's the magic of being a footballer. We mostly don't get judged on our looks or our personalities. And anyway, our man in the cabana was the sort of guy who would take on all-comers.

The only difficulty lay in the fact that our friend was married, with a kid to take care of. Casual encounters were one thing, but a full-blown affair was something different entirely.

It took him a while to realize this. Almost a year in fact. By then the former Miss Shit Tits 2002, or whatever her title was, had become very serious. She was begging him to leave his wife. She loved him. Didn't he love her? Friends were advising him not to buy his kid a rabbit in case his mistress came to the house and boiled it. He thought his brain would boil first, so he broke it all off, and peace returned to his life.

Fast-forward almost one year. He arrives home one day, not a cloud in his sky, and he sees that all his suitcases and belongings are packed and stacked in the driveway. This is not good, he thinks to himself as he proceeds towards his house.

In the hallway, his wife is a sobbing heap. She is holding a large brown envelope. She walks towards him and hands him the envelope.

Bailiffs, he thinks. Oh shit.

But it's worse than that. Much worse.

Michael McIndoe. Every footballer in the village knows Michael McIndoe.

You know that shiver that runs down your spine? There's a type of shiver called the McIndoe. Lots of players wake up in a cold sweat from dreaming about him. They have the McIndoes.

74

Jimmy Bullard even went to live in the jungle because of him.

In our village you won't find a single local with a kind word to say about Michael McIndoe. He was one of our own. Now he is an outcast.

Athletes go broke. It's a fact of life. Tyson bit Holyfield's ear in one of the most iconic boxing moments. Reality bit both of them. Tyson blew $400 million in prize money. Broke. Holyfield got through $250 million. Broke.

You're young and rich and untrained in the ways of the world outside? You get filleted by freeloaders. A huge number of professional athlete marriages fall apart in the years after retirement. I had a 33 per cent chance of being divorced within a year of my last game. That's the figure for footballers. For NBA players it's worse. I'm beating the odds, but then again I have all this unbelievable shit that I'm blackmailing her with.

The thrill goes. The athlete can't do the one thing that gave him a sense of worth and excitement. The marriage goes kaput. Then there is alimony and child support and setting up a new life that is smaller than the life you had. And legal bills. It would be cheaper to have a bad coke habit.

As an ex-player, there is a 40 per cent chance I will be bankrupt within five years of retirement. And I don't even know Michael McIndoe personally. And there are odds that I don't like to think about concerning addictions. There are bad investments and lingering injury stresses which drain money. For footballers there's an 80 per cent chance that osteoarthritis is waiting in the hallway for you with a baseball bat in its hand.

Of course there are your family and friends. When you got your first big contract, you looked after yourself, but you looked after those who were close to you too. But by and large they didn't look after what they got any better than you did. They can't bail you out.

A 2009 piece in *Sports Illustrated* showed that 60 per cent of NBA players suffered financial stress within five years of their careers ending. The figure for NFL players was 78 per cent. Those guys make us Premier League royals look like paupers. And don't forget nearly all of them, at least nominally, attended university for four years before being drafted as pros. Like us, though, they have a short-term earnings spike which begins when they are too young to know and ends when it is too late to learn.

The great Allen Iverson got through $154 million in wages alone within years of his hoops career ending. He is lucky in that Reebok, his sponsor, put $30 million away in a trust for him. But he can't access that until 2030. If he is still around and Reebok are still around, that is.

Athletes are untrained in survival. It's a fucking jungle out there. Football cuts you loose and you realize that it's an express journey from wonderkid to stalwart and on to the crowded terminus of former players with difficulties.

You wonder what you were thinking when you were on £30,000 a week and you insisted on matching the lifestyle of the striker in your dressing room who was on £75,000 a week. The striker was trying to keep up with his mate on the England team who was on £150,000 a week.

So you stop thinking.

When it's all over, dependencies on drink and drugs or gambling often replace the buzz of being a player. So long as

76

you have money, there are more enablers around to help you spend it than there are to help you save it. Many more. So you spend just to stave off the loneliness.

Sweets from a baby. Shooting fish in a barrel. Scoring in a women's prison when you have a fistful of pardons. Nutmegging Robbie Savage. All those things are harder than taking money from a footballer.

I have done it myself. I have sold many investment opportunities to other footballers. I didn't even want to most of the time. Players just solicit you for ways to spend their money.

They think they need the money. They really need the buzz.

The basketball player Michael Jordan once had to explain to a bemused public that the only way he could make a round of golf interesting was to bet at least $10,000 a hole with whoever he was playing with, plus, I suppose, side-bets for longest drive – and 20K says you don't sink that putt.

I've seen the same syndrome in poker schools on team buses.

Footballers are risk-takers. They've beaten the odds just by getting to be professionals. They don't want to invest a modest amount in a blue-chip portfolio that yields a steady 3 per cent. They want to double their wage every week if possible. Surveys show that most people think they would be OK if they earned 50 per cent more than they currently earn. It's the same in the dressing room. Lads tell themselves that if they invest in something and it doubles their money or yields 50 per cent, they will salt that money away for the future and they'll never have to go back to picking potatoes.

When lads came to me looking for chances to spend their money, it was because I had something that the wolf packs of

Wall Street never could have. I was a footballer too. I was a villager. I was one of them. My peers trusted me instantly. They knew that I would never set out to defraud them or to sell them something that I knew to be junk.

I'd say, 'This is your investment, this is your money, it's a gamble, it could go wrong, and if it goes wrong it'll be your fault, I'm not telling you to do it. Capeesh?'

Yes, they'd say earnestly. So how long do you think it will be before it starts paying big?

Maybe never, mate. It's a gamble.

Brilliant! I'm in, mate!

And as soon as they invested they forgot every warning and caveat. They assumed I was running the company on their behalf. I was the CEO, the board of directors, the principal shareholder and the workforce. Me, just one man who also played football.

They were like the kids in the back of the car who keep crying 'Are we nearly there yet?' from the moment you reverse out of the driveway.

Phone calls. Non-stop fucking phone calls.

'How's that business, mate?'

'When's it selling? Soon?'

'What's it worth this morning?'

'How much will we make?'

Same answer every time. I'll get a shareholder update. You'll get a shareholder update. You know exactly the same as me.

This call could be from a player who had blown five times as much on a week in Marbella as he had invested in the company.

78

They never believed me. They believed I had access to something they didn't. The inside track. Jungle skills. Playing football was a relief for me at times.

I can see how it was all so easy for Michael McIndoe. That just makes it worse.

The brown envelope had dropped through the letterbox of my friend's home that morning. Hand-delivered, and not by Royal Mail. The contents were like a museum archive of his affair.

He sifted through it all as his wife wept. Every dinner receipt. Every hotel room statement. Every cinema stub. Every receipt for lingerie, for jewellery, for handbags. It was like a detailed guide to his betrayal. The more items he looked at and the louder he heard his wife crying, the worse he felt.

There was no quick comeback from this. No handy lie or sincere apology that might make it all right. He was going to have to work to restore his relationship. Work and work and work. It would take years to build the trust back into his marriage.

Fuck.

Things got worse though. He felt physically sick as his eyes fell on a list of the text exchanges between himself and this other woman. There were transcripts of the juiciest messages and a record of all the phone calls between them.

He could say that he hadn't meant all the things he'd said, but that left him open. Did he *ever* mean the things he said? Did he mean what he was saying now? Did he mean what he'd said when they got married? What sort of man was he?

He was beginning to wonder about that himself when he got to the bottom of the pile of papers.

79

The bullet that would kill him.

What sort of man am I? The sort who is totally fucked actually.

There is a picture of McIndoe that the papers always use at the top of articles about the guy. He is in Marbella with his entourage of tanned hangers-on. On the beach. Everybody has an orange wristband on, so you know it's a party. The sea is in the background but the gang have their backs to it. All you can see is shades, cigars, bottles of pink champagne and girls sticking out their tits. Everybody is celebrating as if they have just won the Champions League.

It looks so dodgy that it tells its own story.

The articles usually detail the list of the wounded. Who lost how much in McIndoe's schemes. What players. The clubs they were at when they lost the money. The piece then wraps up with the usual prophylactic protection: the Metropolitan Police are examining the scheme . . . no arrests have been made . . . no wrongdoing is implied . . . he has reasserted his innocence . . . (all of which happens to be true as this book goes to press).

Even today, knowing everything that footballers know about McIndoe and schemes like his, most footballers will see that picture and they'll respond like Pavlov's dogs. Salivation and tail wagging and memo to self: book Marbs for summer break. Soon! McIndoe could have put the picture on the cover of his prospectus for potential investors.

As a player, McIndoe was like his investment schemes: he always delivered less than he promised. He needed to get his hands on more talent, not more money. He was OK. He made a living. He survived his limitations to have a journeyman career, playing with remarkable anonymity for a string of towns a double-glazing salesman would find unglamorous. He went from Luton to Hereford to Yeovil to Doncaster and onwards through Derby, Barnsley, Wolverhampton, Bristol, Coventry and Milton Keynes.

His footballing life was like a long train journey through sleet and drizzle. He pressed his nose to the window to glimpse the bright lights in the far distance as the voice on the tannoy said, 'This train serves all dumps as far as Milton Keynes.'

He was the type of player that footballers refer to generally as 'little rats'. Footballing rodents who hang out on the wings, away from the hurly-burly of the game in the middle, living off the scraps that come their way. When most players think about beating their personal best at 'keep-ups', they see themselves performing the tricks with a little rat, not a football.

Of course the phrase 'little rat' has all sorts of other connotations, especially in football. A little rat can also be somebody who lives his life in a generally rat-like manner. If a guy comes to your club and you ask somebody he previously played with what sort of chap he is, and the answer is 'little rat', then there is a good chance he will not be a popular dressing-room figure. He's not sound. Not one of us. Two-faced. Sucks up to the gaffer. Blames everybody else when the shit is flying. Always survives somehow.

As a rule of thumb, then, a little rat on the field will be pretty rat-like off it as well. Which isn't to say that I haven't met wingers who are very nice people off the pitch. This is just a rough guide to the animal kingdom. You'll hear a lot of players

81

today described as little rats in the dressing room and by the wider footballing community. We all know who they are.

I perhaps remember McIndoe best when he was at Doncaster Rovers, where he twice made it into the PFA team of the year. The club I was playing for tried to sign him. I was pleased, but then I realized I was getting him mixed up with James Coppinger, who would have been a good signing. Sorry, Copps.

I'm glad we didn't sign him. It would have been like going out and wilfully catching a virus.

Word of McIndoe inevitably reached our dressing room. A midfielder we had who liked a giddy punt in the investment market came in one day all excited. He was the sort of lad who needed restraining for his own good. Sadly, he had been told that an investment through Michael McIndoe would be channelled towards a company that specialized in gold and property. The returns would be unbelievable. Literally.

Gold and property! Two things that for footballers are as fascinating as beads and mirrors supposedly were to Native Americans before they realized that the people who brought them had also brought the gift of smallpox.

(Smallpox. Now *that* would have been a good nickname for . . .)

Word was that McIndoe would accept a toe-in-the-water investment of £20,000 so that he could demonstrate his investment genius. My friend couldn't get the £20,000 to McIndoe quickly enough.

I shook my head and warned them all.

Two things, lads.

First. Financial returns like that don't exist unless your name is Savvy McSavveson and you are working as Savvy & Savvy's most savvy broker in the Savvy Department and you've just invested in the savviest company of all time, mining pure savvy in the business-friendly republic of Savvystan.

Second, you are footballers. What the fuck do you know about gold, property and stocks? Michael McIndoe is a footballer. What the fuck does he know about gold, property and stocks?

The thing about investments that seem too good to be true is that they are usually too good to be true. From Harvard Business School to our dressing room, those are words to live by.

But my mate arrived at training in triumph a fortnight later. His £20,000 was now £30,000. He did the maths. That was £10,000 in two weeks. It was like 50 per cent of his 20K added to the 20K. Fuck. If only he'd invested £200,000.

I gave a brief supplementary lecture (for free) on the history of failed investment schemes, from instances in Dickens to famous real-life examples. A long history of suckers handing over money, who are used as bait to hook other suckers, and so on. I told my mate and anybody else at risk of contamination that they were just more suckers on the vine.

Some of them said 'Thanks, TSF' and then scurried off to give more of their money away. Four of them invested £50K each as soon as they could.

Players were encouraged to involve other players. That part was beautiful in its simplicity. The village mentality of football is such that we feel more comfortable doing what the other players are doing. That's why it's always a group of players who buy a racehorse, not just one guy who can afford it. It's why a little gang of players might buy Salford City FC.

Before long I was wearing my best 'I Told You So' face.

'He's not returning our calls, TSF. Do you think something has gone wrong?'

No, lads. Everything, I imagine, is going to plan.

At the bottom of the pile of papers that had been hand-delivered in the brown envelope was a picture of a baby boy lying in a crib. On the reverse side it said, 'This is your son,' and there was a birth date.

In court she absolutely cleaned him out. She had to move swiftly and efficiently before his wife got into the alimony business with her wolfish lawyers. The player had paid an initial lump sum in order to bring the regular payment down to the £3,000 a month he was now paying her in child support. Most of his transfer fees and his wages were now being spent on paying for his past mistakes. This week in Marbella was a rare break from the pressures of keeping his head above water.

So, obviously, when he looked out of the cabana and saw her strutting around the swimming pool, he flipped.

As his team-mates, I suppose we generally disapproved of the affair and the stupidity involved, but we saw his side of it.

You live in the village and everybody wants a piece of your shit. We knew that much.

We could have said, 'Well, we're in Marbella, and she's in Marbella, so all's well that ends well.' But we didn't. She was intruding. She was in our space like a predatory lioness. She was spending the money our mate was giving to her every month and using it to suck in more victims. A sexual get-rich scheme, we reckoned.

'Fuck,' I said, as the story wound down to a finish, 'that is bad. But why do you call her Shit Tits?'

I should have been able to figure it out myself. She'd spent £5,000 of his money on a boob job that had gone so badly wrong that initially she'd been left with one boob significantly lower than the other. One nipple pointed towards Tokyo and the other towards California. Silicon Valley no doubt. It was the mammary equivalent of being cross-eyed.

I said nothing but quietly formed the opinion that the ship had sailed on that particular insult. She'd obviously had the imbalance corrected at further expense and, without wishing to betray my mate, she looked pretty fantastic now.

Fantastic and deadly too.

That was the point, I suppose. She was looking great and flaunting it. That was part of her revenge. And in the cabana it made him angry to watch her walking around the pool, looking well and spending the money he was giving in child support on bottles of champagne.

She casually talked to men who didn't know who she was, and wouldn't have cared anyway because she looked fine. My mate felt she should have had a government health warning tattooed across her forehead, but he also felt that she had played him and won big. Financially at least.

He felt like the mug that he was.

I wondered if my mate's hatred of her had anything to do with the son he had never seen. That had to hurt?

Alas. The fact that his son was not in his life didn't even

85

register on the scale of grudges. He explained to me that he'd never even seen the boy and felt no emotion as a result. He referred to him as 'the stray'. He laughed and rolled his eyes when he said it.

I suppose my team-mate hadn't committed any capital offence, but the sensation the whole incident left in my mouth felt as if somebody had emptied my bank account, punched me in the stomach, slept with my wife and run off with my kids.

So same kind of upshot, really. The whole thing left a bad taste. People want our shit and in the village of football we worry too much about that sometimes and not enough at other times.

Probably we are what you believe us to be.

Anyway, it was the beginning of the end of Marbella for me. I got out ahead of the posse.

My other mates at least had company in their misery. It was alleged that the value of McIndoe's scheme had peaked at £30 million. He ended up £3 million in debt but the evidence suggests that he had a very good time getting there.

Of course, if you are a footballer doing a career-long tour of the backwaters and suddenly you have transformed yourself into the top investment guru in the game, then you are going to live with discretion and class, aren't you?

Not a fucking chance. McIndoe went to Marbella. He did Marbs. Big style. He hired a £27,000-a-week mansion. He lashed out £40,000 on champagne at a single beach party. He had the best and biggest entourage of hangers-on and freeloading friends that money could buy. Bigger even than Raheem Sterling's.

These numbers weren't exceptional to other footballers but generally we were using our own money and not somebody else's.

And of course he moved to London. A £4,000-per-week pad in the Mayfair Hotel. Parties, big lavish affairs in the Funky Buddha club, where fools used to go to be treated like shit. He was reported to have rented an apartment in Belgravia for 150K a year and to have run up gambling debts of almost a million in a single year with just one bookie.

And this was the guy other players were handing over their own money to for him to gamble with.

Nobody knows exactly how many players handed over cash. They have found in America that former sportspeople will do almost anything to avoid the public humiliation of declaring bankruptcy. It's the same with having made bad investments. Players really don't want other people to know.

Jimmy Bullard lost 600K. He launched his financial recovery by doing *I'm a Celebrity, Get Me Out of Here*. A lot of other guys, as many as a hundred or so (there were non-footballing investors too, of course), just hoped that somehow they would get their money back, even as McIndoe floated through the bankruptcy courts.

We know that at least five Wolves players lost £2.6 million between them. At one stage a consortium (of course) of players chipped in and handed over a single payment of £1 million. The money dried up in the season that Wolves got relegated from the Premier League. You can imagine the stress levels in that dressing room.

No more Marbella. Skegness-on-Sea for holidays now.

87

But Marbella was suddenly too close and too cheap and too crowded. It was full of what you would now pay to avoid. It had morphed into the Costa del Crime, packed with East End gangsters and Eastern European mafia. Decent people went there for the cheap flights, the hot sun and the chance to eat in places with helpful pictures of the food on the menu and a reluctance to take credit cards. Money still flowed through the place like an underground river, but now it was laundering itself as it went. The Spanish were pretty much victims themselves by then. They'd bought into the scheme, built the hotels and clubs and Golden Miles, and now they couldn't afford to get out of it, so they turned a blind eye and pretended to themselves that nothing was happening.

The last news we heard of Michael McIndoe was that he was being represented by Rollingsons Solicitors ahead of one of his long line of bankruptcy hearings. That's top-line defence for a man who claimed to have lost everything himself. The players who lost so much money when McIndoe's scheme collapsed back in 2011 all scratched their heads and wished they could be broke enough to have Rollingsons represent them too.

McIndoe was declared bankrupt in October 2014. He had told a previous bankruptcy hearing that he had no money and no bank accounts. He was said to be living in Spain.

A lot of people secretly hope that he runs into Miss Shit Tits. They deserve each other. But nobody will be going to Marbella to find out what happens if they do hook up.

The circus has moved on.

PART THREE

Soccerball and Seoul

6

Before we get back to the unsupervised stuff, we should take a little diversion from the post-season pool parties – more of those later – and discuss a couple of pre-season tours. These are like school trips. The teachers come along to mind us. With thirty professional footballers to supervise, it's the equivalent of minding mice at a crossroads.

The first trip takes place in a city in America. I could probably tell you which city it was, but that would give the wrong impression. You would think that we saw something of that city. You would say, 'Oh, I wonder if they went to such-and-such a spot.' You would view it all through the lens of your knowledge of that city. Maybe you would feel sorry for the place.

No, we didn't see such-and-such. And you don't need to know where we were when we didn't see it.

The second trip is to Seoul. Culturally we absorbed two things. One, they do eat dogs. Two, a lot of drink. We absorbed a lot of drink. We did in the US of A too, so let's go there first.

In football we call a tour that turns into carnage a stag do. When the ex-players of this particular club get together now, as we do from time to time, we call that great three-week tour of the land of the free the best stag do ever.

That summer was chaos at our club. The former owner was being hunted down by law enforcement around the globe for tax dodging, embezzlement and a charge sheet of other financial crimes that could jam a woodchipper. They got him. He's still in prison now. Unfortunately, during his year on the run he seemed to have managed to get word to a clone who picked up right where he had left off in terms of running the club.

Our squad had some issues which made debauchery a bit of a foregone conclusion. Firstly, almost every player was over the hill and a millionaire to boot. Secondly, our manager wasn't a millionaire but he was envious of the players who were. He decided to use humour as a cantilever to bridge the gap at certain inopportune moments. Moments like those quiet ones in the changing room just before a match. We were never inclined to build our own cantilever. As the Americans might say, he reached out. We didn't. That's where his problems began. He over-reached out.

He missed being a player. He resented not being as wealthy as the players, and he desperately wanted to be loved. Think David Brent. When we didn't respond to his advances, he blew up. The problem was that nobody bought it, because two minutes earlier he'd been laughing and joking with us as if he were still a player.

Football lesson for you: keep your distance! It's on page one of the manager's guide to winning over players and doing well in the game. Just in case you decide to go into management in the Premier League some day: you are NOT a player any more. You are a manager.

Be prepared to be respected because you are feared and selfish. Don't intrude on the team space with your version of the Muppets' song. All of the successful managers in world football go by that rule. There is no other way to be successful.

If, though, you go down the road our manager went down, then one thing will certainly happen to you. Well, two things. You'll lose your job. That's the second thing, and it puts you out of your suffering. The first thing is the catalyst, the pain that is a symptom of something terminal. The first thing is that you will have your pants pulled down by the squad and a big smiley clown face drawn on your arse. You will be pushed into the centre circle by the players as a full house watches you and the lights man trains the floodlights on your modesty.

Give the squad an inch and generally they will take the city. Who told you it was a gentleman's game?

Ahhh, America. Land of the free. Home of the simple. And when the land of the free opens its arms to the deep pockets of the footballer, things can get interesting.

Tours are paid for by sponsors, so flights are generally pretty painless. Business-class seats come as standard, but some top Premier League teams even have planes chartered for them to Asia or the US with nobody else on board. First class all the way. In the old days, the media would supplement the cost of the flights by sending hacks on board to conduct interviews. (You've seen *Snakes on a Plane*? Yeah?) These days Chevrolet and Samsung simply pay outright for the cost of everything. Bless them.

So there we were, a bunch of losers, in business class with

real business people looking at our tracksuits. They were appalled. They'd worked out that we were a football team of some kind and they were calling their PAs back in the office to tell them to start looking for new employment asap. There is a fucking football team on this flight. Oiks in tracksuits. It's going to be hellish. You should have known. *Always* ask if there will be football types on the plane. This is a disaster, worse than travelling with a crèche of newborns with colic.

Wrong. Wrong. Wrong. Maybe you think we have the intellects of babies, but we sleep like them too. If you see a football team board your plane in pre-season, then you can be absolutely assured of your bliss and serenity. We are banned from drinking. We only watch movies with our headphones on. We don't talk to each other and most of us will sleep for a good few hours because we trained that morning or have training that afternoon. Plus there are thirty athletes on board who want their privacy respected. The only thing you might find odd is that every now and again we'll get up to stretch our hamstrings over the seat. Apart from that, you'll have no trouble here, my friends.

At the time of our landing in Ronald McDonald's back yard, the football landscape of the US wasn't filled with top foreign players like Frank Lampard stuffing their suitcases with dollar bills. Football had arrived, of course, but Major League Soccer was largely populated with whitey natives and a sprinkling of Central and South Americans. The Europeans were still weighing up their options – or waiting till the pay cheques got bigger.

We didn't have time for any of that.

94

'Where's the bang house?'

OK, it wasn't the pilgrims stepping off the *Mayflower* at Plymouth Rock, but it was the first line uttered by any of our party to a local.

The bang house question was asked by one of our midfielders who had a keen interest in getting out and exploring our hapless host city. It was directed to the hotel receptionist. She looked like she was going to cry. She could tell he was asking for the whereabouts of the nearest brothel. But why was he asking her?

In order to give ourselves the best chance of winning our matches and getting fit at the same time, our manager had decided to give us two days of acclimatization. It was a mistake on a par with the city of Troy believing that the lovely wooden horse on the other side of the gates would actually make rather a nice centrepiece, back in the days when Greeks could afford to give gifts.

We strolled out into the night, and I'm pretty sure a few of us never came back. The local bars were rammed with people, and our leaders – the guys who orchestrate – were cutting through the shit and getting to the grit by talking to bouncers, door girls, punters, barmen and so on. All the time working out where to hold a night out.

It turned out there was a suitable place for such a soirée. Right smack bang in the middle of what appeared to be the busiest street in all of North America. It had a roof garden, and below that a nightclub, and below that a private bar with jacuzzis, and below that a lively Irish bar. You could rent the whole place for $10,000 a night, including staff.

We'll take it for tomorrow, my good man. See you at nine p.m. Done deal. Simple as that.

Myself and a small group of team-mates had a few drinks in a pretty cool bar down the street. Most of us were jet-lagged anyway and I was in that space where sleeping actually sounded and felt better than the best hit of heroin anybody has ever shot up their arm.

I headed back to the hotel and to bed. The next thing I knew my phone was going mad. I answered it and a hushed voice came cackling down the phone.

'Mate, where am I?' said the guy on the other end.

'Where are you? *Who* are you, ya prick?'

'It's me, Jimmy, ya knob. I went back with some girl, fell asleep in the cab and just woke up in her apartment. I don't know where the fuck I am.'

Now this was like when Mrs TSF calls me from the car while I'm on the other side of the world to tell me she's lost. It's really difficult to know what to say other than, 'What the fuck do you expect me to do about it?'

The first rule of not knowing how to help as a man: stall them with a classic move that will have no bearing on the outcome.

'Look out the window.'

'OK.'

'What can you see?'

'Your mum.'

'Do you wanna fucking get back or not?'

'OK, OK. There's a pool, and I think a little bar across the street, and what's that? I think it's a petrol station with a massive sign outside. The sign is a big doughnut. And there's a car wash next to it.'

'Jimmy, go back to bed.'

'Why?'

'You're in our fucking hotel, ya twat.'

The following day was really hot. *Really* hot. At least 38°C. Everybody was downstairs in their swimming trunks instructing the hotel staff to drive our two coaches to the beach.

'Hold on, hold on,' said Jimmy as he took a handful of paper from the receptionist. He'd photocopied the address of the place we were renting that night and wanted to hand out copies to girls on the beach. Simple but effective. Very effective, actually.

The rest of America had had the same idea as us and the roads to the seaside were gridlocked. No problem. We climbed out with our water bottles on to the roof of the buses that were inching along at half a mile an hour and proceeded to spray the other four lanes of tinned sardines from twenty feet up. It was great. Everybody began to get out of their cars and a massive water fight broke out on the highway.

Then it got a bit mad. Some of the lads climbed down and began sliding across the bonnets of convertible cars or, in one case, into an open window, past the occupants and out of another open window. People were climbing into our bus in a clever countermovement. By the time we arrived at the beach, we must have had fifty Americans on board with us asking who the hell we were and what we were up to. I must say that the Americans took it really well. I've seen that sort of shit go spectacularly wrong before. It's not an autobahn sort of thing, for instance.

97

Once on the beach we set up camp. A big camp. Right in the middle. It was packed. Along the beachfront were rows of restaurants and rows of people ready to fill them. The sea was cool and blue and the sand was warm. Good warm.

Jimmy, our hype man, set to work handing out these little bits of paper to girls who were walking around or sitting in little sun-kissed groups. Actually he told the two youth team players we'd taken with us to do it, but it's the same thing. Delegation is the key to good management, Jimmy feels.

Youth team players get all the worst jobs. It's a steep learning curve. Oh, you're a bit shy? Tough shit, mate, hand all these out to the best girls you can find right now. I know it sounds like bullying, but I can reel off the names of countless young footballers in the Premier League today who I once played with and I can look back at episodes exactly like that one and say, yep, that was the making of them. That was the day when they came out of their shell. That was when that kid became a man.

A couple of our players were fairly handy at gymnastics. (Stay with me.) We'd witnessed it when they'd scored the occasional goal. Backflips and front flips. The soft sand brought out the gymnast in them and soon everybody was learning how to do backflips. I learned too. I can still do it, as it happens, and I was taught right on that beach not too long ago by a very agile African footballer.

Bizarrely, a group of real gymnasts were already on the beach; four black guys from some university on the other side of the country who competed at college level but who were now on their break. They were amazing. They began tumbling down the beach and performing twists and somersaults. It was brilliant. I've never seen anything like it.

Before long a small crowd had gathered. Then another crowd, until it was just one heaving mass of people. Somebody had a big music system with a local radio station banging out tunes, and the place went off. This was just an ordinary beach in the middle of the day, and it stayed that way until the sun went down. It just goes to show you don't always have to be pissed up to have a good time.

A helicopter flew overhead. It was pretty low and I assumed it was something that you could hire and go up and down the beach in the same way that you can go up and down the Strip in Vegas.

Then the craziest thing happened. The music stopped. Or was interrupted at least.

'This is W-R-A-T and the eye in the sky over Sandy Beach at the bottom of Sixth and Third. As all you sporting fans know, we've got a UK soccer team in the city as part of the South by South West tour and it looks as if today they are out and about on our very own stretch of golden sands right here on the East Side. If you're able to do so, put down your pens, put away your computers, get your bathing costumes on and head on down to the beach right now because this is the place to be.'

All hell broke loose.

The cheers and screams that went up around the beach were hedonistic, and within about half an hour the place was even more crowded. There wasn't a shred of trouble. Not one shred. Just hundreds of people getting to know each other and the police struggling to contain the flow of traffic and setting up road measures in order to filter everybody in.

99

Word started to get around that there was a party happening that very night. It spread beyond the borders of the lucky people who had received the scraps of photocopied paper with the venue's address on. Regulation and control were needed.

'Don't worry,' said Jimmy, 'we'll just let the girls in.'

Ah, problem solved then, Jimmy. Why didn't I think of that? Because I'm not CEO of Stag Do Inc., that's why.

We finished up at the beach and left to head back to the hotel for the mandatory team meal. Team meals are always mandatory. You don't eat as a family together at home but a team is a team. It eats together. Capeesh?

Dinner didn't touch the sides. All of the focus was on getting ready and getting down to the place we'd rented in town. We were as giddy as debutantes.

It's worth noting here that the level of attention that goes into clothing, hair and general appearance where the most seasoned players are concerned is a thing of wonder. They don't care about taking a shit with the door open in the changing rooms or masturbating in the hot tub in the physio room – both keen pursuits at this particular club – but when it comes down to whether or not some random girl will see them after seven p.m. then it's a whole different scenario. The Sistine Chapel got done up in quicker time than most footballers can manage to get ready to go out. I'm fortunate in that my natural looks just can't be improved on.

We made our way back on to the cobbled streets of the city and the vibe was good. Jimmy led the way. He was good like that. Where other people sensed danger, Jimmy sensed good times. It is a rare and extraordinary talent. If he'd ever once

100

stopped to consider bottling it, he could have been a multi-millionaire instead of the bankrupt ex-footballer he is today.

We wandered into our new home ground to get warmed up. One of my team-mates made it his business to fill up the hot tubs. The water came out of a hole in the ceiling. It took for ever to run. Really, ten grand doesn't get an awful lot these days!

Another player introduced himself to all the bar staff and told them where they were going to be standing. It was impressive to watch. It was like my team-mates had been here before. They hadn't, of course. They just knew how to do this sort of stuff.

I did nothing. Didn't know how to. Didn't have the faintest idea what to say or do about any of it. Complete passenger.

A few of my other team-mates went to the nightclub section and told the DJ what sort of music we were after. He nailed it. Absolutely nailed it. A few more of us went up to the roof garden for a cigar. I don't smoke cigars, but I do like being in the company of men smoking cigars. Don't know why. Maybe a glass of brandy. It seems grown-up for a moment.

A few girls wandered in with bits of paper in their hands.

'Oh, wow, so it's you guys, huh?'

They seemed to be impressed. This was good. I had a Corona to celebrate and did my usual trick of hiding from them in case they asked me awkward questions, like what my name was or how I liked their city or what my favourite colour was.

Then it got really busy. Girls were turning up from all over the place. Most had been on the beach that day, and I recognized a few but not many. It was an endless stream. The guys manning the doors had to put queues in place outside. If we had charged, we'd have made a fortune. Damn.

Suddenly the doorman ran in. 'You guys better come outside,' he said.

We went.

It would not have been possible to fit another person on to the street. It was a seething mass of humanity; there were hundreds, maybe even a thousand people, and more arriving all the time. The doorman told us that he'd had no choice but to call the police to sort it out.

'What the hell did you guys say to people on that beach earlier?' he asked.

Just then, one of the cigar smokers came running down and said that we had to come upstairs to the roof garden. Yeah, it's fucking brilliant, there's a helicopter shining a spotlight at the rooftop, so the lads were taking it in turns to have a dance-off while being lit up like Christmas trees.

Clearly the police had arrived from all angles.

When the officers on foot made their way through the crowd and through the front doors and asked who was in charge, I volunteered Jimmy's name.

And Jimmy handled it.

'So you guys having a party, huh?'

(No mate, we're just renting a DVD for the night.)

'OK, and you're from where? And you've paid for the venue, is that correct, sir? Nobody seems to be intoxicated. And are the men somewhere else, maybe with your friend there on the roof garden?'

'No, this is pretty much all of us. Well, a couple might be in the bathroom.'

'So all these women are with you, is that right? You're

not expecting any more men to come down here tonight?'

'Uhh . . . no.'

'OK, well we've got to get that street cleared. It's overcrowded as it is. But maybe I'll stop by later to make sure everything is OK. Sir, you have a good night.'

And he bloody did. Finished his shift. Went home. Got his mates. And came back and partied. He even brought some beer despite the fact that we had enough beer to fill Lake Michigan.

As soon as the officer left to clear the street, Jimmy told the doorman to let in as many of the queuing girls as possible. Which he did with aplomb. Jimmy isn't just a fine businessman. He's a top humanitarian too. No chick left behind.

The cops cleared the street and inside everything was going well until I found myself standing too close to the women's bathroom. While completely off guard, I got bundled into the bathroom by a team-mate who had seen a young lady wander in. After shutting the door he kept his hand on the handle. Fortunately she found it quite funny, and realized that I wasn't behind the stunt. My rosy red cheeks were the giveaway.

'I'll turn around,' I said.

'Oh, you don't have to,' she replied. 'I'm just powdering my nose. Actually I was hoping to talk to you. I saw you pretend to give your team-mate a cuddle while wiping all that lime from your drink down his back.'

'Oh, you saw that, did you?'

'Yep. I thought it was hilarious.'

'OK.'

Her name turned out to be Kaley. I still know Kaley to this day. She's one of my best friends.

But at the time I didn't know things would pan out that way. I just thought that I'd really like to see her naked. Especially as we were locked in a bathroom together. She was attractive in a girl-next-door kind of way. Huge brown eyes and a wicked smile. Instead, I asked her how she'd known we were here. Did she have one of the sheets of paper?

No, she'd only finished work at 5.30 and hadn't had time to go to the beach.

Sooooooo?

'The radio are putting out announcements, every half hour or so maybe. Everybody in the city knows you're here, hun. Jeez, the radio even sent their helicopter to point a spotlight at the building so people know where to head to. So, who the hell are you guys anyway?'

Two mornings later, after finding my way back from Kaley's apartment, where I had slept very uncomfortably on her couch with some sort of animal, I trudged along the hotel corridor looking for food. A door to one of the rooms that lined the corridor on either side opened and a head popped out.

It was Jimmy.

'Mate, can you take Crystal out the front of the hotel for me?'

'Why me?'

'Because nobody will think . . . you know . . . they'll reckon you was talking to her about space or history or something.'

'Fuck off!'

'Please! Do me a favour. If they see her with me, I'll be fucked. You can talk your way out of it. You're smart. Please! For me. I'll time you. Go!'

Fuck sake. Crystal, is it? Come on then.

And off we walked down the corridor, her in the middle and me scraping my face along the wall, pretending that I didn't know her.

I rapidly tapped the button on the elevator a dozen times until it arrived. The doors opened, but just as they were closing behind us an arm shot out and stopped them. The doors slowly reversed and in walked our new chairman, who had flown in that morning.

He had just taken over the club and very little was known about him, other than that he seemed to dress pretty ostentatiously. In a Derek-Trotter-becomes-an-oligarch kind of way.

The lift was not big and rich people do not do the decent thing and share space equally with others. Instead they stand in the middle and make everyone else accommodate them. So we were close.

He looked at me and looked away just as quickly. I couldn't move in any direction, so I leaned away from Crystal instead, which looked odd, but I styled it out by feigning a back stretch.

He looked at Crystal and in a thick foreign accent said, 'Hello there.'

OK. I'm in a club tracksuit and he's just bought the club. I'm one of his own players that he hasn't met yet. Own player. Random girl. Own player. Random girl.

'Hello,' said Crystal.

Well, at least we knew what sort of person our new chairman was.

He turned to look at me again.

No! Don't even think it. No, no, no. Nothing to do with me. Don't give me that look. Is this lift slow today or is it warm in here?

He continued to stare at me. I was later told that where he was from, it was customary for mortals to introduce themselves to God. Not the other way around. But I didn't know that at the time.

I can remember once being trapped in the physio room with one of my old chairmen, who was waiting for the physio to turn up and give him a calf massage. I was strapped up to a machine to reduce swelling in my thigh on the bed next to him.

He had a big wine collection.

I had a big wine collection.

I said to him, 'I hear you have a big wine collection.'

He said, 'Nope.'

Gotcha.

Owners can be funny towards players. They can one-up everything a player has. They are among the few people in football who can do that and they bloody well know it too.

You're a player. I'm the owner. That is all the relationship will ever be. You want to talk about wine? Go down to Oddbins.

The lift continued descending and the silence was getting painful. Moreover, I didn't know this Crystal girl and she didn't realize that this was our new chairman. She could have said anything at that moment. Anything.

I had to break the silence and start a conversation so that she wouldn't.

Think.

Think.

Think.

'Soooo . . . did you . . . do you . . . think that . . .'

BING!

Oh, thank Christ.

The lift doors opened and we allowed the chairman to get out first. You do that as a player. It is a sign of respect in a world where very little respect is afforded to anyone. It also gets you nowhere. We may as well refer to it now as a tradition, such is its pointlessness.

I scoured the lobby. It was clear. Surprisingly. I put my head down and performed a walk not too dissimilar to the gait used in those walking races that you see in the Olympics, dragging Crystal's slender body behind me. It must have looked like I was a spoilt grown-up brat who had just been told he couldn't have a treat and was now dragging a blonde dolly in a huff to the next room for a good sulk.

Wrong. I'm a footballer. Different thing altogether.

Our little dance caught the eye of the receptionist. 'Ah, just the person,' she said. 'Can you take a look at this room service bill please, sir?'

'Yeah, that's definitely a room service bill. I'll talk to you later. Thanks then!'

Crystal and I shot through the sliding automatic doors and outside. We were almost free.

'Soooooo . . . I need some money for a cab,' she said.

Didn't he give you any? No, he didn't. Of course he didn't.

'OK, here – what are these ones? Why does all your money look the same? How much is that?'

'That's about three dollars.'

107

'Well, how far are you going?'

'As far as you like, honey.'

'No, I mean . . . fuck sake . . . here you go. Is that enough?'

It was enough. It was everything I had on me, which was about $150.

She leaned in and kissed me on the cheek. 'You're much nicer than your friend up there.'

You fucking got that right.

'OH YEAH???' came a shout from behind us.

Disaster.

Half a dozen of our most 'loyal' fans, smoking off to the left behind the palm trees. I hadn't seen them. They'd seen everything. They'd seen me giving a blonde girl $150 and they'd seen her kiss me on the cheek.

Now, just to set the scene. The day before, I and a team-mate who was a legend at the football club, having been there for some years and achieved significant success along the way, were out in a bar when we should have been resting in our bedrooms. We weren't getting pissed up; we had decided that the hotel food was horrific and that we were going to the rib shack over the road to get a steak. And a beer. Maybe two beers.

Our 'loyal' fans, who had flown out to watch the tour, were staying in our hotel. They knew when we were supposed to be training, playing and resting. They knew when we were supposed to be doing something and when we weren't.

My team-mate and I sat there drinking Samuel Adams and eating steaks from cows that had to have been fifty feet tall when they roamed the prairies. Then the door swung open. In walked half a dozen of our fans. They clocked us and they knew

108

that we weren't supposed to be there. They're a bit maternal that way.

Now we have a problem. The fans have taken back control of the game. They're holding the ball and the power has gone to their heads. You can see it rising from their stomach to the cortex and swishing around their eye sockets until their heads spin around. Power.

We did the only thing we could have done in that situation. We bought them each a beer and a Jägermeister with Red Bull. Then another round. We even struck up a conversation. Players hate doing this with fans. The common ground for both sides is the football club, but generally fans ask stupid questions that place players in an awkward position, like 'Why is the manager playing X?' That's one of our team-mates you're talking about, you dozy prick. And we take that as a sign that you don't know anything about football. It's uncomfortable all round.

However, we persevere, and before long we're actually laughing with them. Mostly about Americans and their culture and the strip club that they had been to the night before.

Then, BANG! The door swings open again. One of our coaches looks at us and curls his finger. 'You two, come with me.' It's like the sheriff has walked into the saloon bar in Dodge and found two of the baddest hombres in the West.

Now this sheriff was actually a good guy. He was a coach because he was soft. He'd never be management material. He didn't yell or bark, but he had to look authoritative at that point. Not in front of us, you understand. In front of the fans.

We got outside and began walking back over the road to the hotel.

'How did you know we were there?' I asked.

'You know that fan with the odd clothes and the tattoos?' said the coach.

'Yeah.'

'He slipped out while you were ordering them beers and called the hotel and told them to tell the gaffer that you two were in there.'

Motherfucker. Horrible, horrible, busy, pathetic mother-fucker.

And people wonder why footballers don't want anything to do with fans.

You know what saved us? We weren't getting pissed up. We were just having a couple of beers and a steak. And even that was too much for some people to swallow.

So I was nervous when I turned to walk back into the hotel after booting Crystal into the back of a cab.

'And what were you two whispering about?' asked one of the fans.

'Nothing much,' I replied.

'Didn't look like nothing to me,' said another, stubbing his cigarette out on the floor.

'Well, it was something,' I said. 'Actually, it was something really fucking big.'

'Yeah? What was it?'

'OK, come over here then. I don't want anybody else to hear it because it's pretty huge. Mega actually. Almost too big to think about.'

They came over, salivating, leaning in with their tongues out.

'We were talking about space.'

*

Two days later, Mrs TSF called. 'Apparently you're talking to strange girls outside hotels?'

Fans are like the fucking Stasi.

It had been all over the internet back home. Those same fans that grassed up my team-mate and me in the bar to our manager had put out this crap as a pathetic tour diary entry for a strand on the fans' forum that they had set up for equally pathetic losers to read back home.

Mrs TSF doesn't read such drivel. She has always known better than to look at fans' forums. But she does have a couple of busy mates who are envious of her escape from the shithole of a village where she grew up, and who make it their lives' work to undermine her happiness at every opportunity. Her phone had rung the second her husband's name had appeared on the forum. Talking to a girl outside a hotel in America, eh? It's pathetic. The jealousy Mrs TSF has had to put up with over the years is pathetic. But it does flush out your real friends. I'll say that about jealousy.

She knows me, does Mrs TSF. Even better than that, she knows the player who asked me to lead Crystal out of the hotel for him. So when I explained what had happened, my words were earnest and unfaltering. And my team-mate's reputation with the women was so legendary that it was obviously true. Jimmy was a cross between late-period Casanova and the Artful Dodger.

'One thing then,' said Mrs TSF. 'Why did you give her a load of money if she was his problem?'

'Doesn't matter,' I said. 'Water under the bridge, my darling.'

111

*

The tour continued. The football was abysmal. We were shit, the teams we were playing were shit. The highlight was watching alligators trying to eat footballs that had been ballooned into their pond behind one of the training goals. We entertained ourselves with alligator jokes. Bring me a gator sandwich and make it snappy. What do we do if he chokes on the football? Give him Gatorade.

On the first day one of our coaches had tried to fish one out with a long pole. (A ball, not an alligator.) One of the receptionists from the sports hall where we were training came sprinting out to ask if he was fucking crazy.

But he wasn't the only stupid one. Oh no. I give you . . . me.

I hate golf. But I hate being bored even more than I hate golf. So when three of the lads asked if I wanted to play golf with them at some flashy club, in the absence of anything else to do, instead of telling them I'd rather lick my own arsehole I said I'd be absolutely thrilled to join them.

We turned up, and actually the place wasn't too poncey. Maybe it was because we each had to spend $500 buying the correct attire and another $300 each to hire the clubs. Anyway, it was something to do. We hired two buggies and headed out. The refreshment buggy was prompt and indeed full of refreshment. The ice-cold Budweiser in aluminium bottles was a treat none of us had seen before.

Now there is a rule in football. If somebody hits the deck in training and stays there, then the next person the ball comes to is perfectly entitled to have one free shot at that player. Not stupidly hard. Not at the face. Just hard enough and with the

112

right levels of condescension in the accompanying banter soundtrack.

In the warm-up before a match the previous season I had gone to ground. I'd turned around just in time to see Jimmy shouting 'Whhheeeehhheeeyyyy!' while hitting a solid side-foot at me. Most of the players take their opportunity with a side-foot, because just in case the player on the ground does get the arse, it can always be said that you're a pussy, it was only a side-foot.

The fact is, most professional footballers can hit a side-foot harder than you guys can hit a ball off the front of your foot. So as I tried to clamber back on to all fours, the ball is upon me. It hits my thumb plumb on the top and dislocates it. The physio puts it back in with me holding back tears – it is as painful as people say – and since then I've been able to get to about nine holes on a golf course before the thing starts to pop out again.

So I'm drinking and driving the golf cart instead, to preserve the life of my favourite thumb. And as I drink, the pain wears off just as we come to a beautiful and, importantly, dead-straight par five. I can't resist.

Now, unlike a lot of footballers I'm shit at golf. My coordination stops at football. I can't dance, can't play tennis, can't play golf. But I hit a glorious drive down this particular par five. Then I hit a magnificent second shot, like an arrow. It flew over the hump towards the top of the flag, and I was thinking it had to be on the dancefloor, sat just under the flag, awaiting my permission for it to throw itself into the hole.

We walked over the hump and there was no ball. The green backed on to a vast lake. Was that lake always there? I did

113

the man-jog that you do when you've forgotten where you've parked your car. This can't be happening; somebody get God on the phone, quick!

And there it was. Right on the lip of the green, with ten million cubic tonnes of H_2O about a millimetre behind it.

I couldn't leave it there. If I sank this, it'd be an eagle, and apparently that's really good. So I took my right shoe off, and my right sock off, and I plonked my foot into the lake while working out where best to chip this ball to, for what would surely be one of the most memorable moments in the history of golf.

'WHAT THE FUCK IS THAT?'

On my life, as I sit here today typing these words, there was a fucking great alligator about to take a keen interest in my right leg. And by great, I mean gi-fucking-normous. Its eyes were above the water, floating right towards me. It was only about two metres away when my team-mate spotted it.

It is no exaggeration to say that I shat myself. I leapt in the air and ran all at the same time, like a cartoon character. Except in the cartoons they don't shit themselves.

It was frightening. With a sharp swish of its tail, the beast slunk back to the middle of the lake, where it stayed, probably laughing to itself underwater.

Of all the stupid things that come in and out of my top five stupid things of all time, that one has remained a constant chart-topper.

I really liked that group of players, but we were so bad on the pitch. We had so many things going against us – some of them our own fault, some of them external matters we couldn't control – that we were never going to achieve anything impressive on a Saturday at three p.m.

By the time the end of the tour came around, I think most of us were ready to go home; it had been day upon day of going out, running, training, playing, repeat. It was tough. We had played hard and burned the candle at both ends. And because of that we had become losers as mates, if not as a team.

At the airport our flight was delayed by an hour. Then another hour. Then another hour. It was painful. You know what it's like. Finally, we got on board. At least we had business-class seats and could sleep.

We settled into our seats. Champagne, sir? Couldn't possibly, I'm afraid.

And then . . . BANG!

We never found out exactly what it was or who it was. Just that one of the ancillary vehicles that dart around a plane as it's loading up people and baggage had managed to hit the plane. How the fuck you drive smack bang into a bastard great plane in broad daylight is beyond me, but there you are.

So we got off and waited in the lobby for an announcement for another three hours.

This was around the time of the planking craze and we passed the time by taking it in turns to plank the escalator handrails from top to bottom. It was funnier than it sounds. Then we had a dance-off. Or rather, we made the youth team players have a dance-off. That was amusing, because many of the other delayed passengers gathered round in a big circle to clap along.

Then it flashed up. CANCELLED. Now that puts thirty players and ten staff in a bind. How do you get forty blokes into a hotel room, and who's paying?

There's no punchline by the way.

The UK is asleep. The chairman has flown back to his native Diarrhoeastan on 'business'. There are no more flights to the UK until at least noon the following day.

Hobson's Choice. Except here there is no choice as such. We're either fucked or we're fucked.

And then we were saved.

In order to avoid bad publicity, the airline sent a representative to talk to our manager, who advised him that a five-star hotel not too far away from the airport would be laid on provided we got on a bus that was waiting outside and didn't mention it to any of the other passengers.

We did as we were told and arrived at what was a very acceptable hotel some thirty minutes later. I mean, it was a business hotel for business people on business. But it was very acceptable.

The manager told us that because we didn't know what was going on with the flight, we could have a night out. Ordinarily that would have been music to our ears, but the day had been exhausting and everybody just wanted to go home.

We sloped off to our bedrooms in pairs. I was sharing with Jimmy. The rooms were clean and fresh; the beds looked inviting. Jimmy threw his bag down, walked to the window and pulled back the curtains. It was dusk and neon lights were bursting into life ten storeys below us.

'We're in America, mate.' Just in case you're wondering where you are.

'Jesus, I'm fucking knackered,' I said.

'Look at all those signs down there,' said Jimmy. 'We could go for a quick beer, couldn't we? We've never been here before.'

'Not me, mate,' I said. 'I'm absolutely knackered.'

'Look at that,' Jimmy continued. 'McDonald's, Dunkin' Donuts. God, those Dunkin' Donuts are everywhere, aren't they?'

'The last thing I want is food,' I said. 'I just want to sleep.'

'Cheers Bar. Ha! They've got a Cheers Bar here, like from the TV! And what's that one? H-O-O-T-E . . . Hooters!'

'Come on then, just a swift one, get your shoes back on, it's already ten p.m., where's the fucking room key? Hurry up.'

Hooters was of course suitably disappointing. But we enjoyed a few beers none the less, and talked about life and our plans for world peace. Over breakfast the next morning I remember telling two of the Hooters barmaids that we were booked on a plane back to the UK that afternoon and they lamented the fact that we wouldn't be able to go skydiving with them like we'd promised the night before.

Some things are unavoidable.

At the airport there was a bombshell. If that's the right word. The air hostess at check-in informed us that our seats were no longer business but economy. Business was full. However, there were six first-class seats. The management duly took four and donated two to the players.

We were all set to vote in democratically elected representatives when a player who had been at the club longer than time had existed launched an impassioned plea.

117

'You're always telling me what a legend I am – now is the time to respect the legend!'

Everybody laughed, and he got one of the first-class seats.

I put forward Jimmy for the other seat because of his sterling efforts off the pitch in the US. Everybody agreed. It was a landslide.

And what did Jimmy do? He gave it to a youth team player an hour after take-off, as a reward for handing out the fliers on the beach to the girls that came to the party.

We secured relegation the following season with consummate ease, but many of the problems for those players were just beginning. It was the beginning of the end for most of us. And we would never have it that good as footballers again.

I hated that club. No, that's not quite right. I hate that club.

But I loved those guys. No, that's not quite right either. I love those guys.

7

Parts of Asia are odd. The other parts I haven't been to yet, but I'm betting they are odd too. Our humble club was invited to take part in a tournament in that part of the world. That was odd in itself, but we headed off courageously.

It was South Korea, for those of you studying Asian geography, demographics and affiliated culture. Now, pay attention. You just may learn something that isn't in your $100 textbook.

The oddest thing about these countries from the footballer's viewpoint is that they don't even know they are odd. The British Empire never got to South Korea and you can see how they lost out. No Wetherspoons. No Dixons. No pound shops. No Argos. No Boris Johnson. Our hearts went out to them.

We had an Asian player in the squad. We had never really considered his Asian-ness until we got there and found that he was the leader of a mass movement. There were Asian people everywhere and they seemed to worship him. He was actually the reason for us being invited to compete in South Korea to begin with, such was his fame there. The rest of us found that just a little bit crushing.

What's more, we were competing in a tournament with a collection of seriously heavyweight clubs drawn from all corners of the globe. They told us the globe had corners even though it was obviously round like a football. But we were footballers and we saw no reason to argue, other than to bicker about who among us was best at taking corners.

The other teams all had great pedigree in their respective countries and came to South Korea boasting names that you might have conjured with when playing *Championship Manager* at three in the morning, you sad bastard. Let's just say they were seasoned pros. A couple of them actually stood out to the point that when we got home, we tabled a £5.5 million offer for a holding midfielder from a South American team. Let me blow my own trumpet here and invite my Big Band to back me up. We tabled the bid because I waxed prosaic about the midfielder to our scout. The scout watched the video back and then went and convinced the manager to go for him.

Yes. You can have that kind of power as a player at certain moments. It's a nice thing. Just don't let it go to your head. You know how Sir Alex Ferguson was persuaded to buy Cristiano Ronaldo by Roy Keane after United played against Sporting Lisbon? See where this is going? See what I am saying? Fine.

Back in Blighty, our physio had given us a pep talk before we headed off into the unknown. 'Lads, it will be bloody humid, and you'll be properly jet-lagged. I've got some sleeping tablets here. Any questions?'

Five seconds, ten seconds. Finally a question from an Irish lad at the back: 'They won't make you drowsy, will they?'

Jesus fucking Christ, have a day off . . . You couldn't be any drowsier, mate.

Tragically (and I do mean tragically, despite the *Guardian*'s warnings in the 'How To Write Real Proper' section that I should only use the word 'tragically' if somebody has died), I had a deal with multiple airlines which basically allowed me to upgrade to 'the best available seat'. And the best available seats were always in first class. Obviously. It was a dream of a perk given to me by a bank that used to be deeply in love with me. Now they stab me in the back, and when I turn around they stab me in the chest.

The deal was pegged to their credit card, which had a limit of £100,000, reserved for their most beloved clients. And Premier League footballers too, it seemed. The understanding was that when the football ended, if you needed to grovel at the counter, you would be joining the queue with all the other plebs. Always read the small print.

I waved my card at the lady checking in the bags and was informed that there was, happily, one first-class seat remaining. I say seat. I mean modestly sized trailer home. I mean futuristic pod. You people sit in seats. I recline and am fed grapes by nymphs while in my pod.

'I'll take it,' I said, welling up a little.

Now then. We are a team, and when I look back, it was a most stupid, selfish and shitty thing to do. The thing about being in the pointy end of the plane while all your mates are in steerage is that it's only funny to you. In cattle class they don't get the joke. I know that now.

In fact, even in business class they don't get the joke once

121

they realize there is a class above them that they are barred from. And the lads were in business class. Spare them your pity. It's not like thirty of them were being forced to travel to Asia clinging to a log. But they carried on as if they were.

Basically, being in first class made me look like I was Billy Big Bollocks (coincidentally, my pet name for myself), and some of the lads resented that.

Possibly it didn't help that when I peeled off up the tunnel to the left as we were boarding, I waved a cheery '*à bientôt*, chums' to the lads as a harem of lovely stewardesses rushed towards me to see if there was anything I needed.

I was determined to make matters worse during the flight by occasionally nipping downstairs to peek my head through the curtains and smile down at them all, while scrunching my nose and waving my hand in front of my face, as if the stench of poverty wafting towards me was just too much. I would then retreat upstairs to the pampering I deserved and think about some day organizing a charity record for footballers trapped in business class. Bono, I want you to sing the line one more time. Tonight thank God it's them instead of you . . .

Two things got me through those difficulties with my team-mates.

One. The principle of the thing. Air travel is painful and tiring. One gift horse that should never be looked in the mouth is the opportunity to upgrade the seat. Arriving in Asia refreshed, fed and watered is the professional thing to do.

Two. I didn't really give a shit.

When it comes to first-class travel, I am in fact an old-fashioned socialist. I earnestly hope that some day all of the proletariat will travel in first class. Nothing is too good for the workers. Only when that happens will I rest easy in my pod on the floor above business class in the First Class Executive Premium Plus Deluxe Party Member Only cabin.

Anyway, enough of the firebrand politics. I took my place in a row of three spaceship-style capsules laid out on the top deck. This, for you plane nerds, was one of the first A380s, by the way. I reclined and thought fondly of the rest of the squad huddled and seething down in business class. Travel was broadening their minds. They were beginning to understand words like meritocracy and ha ha ha.

I felt quite relaxed. I glanced to my left. Fucking hell. And to my right. Jesus Christ.

I was sandwiched, empodded, trapped, stuck between the manager and the assistant manager. Nice people, I'm sure, but conversationally a rock and a hard place.

We all glanced at each other as if we'd run into each other in a cheap massage parlour. We came to an unspoken understanding that we would never speak of this moment again.

'Hello,' said the manager. 'Didn't expect to see you here.' Master of the understatement, the manager.

Our assistant manager was more withering. He leaned over and whispered, 'What the fuck are you doing here?'

Honesty was the best policy. So I lied.

'They upgraded me, totally out of the blue. What a crazy world we live in, huh? What can I do? Gift horse, mouth . . . and all that.'

Hmm. So. What's your excuse?

As an experience it was more awkward than the time I'd

turned up to do a talk on behalf of the club at the local cancer hospital, with explicit instructions to speak about the benefits of living healthily and exercising regularly. Only to discover that it was a hospice and none of the audience had longer than three months to live.

No wonder they had told me not to go on for too long.

I told my audience a fairly lively story about what certain members of our squad had got up to in Las Vegas instead. It seemed to cheer them up. I offered to come back in four months and tell the story again to a whole new audience.

The seating arrangement totally ruined the flight for everyone. And by everyone I mean me. You don't sit and chat with your manager for eleven minutes if you can help it. Not unless you have something urgent to say, like you want a transfer or you're not happy being on the bench or you killed somebody on Saturday night or you have given his wife herpes.

Eleven hours?

I repeat. Eleven fucking hours.

Not a single word, other than to tell the air hostess for the fifty-fifth time that we wouldn't have a glass of champagne, thank you. Heaven forfend! We're professionals. Take it from our sight, wench. When all any of us wanted to scream was, 'Yes, for the love of all things holy in Reims, we will have the champagne, and leave the fucking bottle too.'

Eleven bastarding bastardly bastardful fucking hours.

I hadn't even taken the sleeping tablets. I wanted lots and lots of sleeping tablets.

Despite being thousands of miles from home, and generally being prone to terrible bouts of depression when travelling with any club I played for, I felt like kissing the tarmac when we eventually touched down in South Korea.

What struck me immediately was just how westernized the place was, if not the people. The people really needed to catch up. As I say, the thing about these places is that they don't realize they are odd and foreign. The people genuinely looked at us like we were aliens.

It turns out that Seoul is not a charming Cotswolds-style village. We looked at the city as you would view New York or London, except that if you climb high enough in those two cities you can see the edges. The rivers and the green spaces. In Seoul you couldn't see the edges. You couldn't see anything other than more high-rise buildings stretching for miles and miles in every direction. It sprawled. Like a fat man on a bean bag.

We arrived at our hotel, right by the Olympic Stadium, still with its rings, shiny and high above us in the sky. The humidity was awful. The worst I have ever been in. Stifling. No sane human being would ever schedule a football tournament here. But football is not run by sane people. It is run by cattle rustlers, grifters and gunslingers all looking to rip each other off. From top to bottom. Google 'FIFA' if you have doubts.

Our resident South Korean player couldn't leave the hotel in the conventional manner after we arrived. He had to be smuggled in and out. The five thousand locals lining the street for him when we arrived ensured that. It was like Michael Jackson in Paris. (The city, not Hilton.) He'd come to the window every now and again and give a little wave and the adoring fans beneath would let out a high-pitched scream as if he were all four of the Beatles. I half-expected him to grab hold of one of our more slender players and hang him over the balcony.

For most of the other players, this level of fandom was unheard of. Some of us pretended to be cool and patiently signed autographs that people hadn't actually asked us for. In fairness, the Koreans were polite enough to go along with it.

I know now that when you see TV shots of players walking past lots of fans in faraway places on pre-season tours, most of those players are just bemused. They put headphones on and carry their washbags up over their eyes, while pretending to take it in their stride. The reality is, they don't know what to do about any of it.

One day we were packed off to a shopping mall where they had set up a long table like in one of the Fairy Liquid commercials in the eighties, except this one featured a never-ending supply of teenage Koreans who came trundling through, each wanting an autograph and a picture from every player. Thirty of us. Some of the fans were crying. I promise you, they were actually crying. Prior to our plane touching down they had no fucking clue who any of us were, and to be honest, now that we were sat there, I still wasn't sure that they recognized any of us. It's a powerful brand the Premier League.

Six bloody hours we sat there. I learned the ancient art of what they call 'mind over cramp'.

Training was exhausting. More so than usual. It was so fucking hot. Even the rain was hot. I was hot. Everything was hot. We played our first game and I lost a stone. A fucking stone.

That is unheard of in the Premier League. This game was played at night and I still lost a stone.

A stone I lost. In one game. That isn't healthy for anybody, no matter how well you recuperate or how many sports scientists pump you full of strawberry-flavour gel and sickly sweet electrolytes.

Before that game I also managed to fall asleep in my hotel room. I just closed my eyes for a second. That's all it was. The next thing I knew, the chief scout was ringing. Where the fuck are you? Get down here now, we're all on the bus. The worst feeling in the world. Your arsehole falls out. Every player experiences being late for the bus at least once in his career. The point is that when it happens to you, make sure you apologize and take it on the chin. There is no styling it out. You're a wanker for the rest of the day. Deal with it. I didn't, and paid the price for it.

The tournament was fun though. It was fantastic to play against different footballing cultures. Two of the teams were huge in world football, far bigger than us, but we gave everybody we played a real game, and not just in terms of our physicality. Tactically we gave a fantastic defensive and attacking account of ourselves, and there was mutual respect on both sides in each game at the final whistle. I really feel that the South Americans in particular were surprised by just how controlled this English bunch were, not the cloggers they'd been led to believe. A few of them can actually play. And their fitness? Forget about it.

It happens in football sometimes. Twice I have been applauded off by opposition fans. In fifteen years. Twice. And believe me, I have dished out more than my fair share of hidings. Taken a few too. But those oh so rare moments of mutual respect among footballers at the final whistle, when both teams are able to embrace and tell one another in broken language that they appreciate the effort, courage and skill of their opposite number, are to my mind at least one little oasis in a vast desert of hostility. Win, lose or draw.

One opposition player came up to me at the final whistle and asked for my shirt. It is not an overstatement to say that I was honoured to have his. At one point in the game I'd played a back-heel that sent one of our players clean through on goal. At the next break in play, this player tapped me on the back, and when I turned around I saw he was applauding me, saying 'good, good'. It's heart-warming, honestly, because it's rare among players. Very rare.

I'm so glad that I had the chance to take part in that tournament. Sometimes it comes in handy having a resident Asian player in the squad.

What was not fun was one of the nights out we had in Seoul. After the most mind-numbing recovery day in the history of modern football, we were told that we could go out the next day after training. And our South Korean player took it upon himself, and on behalf of his nation, to show us around.

'We go to some fun places, but we eat nice food first, OK?'

Voice from the back: 'Just so long as it's not dog.'

Cue laughter.

Resident Asian: 'We go to restaurant with dog but you don't have to order dog, do you?'

Laughter ends.

They really do eat fucking dog. You see a dog cut in half and hung up in exactly the same way as you see those ducks hung up in the windows of restaurants in London's Chinatown. Except you never think in London that the duck might once have been Donald or Daffy. But every hanging dog carcass makes you think of Lassie, or Eddie from *Frasier*, or . . . no, no, not poor Scooby Doo!

I shuddered and swerved the dog, longing to get back to England for a good old-fashioned Tesco burger cut with 29 per cent horse meat. I went for the grill instead. There were big pits of flames with a mesh on top, and loads of raw beef strips that you seasoned and then chucked on to the grill. We all sat round like pigs in shit. Healthy and tasty.

(True story. When we arrived home, I and two other players looked into opening a restaurant exactly like that one in Seoul, but were thwarted by restaurant licensing laws which wouldn't permit 'an open fire at the customer's table'. Maybe they thought it was the slippery slope on the road to serving dog. Maybe if a customer went up in flames he would go 'woof'. And no, we weren't going to call it Rover's Return, or the Pound Shop.)

Anyway, that night descended into the sort of night that footballers sometimes experience. Or else we footballers descended into the sort of night that Seoul often experiences.

We found ourselves in a nightclub which as the night unfolded seemed to be the set for the most distasteful game show ever invented. The following paragraphs don't contain any jokes.

Here's how it worked. There was a big restaurant downstairs. So far, so normal. Above the restaurant, it was as if you were looking up at the floors of a hotel. Maybe six storeys high, and every corridor full of doors, exactly like you would find in a hotel. Behind each of those doors (and this is the equivalent of a Saturday night down the Dog and Duck by the way) was a big table with bottles of booze on it, and a horseshoe-shaped seating arrangement around it. There was a small toilet in one corner behind another door, and in the other corner was a karaoke machine. The lads – groups of mates, or in this case a football team – sat around the table. Outside on the landings were porters who looked exactly like bellboys – same attire, stupid hat, glove under one lapel, etc. Central casting jobs.

Here's where it gets grisly. The job of the porters was to grab girls who were walking around and put them into the rooms. They had to remember which girls had been in each room, and who was in each room in terms of tourists and natives. Other than that it wasn't much of a strain intellect-wise.

Sometimes the girls were happy to be taken to a room, and sometimes they were a bit fussed, so the porters literally grabbed their upper arms and frogmarched them to the door, opened it, and chucked them in, like zookeepers tossing meat to lions. I mean, they pushed them forcibly into the room.

The girls would then look at the lads sitting around the table to see if they liked the look of any of them. If they saw a lad they liked, they would come over and sit down with him. If they didn't, they'd walk out, only to be thrown into another room. If they sat down next to you, you were obliged to say hello and offer them a drink. If they said no to the drink, it meant they weren't feeling your inner beauty. If they said yes, you had to ask which drink. Whisky. Then you were close to a home run. If they drank it, you were three-quarters of the way.

Ditto if after you'd chatted for a while she offered to sing you a song on the karaoke. Then you were pretty much in.

If you were receptive to her performance, you had to put some money on the table. Simon Cowell style. Sign the act. Seal the deal. Maybe the equivalent of £5 or £10. And that had two meanings. The first was that you were prepared to pay for a taxi back to your place with her. And secondly, the amount told her how far away your place was. The more money you put down, the further away you lived, and maybe she would be likely to go back with you if you were living out in the sticks. If she took the money off the table and put it in her purse, that meant she wanted to come back with you and was ready to go asap. She was keeping the money safe for you in her purse in order to pay the taxi driver. I offended about three natives mortally before I got the hang of it.

So far, so pretty OK. The gimmick of throwing the girls into the room was pretty odd and a bit worrying, but once inside, the girls seemed to know what they were doing.

Then two American girls got thrown in. They were from California. They were on an exchange year at the University of Seoul. They lived together not too far away and were working part-time in a hospital over the road while they studied. They had been to this place loads of times to buy dope.

They were crying. I asked what was wrong and one of them turned to me and said that she had just been raped upstairs by a group of men. She said that they were part of a very serious local organized gang. How did she know this?

131

Well, they were the people she usually bought her dope from.

I wanted to call the police. The girls wouldn't let me. I told our local celebrity player. He basically said 'shit happens'. I told him to get the manager – the manager of the nightclub, not our manager – but he said there was no point, the management wouldn't do anything, they'd be too scared. More than likely he was right.

So I tried to call the police, but one of the girls snatched my phone. They were terrified. They said they wanted to go home but were too scared to walk back through the club and downstairs to where the taxis were. Every time they had tried to leave, they kept getting grabbed and thrown back into rooms by the porters. I told them I'd walk them out, and just for extra security I asked two of the lads to come with me, which they did. Always grab the centre-halves. They're the scariest players in any squad generally.

On the way to the lifts, the porters were still trying to get hold of the girls, so one of the centre-halves pulled them away. I can't remember the lift but I do remember that once we had made it outside, one of the centre-halves was trying to tell me that we should go to the police. The girls were absolutely steadfast that they wouldn't go.

We got them to the taxi. I made one last desperate plea to the girls to let me come with them to the police station but they just wouldn't hear of it. I paid for the taxi and they left. I never saw them again.

I talked to the guys about the three of us just heading down to the cop shop to report the incident ourselves. The wisest among us, the team's moral leader, said that sad as it sounded, he felt that if we went to the police they would try to pin something on us, anything. We were strangers in a strange land, and until you get a feel for a place there's always a danger that you could make an easy victim. We would be three footballers telling a terrible story about something that had happened to a couple of Californian girls who wanted no attention whatsoever. For one thing it was a media shit-storm just waiting to happen.

I honestly didn't know what we could have done. If the girls wouldn't let us take them to the cop shop, or tell the management, or look after them, then what could we have done apart from making sure they got home OK? The girls said the police would do nothing so it didn't matter. We must have stood there for fifteen minutes trying to persuade them but it was no good.

One of the guys wanted to go to the room of the alleged rapists and have it out with them there and then. Of our limited options, taking on a gang seemed like the poorest choice by a country mile. I felt his anger though.

I'm still not really sure what we were supposed to do but I do know that when I told this story in my first book, the bit about the American girls was edited out. When I asked why, I was told that it made me look bad. As I say, I'm still confused about that night. What happened? How? Why no police? What *were* we supposed to do? *Do* I look bad? Maybe from thousands of miles away. I'm not the point of the story though.

The world is a fucking horrific place sometimes and it can be fucking hard to know how to deal with it at certain moments. I did the best I could, but I felt utterly helpless and hopeless none the less. I still think about those poor girls. When things

133

go bad, places like South Korea seem an awful long way from home.

The tour continued, but it too was less than happy. Unfortunately, as is often the case in football, only in times of hardship does a team realize how much effort goes into playing in a country with 80 per cent humidity against opposition that are conditioned and better at playing a slow tempo and conserving energy.

And hardship did come. That pre-season tournament killed us at certain moments in the campaign. When we wanted to find the next gear in matches where we were dominating or needed to get back on terms, we couldn't. We lost games we might have drawn, we drew games we should have won.

I stand by my theory of recent years, on the demise of English dominance in Europe, that it is extremely difficult to take a squad of unconditioned players to far-flung places around the world – sometimes Asia and the US in the same pre-season – and when they return expect them to play two games a week, plus internationals, with no winter break. It is crazy. It isn't right. The greed of our elite domestic clubs is matched only by the exploitative demands of the Premier League and the insatiable appetite they have for selling TV rights.

I get business, I really do. I love business. But there comes a point, doesn't there? I can envisage NBA players sticking one hand on top of the other to make a 'T'. 'Come on guys, huh? Timeout? We're dying here!'

So by the end of that Seoul tournament we were more than ready to go home. Away from the games, I was actually in a fierce state of depression. A real bad lull. This is the point when I first told somebody in football that I was suffering with what I felt was depression. I say that because I hadn't actually been diagnosed by a doctor, but I felt it. I mean, for fuck's sake, you just had to look at me back then to know that here was a guy who was not functioning like a normal human being.

Some people suffering from depression say that they hate being away from their family. I didn't. Some say that it is the emptiness of their lives that drives them down the rabbit hole. Not me. Others will say that they can't cope with the thought of everyday tasks, the menial chores and the regularity of life. No. For me it was the boredom. I fear doing nothing like other people fear a terminal diagnosis. I feel it after ten minutes. If an hour then passes I panic that I haven't yet come up with something to do. Then my brain tells me that it might go on for several hours, a whole day, a week . . . and what if it goes on for ever? And before you know it, BANG!

That's how easy it is for some people to slip into depression. And let me tell those of you who don't know how hard it is, once you're down there it can be a long, long climb back out. I know it sounds crazy (probably not the right word) but it feels like being possessed by somebody else. It feels like somebody has climbed into your body and refuses to get back out again until he's dragged you down with him. It's like somebody whispering in your ear over and over, 'It's all a big nothing, we're all going to die one day anyway, what's the point? Just close your eyes and come with me. It'll be easier.'

That's where I was in Korea.

I first told a scout. He was old school, probably still is, but he was one of us too. Great banter, great guy. He listened; he didn't understand, but he listened. He told me that it would be too much of a strain on me to tell the manager. The fact that I was almost crying when I told him probably drew him to that conclusion. So he stepped up. He told the manager. The manager asked to see me in the lobby. He was fine. He told me that if ever it got too much, I must tell him. Because he had other players who could play instead.

Seriously.

But I'm not surprised. We didn't bloody understand these things back then, not really. Nobody did. And even those who had a vague understanding or had heard the word 'depression' didn't want to talk about it. They were football people. They were wholly uncomfortable opening up about their emotions or their deepest thoughts and beliefs. If you had a problem, well, go to a professional and get it dealt with, and hurry the fuck back because there's a game tomorrow afternoon, you selfish prick.

Christ, what were we thinking?

There was no doctor. I survived. We brushed the whole thing under the carpet. The only time the manager ever asked me about it was when we were playing round-robin games in training, where there are three teams and the team not playing has one touch around the outside to put the ball back into play with a pass. He'd walk around the pitch towards me, slowly.

'Are you OK?'

'Yeah, gaffer, yeah.'

'Good. Let's have a big performance from you on Saturday then.'

And that was his way of asking me if I was dealing with my issues on behalf of the club. For a while I did. But fuck knows how.

I was in an awful state when the time came to go home from Seoul. We hadn't won the competition. We hadn't expected to. I can't actually remember who did. I could google it but I'm not sure that I give too much of a fuck to be honest.

I had a big decision to make on the return leg: to sit in first class or, well, not to sit in first class. I decided not to. It was my little way of trying to build bridges with the lads and the manager, who had been furious with me for not apologizing immediately when I was late on to the team bus before our first match. He had made an example of me in front of the squad and even dropped me. I was feeling very low, fairly useless and more than a little sheepish. I also felt anger. It was a genuine fucking mistake, but I should have apologized immediately. He was right about that.

So I sat in business class. I know, I know. I know I sound like a prize wanker.

What is that thing that various monks do when they whip themselves? Mortification, isn't it? Is it to cleanse the soul of the sin or to prevent the sin from occurring at all?

Either way, I let that business-class seat whip me all the way home.

Eleven fucking hours.

PART FOUR

Next Stop Ibiza

8

There's an alternative title that I considered for this book: *I Know This Sounds Bad, But . . .*

So in that spirit, can I make a short story long and introduce one of my best friends. Sync we call him. To know Sync is to love him. He's funny. He's half-mad. He's fun. He's loyal. He's like one of those sorbets they give you in posh restaurants to clean and refresh your palate. Sync does that to your brain.

So, I know this sounds bad, but . . .

Sync used to match his jackets to his Lamborghinis.

He had a white Lambo and he also had a purple one. He had leather jackets to match. He then traded them both in for a brand spanking new black Lambo that cost him about £250,000. He got a black leather jacket to go with it. He looked the fucking nuts. He was his own accessory.

It's the purple jacket I remember when I think of the early Ibiza era. It's that purple jacket which forces me to tell this story before we even leave the runway for Ibiza. Ladies and gentlemen, TSF Airways regrets to announce that our scheduled flight has been delayed . . .

Now, when you walk into a dressing room as a new signing, it takes time to suss out the lie of the land. You observe who is in what clique. You get a feel for who feels threatened by your arrival and who is glad that you have joined. You know that when word went out you were being signed, these lads discussed you in scathing detail.

'Sorry. Don't like him. Don't rate him. Not what we need.'

'My mate played with him for two years. Says he's a good bloke.'

'I heard he's a tosser. Reads books.'

And so on.

Sync walked into our dressing room and he was just himself from the first minute. For better or worse. It was like the door had been opened and this fresh breeze had blown in off the Mediterranean. It reminded you of sun and sea and good wine. He just walked in the door and from that moment he never sought anybody out, people were drawn to him.

Now ours was a good club in an unfashionable area but we had very decent players and money had ceased to be a novelty for most of the lads. Still, nobody had ever seen a guy drive up on the first day and step out of a purple Lamborghini wearing a matching leather jacket. He had accessorized further with a pair of purple trainers.

Footballers never rush to judgement though.

'Fuck me,' somebody said, 'he's a bit busy. Take a look at this, lads.'

So when Sync had changed and hung the purple leather jacket up, Matty reached for it from the peg and signed his name across the back in biro. Then he passed the jacket and the biro along for everybody to sign as if it was a petition from the lads.

He had ruined the jacket of a guy he hadn't spoken two words to.

When he came to me, I shook my head. 'Matty mate, I'm not signing that. That's not me, mate. It's not my banter. It would be easier for everyone if you just say that you never asked me.'

Matty had been half-expecting a refusal so he moved on quickly.

Lo and behold, when Sync saw his jacket, he shook his head and smiled, but he made a mental note of who had signed the jacket and my name was not on it. I watched Sync like a hawk when he came in and saw his defaced jacket hanging on the peg. For just the tiniest fraction of a second his face darkened and then he turned around with a grin on his face and defused the whole situation brilliantly.

Like a lot of very bright guys in football, Sync camouflages his intelligence with humour. When you are very sharp, you don't want to be the guy who keeps saying 'well actually . . .' when the lads are happily bullshitting about something nobody really knows anything about. A lot of the really smart clued-up guys never really get credit for that, and it suits them just fine.

So Sync made an instant mental note of who had signed the jacket and who hadn't and years later, when we were fast friends, he mentioned that morning. He had been pissed off, of course he had. Making shit of another guy's stuff is a lazy, low form of banter and it gave Sync an even lower opinion of the lads than the opinion the lads had formed of Sync when they saw him in matching jacket and Lambo. But he was smart enough to grin and bear it and to remember the names. If he'd shown a weakness, if he'd let people know that he was angry, he would have got no peace.

You never actually reveal anything about yourself on your very first day – that's a big thing. That could set the tone for the rest of your stay at the club. Sync was famous enough that all of us had pre-formed opinions of him anyway. And then he showed up in the Lambo and the jacket. First thing? Target that jacket.

He had shown enough for one day without letting the lads think he was taking anything too seriously. So he'd just laughed and he was fine after that – a big addition to the team and the dressing room. He was a lovely lad, great to go out with, a decent footballer, great in the changing room, great with the lads, lots of banter, a bit mad. In short, he was one of us.

He and I played in the same position, but when he arrived I was glad to see him. I had hit a bad run and confidence was low. Mrs TSF and I were unhappy with where we were living and I had decided that this wasn't the club for me after all. A new player coming in, a very good one at that, meant that either my job on the field would change (and mentally I needed change) or I would be sold on. Either way I would be happier.

As it happened, I was wrong. My role changed and I did well, but the gaffer never came out and said, 'TSF is playing a different role for us at the moment and he's doing it well.' It's amazing, but when a manager says that, pundits and punters alike nod their heads and say 'yes, yes, of course we had noticed that too'. But they hadn't. People just said, 'Well, he's not doing what we thought he would do. This isn't what it said on the tin.'

So when Sync arrived, I was pleased to become his mate but it actually left me in a Catch-22 situation. I was doing an effective job but it was a job I hadn't been bought to do. The manager was saying nothing to me or about me though, because he and I didn't like each other. I knew that he knew that when he bought me he had bought a brand, and he was going to sell me when it suited him as exactly the brand he had bought. He wasn't going to answer the phone to other clubs and explain that I wasn't what they were looking for, but if they were looking for something a bit similar you could mess with his wiring, etc.

Nobody buys a Lamborghini and sells it on the basis that as a Volvo it's pretty good. Do they, Sync? So I was trapped there, and Sync was the light relief.

We were flirting with relegation when Sync arrived but he was oblivious to that whole situation. No stress. No bother. Just give me the ball, lads, and we'll be fine. We rose up the table and even a guy like me, wallowing in the misery of my own situation at the time, was glad for him.

When we went out I would hang on for dear life. Going out with Sync is like riding in the first carriage of the baddest roller-coaster in the park. It's fun, it's scary, and there's a voice in the back of your head screaming, 'This thing is going to fly off the rails . . . HELP!'

In time we both fell out of favour with the manager and we got to spend a lot of hours together on that rollercoaster.

Mrs TSF had gone down to Ibiza with the minor TSFs at the end of one season and I was due to join her down there. I had a few end-of-season things to clear up and she was going ahead as the leader of our small expedition force to report back to me on whether the wine was chilled enough, the towels were crisp enough and if there were any couples horseriding on the beach whom we could photograph in silhouette and say, 'There we are again, another island, another thoroughbred. Ah!'

Her plane had hardly got its wheels off the runway when Sync rang.

'What ya doing?'

Rookie error here on my part: 'Mrs TSF has just left for Ibiza, so I'm rattling around in the house here.'

'Let's do something. What ya wanna do, mate?'

I know he means London. I'm not a big fan of London, so I try some damage limitation. 'We could go to Windsor. Few quiet glasses of wine.'

Sync drinks Sauvignon Blanc like it's mother's milk. Except he drinks it by the barrel. If you drink with Sync, you drink Sauvignon Blanc.

I'm thinking about a nice restaurant down Windsor way called Brown's. It has a lovely terrace. You can almost throw your corks into the Thames as it moseys past. We can watch the world go by, Sync. What can go wrong?

It's about midday. He's texting me that this is going to be amazing. I'm texting back saying yes, nice quiet afternoon by the river. It should be good.

Then the Lamborghini screeches into my drive. Sync is out of it before the engine is switched off. He hasn't even bothered to coordinate his clothing with the car.

'Come on, mate, where's the taxi? Where's the taxi?'

He won't countenance either of us driving to Windsor. He's probably right, so we call a cab.

Windsor. Perfect table with prime view. Just sitting there. Bottle after bottle. Sync has instructed that a new bottle be brought along in an ice bucket every twenty minutes. Just in case. The two of us bitch about what is wrong with football and how hard our lives are. Girls with nothing else to do flit around the table like butterflies, filling their glasses from our bottles, talking shit to us.

'Who are you?'

'What do you do?'

'For real?'

'Wowsers!'

A woman I know, Vicki, lives nearby. I can see her house just a little way up the river, so I text her that if she's around she should join us. By the time she arrives, the ice buckets of wine are beginning to stack up. She puts a good dent into the wine lake, in fairness to her, and after a while Sync has a brainwave.

He enjoys a nice shisha pipe. As a footballer he was probably ahead of the curve in this preference. Anyway, the sun is thinking about calling it a night, the afternoon has passed very quickly, and no clubs are open yet. So we say, why not? We could go for a shisha while we are still wine mellow. There is a definite feeling that if we don't go now we will be slobbering drunks pretty soon.

The heat has gone out of the day and we walk to this place, sit down and order a shisha. I have an apple. Sync, a man of habits, always has apple flavour too.

There is a woman at the shisha place who doesn't like her own hair. She is saying this out loud like a mad lady. Vicki says, no, you are wrong, your hair is lovely. Come and join us.

147

She joins us. I say to Sync about this woman that I'm getting a strange vibe, something ain't right. We stay for another couple of hours. About eleven o'clock the shisha place wants to kick us out. They want to go home. Then, out of the blue, Vicki falls back in her chair and the woman with the controversial hair gets on top of her and they have a full-blown snog, grope and the rest of it for about two minutes.

I look at Sync. This shisha shit ain't bad, is it?

Vicki and the mad lady disengage. Sync says let's go to this club called Vanilla. Conveniently, it's just round the corner. I phone through to order a VIP table and all the rest of it. Please have plenty of vodka, Red Bulls and Coke on the table. Lord Sync is coming.

We are the only people in the place. Sync sees this as an opportunity. He starts dancing and doesn't stop for half an hour. When he is done, the place is beginning to fill up. Let's go somewhere else, he says, this place ain't the greatest.

Me and Vicky walk outside. Then we notice that Sync is missing. We go back in and Sync is at the spot where you get your hand stamped. There is a small solid desk there, about four feet by a couple of feet, and Sync is pretending to be the guy who you pay before going in. There is a big queue and Sync announces that there is a change of plan tonight. New management. New theme nights. No entry fee tonight, but you gotta win an arm wrestle with me to get in.

Sync likes to boast that he was taught how to arm wrestle by some arm wrestling ninja he met on his travels, and since then he has been unbeaten at arm wrestling. Nobody in the queue complains about this new policy and they all stay to arm wrestle; even the girls are arm wrestling him. The losers just walk out like sheared sheep. There are no winners apart from Sync. The club is losing thousands of pounds.

Management appears suddenly. 'Er, what's going on here? Oh, Sync! How are you, mate?'

'Yeah, really good. I'm just messing around having a few arm wrestles.'

Just a few arm wrestles. Not a few arm wrestles and then sending your paying customers home.

We walk out and find a Wetherspoons. We sit outside under the heated lamps and have a few more drinks. Vicki says goodbye. She has to go.

I know what's coming next. I have bombproofed myself for this. When the day out was proposed, I sent several texts for the record.

'Few drinks and home, mate. No strippers.'

'Having a bit of bother with the financials. Pressure from Mrs TSF. So no strippers, mate. Anyway, you know I hate that shit.'

'Gotta be somewhere in the morning. So not a late one, OK? No strippers.'

Sync replied. He went on the record. 'No worries, mate.'

Now Sync says: 'Let's go see some strippers, mate.'

I look at him through narrowed eyes. 'OK.' Those texts were three hundred and seven bottles of wine ago.

We jump in a cab.

First strip club? Closed.

Second strip club? Sorry, sirs, you are too drunk.

Third strip club? Come on in.

A Thai girl walks straight up to Sync. He seems very pleased with this. I tell the other hovering artistes of strip that this is my worst nightmare and they are characters in it. I ask them please not to talk to me. I don't want anything to do with any of this, so just leave me alone. Really sorry. That's just the way it is. Admire your work, by the way.

I sit down. You can't take your phone out in these places. I become very conscious of how many times an hour I just check my phone. There is nothing to read either.

Soon one of the girls sits down beside me.

'What are you doing?' she asks.

'Nothing. I just don't want a lap dance. I fucking hate it. I'll buy you some drinks if you sit and talk to me so no one else bothers me.'

I look around for Sync, so I can point out my friend the paying customer. Last I saw he was totally lettered on a dancer's pole, spinning around and around until security came and peeled him off. Before that he was behind the bar pretending to be Tom Cruise shaking up cocktails. Now he is gone.

Oh well. Football friendships are transient. We move on.

The girl is from one of the many parts of Russia I have never heard of. Having spoken to her, it is also one of the many parts of Russia I will never buy a summer cottage in. She gives me her entire autobiography and for fifty-nine minutes it is riveting, but on the hour mark I begin looking around for Sync again.

A guy comes over. Apologetic in the sort of way these people are when they have serious weight and muscle to call on.

'Listen, the bill is racking up significantly here,' he tells me.

'We can't let you go through to the end of the evening. Just in case you and your friend do one.'

I ask how much is 'racking up', and is that a trade term in strip clubs? He says four grand and counting. I see his point, even though I've only had a couple of glasses of wine in the ninety minutes or so we have been here.

'Don't worry about the money,' I say to the guy.

'I do worry,' he says. 'That's my job.'

'He's pretty rich,' I say, trying not to turn into a wanker.

'Maybe he is,' says the guy, 'but we need some kind of payment. In case we get pretty poor.'

'OK,' I tell the guy, 'I'll get him to sort it out if you can find him.'

Sync is with the Thai girl when he is found. Another girl has been bringing him a succession of mounting bills (another trade term?) and he has found each one funnier than the last.

About half an hour after being located, he comes down the stairs. His retention isn't great right now. I see him dancing around again. My brain won't quite compute what I am seeing. He's drunk. He's dancing. He should be sorting the bill.

Ah, that's it. The bill is stapled to his ear. I move towards him; he isn't going to move towards me. Yes, he has four staples holding the bill tight to his ear.

The Thai has a newsflash for me.

'Your friend is fucking mad. He is off his head. In a real good way. I love him. I totally love him. I will get him some antiseptic for his bill. I mean his ear.'

I am a trained medical professional. I poo-poo the antiseptic. This is medicine on the run. We are in the field.

151

'Vodka will do the job.'

Vodka is found. Sync has no interest in having vodka poured on to his ear. I am told that the staples were self-inflicted. Makes sense.

The bill stuck to his ear is an older version. The newest version is up to six grand now. Time to pay.

Two questions. Has he put down the deposit for a house with the Thai girl? Am I going to have to tell his wife?

We go outside. Sync hands me his card – serious plastic – and says get some cash out for the taxi home. He thinks there is money on the card still. Then we'll call it a night.

There is a petrol station next door with a cashpoint. I buy a sneaky bottle. And while getting some cash out, I have a sneaky look at his balance.

Fuck me. *Fuck me.* Three million quid just sitting in there.

He thinks there's enough for a cab. There's three mill!

Even as a footballer I am shocked.

A cab has turned up. Sync has vanished. I'm sat there making small talk. Not my strength. I keep telling the cabbie to hold on, my mate is just around the corner. He's settling up a bill or something. The cabbie is giving me the 'heard it all before mate' shrug of indifference.

Suddenly Sync comes tearing around the corner and takes a full dive straight into the taxi – head first through the door, which had conveniently been open, awaiting his arrival.

'Wait a minute, wait a minute,' he says, giggling.

'Why?' I say, not giggling.

'Just wait, mate, just wait.'

A moment later a modest herd of immodest strippers comes

running around the corner and jumps into the cab on top of him. Sync valiantly shouts out my home address just before he sinks under the waves of flesh.

We're off.

Just what I need. Sync is bad enough. Sync plus five strippers in my house is apocalyptic.

I have a home cinema and a snooker table downstairs in the house. The big screen goes on. Music is blaring. They are dancing all over the chairs. There is one of them (not Sync) on the snooker table doing a striptease.

I'm exhausted. Frightened. Drunk. I just head up to bed, pull a pillow over my head and sleep.

Next morning I check the phone for the time. It's late. Too late for me to live. Late to the extent that I have ten missed calls from Mrs TSF in Ibiza. Ten missed calls and lots of terse texts.

Always sweep the minefield before you stumble across it. I go downstairs to check the damage before I call Mrs TSF back.

Music is still booming but everyone is asleep. It's as if there has been a ghastly stripper massacre. Strippers are lying everywhere, limbs akimbo. Knickers and bras scattered everywhere like somebody has run amok in Ann Summers.

I turn the music off. Have to make a plan. Have to drink water then make a plan.

The Thai girl appears.

'What's wrong with your friend?'

First thought: Sync is dead. She has found him. He isn't breathing. He is white as yoghurt. She is asking what is wrong with your friend because she knows. His heart no longer beats.

153

This is upsetting. Mainly because neither my career nor my marriage will be helped by the headline 'Five Strippers, Dead Footballer Found at TSF Pile'. My agent is good, but not that good.

Oh, and poor Sync. But at least he passed happily, leaving me to clean up his mess.

'He won't fuck me,' she adds.

'Oh. Is that all?'

'Is that all?'

'Wrong guy. He goes out, drinks, flirts, spends money, has the craic, has a dance, has a chat, but he won't ever do that. Don't worry. It's not you, it's him. His code.'

'Oh.'

'He hasn't shat the bed or anything, has he?'

She tells me she managed to get the staples out of his ear. She poured some vodka on him. She found a bottle in the fridge.

Now, this was an Icelandic vodka that was horrendous and a gift, and it had been in my fridge for like a hundred years before being called into service to provide an antiseptic for Sync's ear which had a bill for strippers stapled to it. Of course.

What to think? Thank God Sync's ear won't be septic?

Nah. Who cares?

Or . . .

Mrs TSF will notice that missing bottle of Icelandic plonk instantly and she will know that something very dark and very weird has gone down in this house.

Shit.

Things to do immediately: Check eBay for more Icelandic vodka. Call Mrs TSF.

Not in that order.

She answers on the first ring.

'What's the problem? I've been calling you for hours. Please tell me it's something really simple like you need cash wired over or you have lost a remote control. Look, I really need you out here.'

'What was that?'

'I really need you over here. The little TSFs are driving everybody mad, even me. I can tell the others are getting fed up. I'm sticking out like a sore thumb on my own. I'm drowning. I need you to be here.'

'OK.'

'Good. So I booked you on an early-afternoon flight out from Stansted. Just pack a bag and get your useless arse over here.'

She ends the call. Of the three big London-area airports, Stansted is the furthest away. That's not a problem, except the big hand and the little hand are telling me that it's somewhere between half nine and ten o'clock now. The flight is at one o'clock.

And there has been an unlicensed stripper massacre in my wife's home. And Sync is in a Sauvignon Blanc coma. And there is more underwear lying around, it seems, than there are strippers. Shit. Suppose they have been messing with Mrs TSF's lacy smalls? Oh God.

'Right, Sync. Come on, mate.'

He doesn't move. I call on my medical training again and slap him hard across the face a few times.

He comes to.

Before I use the stick, I offer him the carrot of water and

paracetamol downstairs. He is unfocused though. He spots the iPod. Puts it on. More music going full whack. He starts having a little dance. A stripper comes alive and starts dancing too as if she has no control over what her limbs do.

'NO! NO! NO! There is a bit of a situation here, you fuckers. You all need to get the fuck out of my house asap. I have to go to Spain. Important business. International shit. You, five hung-over strippers, and you, drunken footballer, are all that stands between now and the end of the world.'

They start picking up bits of stuff, turning things inside out like they are archaeologists and they need to be very careful. Look, this seems to be a stiletto-heeled shoe. Was there another one? Was this once part of a pair? Are these knickers or some sort of primitive dental floss?

I'm getting more and more agitated. I keep force-feeding them all water. They'll either sober up or their bladders will burst simultaneously and I will end it all by drowning myself in the flood.

Finally I call a taxi and count the strippers into it. One. Two. Three. Four. I thought there had been five. Maybe one already left. Anyway, goodbye and thank you all for coming. Or in your case, Thai lady, for not coming.

They're gone. I run back indoors and tell Sync that this is now very urgent. 'You've got fifteen minutes, mate. Otherwise this isn't gonna end well for me.'

He gets it. I go back to cleaning things up. He does the same.

After a while, I listen out for him. I hear nothing. The draught tells me that the door into the garden is open. Sync is now lying bollock naked on the front lawn, passed out, face down like some ironic garden ornament piece which came in a controversial second for the Turner Prize.

I haul him in and get him dressed. Any neighbours or passers-by who are rubbernecking on these tender moments will have to be killed before I catch the plane. More hassle.

'Come on, Sync, mate, come on, pal, let me help you. Oh, there you are.'

The fifth stripper has appeared, acting like she is surprised to see us. She is like a character in a play who you assumed had died before the final act. Now here she is. *Enter stage left. Tits glittery.*

She needs to get home. In fact, he tells me now, so does Sync. He's just remembered through the miracle of checking his phone that Mrs Sync has arranged a family gathering over dinner with her parents, the kids, the whole shebang. Completely slipped his mind until now. He takes on this annoying tone. I'm waiting for him to say, 'Huh, you think you got troubles, mate . . .'

I've dispatched 80 per cent of the strippers in a cab and didn't think to call another one for Sync and the unpredictable rogue element of the stripper community. So I get the car keys. I drink a glass of water for luck. I usher Sync and the last living stripper into my car. The house is in a state of dishevelment but it's not going to be improved significantly by my hanging around. I throw a small bag into the boot and we all drive off.

'Sync, mate, where am I going? Where will I take you?'

He turns to the girl and says, 'Well, what are you doing now?'

Death wish stuff.

157

She says, 'Well, you can't go home looking like that.'

'Drop me at the train station,' he says. 'I'd better get home.'

Fine. The train station is half an hour in the wrong direction, but it's better than having Sync and a stripper come to Stansted with me.

We pull in at the train station. Funny thing: there is a spa there. Sync says to the girl, 'You're right, I can't go home like this. I need to go into this spa. Wanna come?'

They get out and walk gingerly towards the spa together like they are an old couple. If he doesn't get back home by four for this dinner, he is dead, and it's not my fault. I will get the blame. That's because he will blame me. But it is not my fault.

I said, on the record, NO STRIPPERS.

I'm feeling good though. I'm still drunk but approaching the familiar badlands of Inner Hangover. I'm late, probably in trouble, but in a short space of time I have got Sync and five strippers out of my morning. I'm getting shit done.

The phone rings. Mrs Sync.

'Is he with you?'

'Well, I just dropped him at the station.'

'So I'll see him in an hour. Why isn't he answering his phone?'

'Why? Well, we had a bit of a night of it. And there is this spa at the station, so I suggested to him that we both go in and freshen up. He's checking it out and I'm parking the car.'

'A spa at the station? OK. Hmm.'

'He won't be late, I'll see to that. Trust me.'

So now I'm drunk, speeding, in trouble and lying to Sync's missus. I text Sync to let him know the precise lies I have just told for him. I tell him to get home or his balls will end up in the mincer and it will serve him right.

Stansted. The check-in desk is shutting down. The flight is closed.

Question: What value can you place on a man's dignity?

Answer: Fuck all if he is in trouble with Mrs TSF.

I beg and whinge and cajole and cry and carry on and throw tantrums and pretend to be having a series of cardiac arrests until they bring out this little buggy and let me sit on it. I am weeping with gratitude. Young Senna floors the thing right to the flight gate. Wheelie turns, the works.

Now they are saying the plane is closed. They've shut the door. I start acting up again. Surely the door opens? They're not entombed in there for eternity?

Senna gives his colleagues a look like, guys, you really don't want to see this.

I'm saying, look, please, please, please, I have come through security (like I've escaped from a Siberian gulag on foot) and I have nowhere to go. Please let me on the plane. I may die.

They've seldom seen a grown man cry. It shocks them. Or they contain their laughter till I am gone. Either way they let me on the plane.

I'm the guy who is last on board. The guy who has held everybody up. The guy reeking of booze. The guy who has to ask people to get out of their seats so he can get into his seat. If this plane goes down, they are going to club me to death, use me as a flotation device, and then eat me.

And when I am sitting down at last, throwing apologies

around, I am the guy getting a text message when everybody else has shut off their phones.

Ping! It's from Sync. It's long and jumbled.

'No worries on Mrs Sync mate don't worry I'll say we were at the spa together blah blah blah. I just remembered something mate blah blah don't go off on one. The stripper girl with me says there is a pair of her knickers in your family bathroom in one of the drawers, dunno why mate, thought I should tell you. Mate, great night, hope you got on the plane alright. See ya later.'

The plane is literally being pushed out towards the runway by all the holidaymakers who have been delayed on the flights behind us. Inside the plane, the hate being directed at me is pouring out of all the little overhead air vents which have been trained in my direction.

I am bolt upright in my seat, eyes wide open, white-knuckling the ends of the armrests. I've come through all this and there is a fucking time bomb in my house?

Ten minutes late, you fuckers? You people think you've got problems? There is an undetonated pair of stripper knickers in my family bathroom. The family who use that bathroom will arrive home together, and one of them as always will be in the direst need of that facility . . .

I am going on fucking holiday to Ibiza. And then I will be killed. Where is your humanity? Your compassion?

So that was my introduction to Ibiza.

(Note: By the grace of God I picked the right stall in the post-Ibiza Gotta Pee Right Now Handicap Stakes. No stripper knickers ever darkened our drawers again.)

9

I love England in the summer; nowhere is as green or dappled. I love Provence. I love Milan. Not many people love Milan; I guess it depends on whom you know there and the memories they've given you. I adore Seville and I love Barcelona. I really love Barcelona. But my heart is nailed to a little island in the middle of the Mediterranean.

Some people call it a shithole, but they have never actually been there, or they have seen too many cheap tabloid documentaries. Maybe they have been but they went to the wrong area. The Romans called it Ebusus, others call it the White Isle. I'm happy to call it Ibiza. Unless the flights to Ebusus are cheaper.

The Romans knew how to let their hair down and they knew exactly where to do it. The Mediterranean literally translates as 'the middle of the earth' because for centuries it was the centre of civilization, and for a few fleeting moments in the history of football one corner of the Med was at the epicentre of everything we footballers didn't want you to see.

That corner was Marbella though. The game moved on. This is Ibiza, and there, things were different.

My love for Ibiza needs to be put in context.

I love Ibiza, but not in the way you might think. I'm not Mr Congeniality. I don't like people talking to me and I don't like sharing my holidays with strangers. Show me the noisy splish-splash of a communal pool teeming with bikini-clad intellectuals posing against a five-star backdrop and I would rather swallow my own tongue.

I have been to these places because I was a footballer and I thought at the time that I had no choice. I went to the beach parties, the casinos and the nightclubs because I was curious and there was nothing else to do. Now that I have the choice, I'd much rather be in a villa surrounded by family. No pressure to do anything other than wade through my thoughts. The family send up a flare if they see me wading in too deep.

When I go out, my tastes are simple. If you can give me a newspaper or a magazine, a beach shack, a vat of rough rosé wine, a lunch that lasts four to five hours, people who won't bother me and a view of the sea with the sun-worshippers bobbing up and down in the distance, plus my phone, then I'll marry you and take you away from everything you hate about your life.

The world isn't fair but my offer still stands.

When you're starving yourself of the good things in life, things like decent food, wine, sunshine and general happiness, for ten months of the year over a fifteen-year career – the best years of your life, so they say – then you can be forgiven for being selfish when in your own company.

During those ten months of the season there are quite a few moments that are so tedious that you feel yourself slipping into a coma. But when you wake up one morning and you're thirty-five years old and the circus has left town, you miss even those moments. Still, you were right at the time to save up those moments and trade them all in for the right to a good holiday at the end of a season.

Tedious? Surely not.

Look. Nowhere on earth is as boring as the team bus. The team bus should be outlawed under the Geneva Convention as a cruel and unusual punishment. First of all it is not a 'team' bus. It's just a fucking bus. You get in and you look out the window with your zombie stare and listen to the same jokes that you've been listening to all season and you wish you were dead. You think you might like to take out a book, but that would be too disturbing to your fellow passengers. You can read newspapers or magazines. Books are uppity.

When I saw some West Ham fundamentalist fools stoning the Manchester United bus outside the Boleyn Ground last year, I actually felt a little pang of envy. It must have been the most exciting thing ever to have happened to the United players on a team bus.

The bus does nothing to forge relationships or bring players together. It is where matchday squads go to die for up to six hours of a perfectly good Friday morning. Unless of course you're at a club that can afford to fly to every away game, in which case you spend most of the journey praying that you don't die together. Or alone.

Us boys on the bus are simple folk. Our income often outstrips our tastes. We are easily bored. We are twitchy like greyhounds. Except goalkeepers, who are the Eeyore figures

163

on the ark. (The laptop keeps insisting that by Eeyore I mean Eyesore. Well, good shout. That too.) So imagine the excitement when a culinary breakthrough hit our world.

Let me explain something to you. Lots of players like to bring their own little snacks on to the team bus with them. It helps break the trip up. The trick is to pack something that nobody else likes so you don't have to share your stuff around. A lot of chocolate is banned, and so are sweets like Haribo. Little-known fact: Haribo was invented by the Germans to fuck our football up. We are wise to that. You can't really have your players getting sugar rushes on the bus and then having a comedown crash all at the same time. Bayern wouldn't do it. The Germans have invaded entire countries when they are sugar high. It's not good match preparation.

You have to be smarter. You have to hunt and forage (well, get the household staff to hunt and forage) until you find something to stuff your face with, some snack that nobody else really should like or covet. It also has to be harmless enough to ensure that the shifty new nutritionist won't turn snitch and denounce you to the manager for eating crap.

So, make general over-the-top *X-Factor*-style fuss for, ta da, the remarkable contribution to world cuisine that is . . . the yoghurt-covered raisin.

You can't argue with yoghurt. It unites the cultures of the world. Turkish players spread it all over the chef's signature lasagne in great swathes. Seriously, I've seen the fuckers do it. Brazilians pour it on their breakfast cereals. The Chinese drink it. Greeks flog their own yoghurt in order to kill the bacteria of bankruptcy.

Footballers on buses like to take their yoghurt wrapped around a raisin.

And how can you be anti-raisin? When was the last time anybody got angry with a footballer for eating fruit? Save for Dani Alves when he ate that banana.

So we got swept up in a gastronomic revolution, the like of which comes along maybe once or twice in a career spent on 'team' buses. The yoghurt-enrobed raisin was our snack du jour. Players were popping them like ravers pop Ecstasy in the frenzy of an Ibiza nightclub.

Which neat segue brings us nicely to the isle of Ibiza, which had suddenly become the yoghurt-covered raisin of holiday destinations for footballers. We were too rich for Marbella. Not rich enough yet to have our own pads in the places where old money had been hiding out for years, but TV money would fix that. Soon nowhere would be safe from us.

A small group of us liked to think of ourselves as independent thinkers constantly swimming against the tide of football conformity. So two team-mates and I took off post-season to Ibiza, stashing so many packets of yoghurt raisins in our gear that we could have been done for trafficking. Or just plain weirdness.

Which in Ibiza is a tough charge to make stick.

In Ibiza there are cool people and there are young people who only come out at night. There are impossibly wealthy people, there are sportspeople including footballers, and there are even one or two hippies still to be found. My parents take an Attenborough-ish delight in spotting hippies whenever I take them to Ibiza. I even thought about getting them a hippie for Christmas one year, with a stern warning that a hippie is for life not just for Christmas. I knew, though, that we'd reach a point where the poor thing would have to be put down.

Apart from the cool people, the young nocturnal people, the Adonis-like footballers, the hippies and my parents, there is another common breed among the fauna of the region. The common-or-garden wanker. Ibiza's equivalent of the grey squirrel.

There are loads of wankers on Ibiza. The island is their mecca.

The Blue Marlin bar is their holiest place.

I'd heard amazing things about the Blue Marlin. It was said to be such a cool beach bar that its very existence ended mankind's need for there to be any more cool beach bars.

The Blue Marlin was said to be a destination to tick off, a bucket list staple, a pilgrimage, a rite of passage. Comprende?

You can guess what's coming next, can't you? I didn't like the Blue Marlin at all. My bucket list includes the line Never Go Back to the Blue Marlin While Still Alive. In fact, my going there was the first recorded instance of a blue marlin reeling a human in and filleting him.

For my money (and the Blue Marlin has quite a bit of my money now), the Blue Marlin is a place that thrives off myth. The reality is much tamer.

Remember that scene in *Stand By Me* when Gordie is chased by the 'killer dog' Chopper? He scales the junkyard fence just in time, he thinks, to avoid Chopper consuming his balls like a couple of yoghurt raisins. When he jumps down on the other side, he looks back through the chainlink fence to see an excitable Labrador rolling playfully in the dust. He'd expected to see a snarling wolf. 'That's Chopper?' And Gordie and his friends start waving their arses at the goofy dog.

That's basically the Blue Marlin experience. Folklore is one thing. The reality is something else.

My first thought, when I saw that the Blue Marlin had a stony beach and the nerve to charge €15 for a bottle of Corona, was to regret not having stayed back at the villa with some yoghurt raisins and a good book. But down these overpriced streets a young football man must go. The price is the price anywhere you go in the world. I can live with that. But generally the top destinations have the best locations. Like a sandy beach for instance.

I think beach, I think sand. Nice places on nice sandy beaches can charge me €15 a bottle and I won't grumble. If there's a sandy beach, I might drink a few bottles and then kick off my shoes and walk along the sandy beach.

Stones? Not so appealing. My disappointment was palpable. 'What the fuck is this?' I asked.

You see, the Blue Marlin is where gymsexuals go. The gymsexual is a man who prefers to have sex with a mirrored gymnasium wall than with a woman. The gymsexuals like to go to the Blue Marlin so that they can look at their reflections in the sunglasses of beautiful women. Self-voyeurism is their preferred choice of erotic experience.

I hated it all the moment I got there. It seemed that everybody in the place hated me. I was giving off the air of a man who really, really did not want to be there. I was surrounded by people who desperately wanted to be there, but didn't want to look like they cared. We made each other feel edgy.

Now, full disclosure. Footballers use the gym a lot. When we are injured, we spend our working lives in gyms. And there are two things that are as true today as they were millions of years ago; two essential truths of the human condition.

Footballers hate the beefcakes that use the gym.

The beefcakes who use the gym hate footballers.

At the Blue Marlin it appeared to be Beefcake Monday. Two beefcakes allowed in for the price of one, but never side by side, obviously.

They don't spend any money inside because their big beefy hands won't fit into the pockets of their ridiculously strained trousers, but they are loud and their biceps are in your face like an old stripper's tits. Every time they laugh, they look around to see who's looking at them. They roll their sad shorts up to their groins, where the 'roids have shrunk their balls to the size of, yes, yoghurt-covered raisins. They spread out in a way that intimidates others and invades their space. They colonize. It pisses me off.

Obviously I look as if I have been chiselled out of rock myself. My face may cause many people to hate me, because straight off I am too pretty. My demeanour that evening, though, was the classic bulldog-who-has-just-licked-vinegar-off-a-nettle look. I put on a face like a baboon's slapped arse and I didn't mind showing it.

Now, I've been in arguments all over the world with people of all walks of life, not because I'm a massive arsehole, but just because people tend to want to argue with me because I'm a footballer. And I am just enough of a massive arsehole to respond.

What I didn't clock straight away, mainly because I don't give a shit about stuff like this, was that the gymsexual beef-cakes were uneasy. The social hierarchy of the Blue Marlin had been disturbed. An alien species had been introduced to their habitat and they hadn't the brains to know what to make of it. The fact that we didn't feel the need to do the peacock walk among the loungers full of beautiful women upset the beef-cakes no end. It challenged their primitive egos.

If we'd been anywhere else, they would have performed the traditional baiting ritual of the empty-headed bully and kicked sand in our faces. But the Blue Marlin? Those stones could ruin a good pedicure.

So instead the trouble came to us in an incredibly subtle way.

Suddenly our €15 Coronas were being knocked off the table, 'accidentally'. And the stares that followed were the stares that said, 'What are you going to do about it?' Classic signs of gorilla aggression followed. Grunting, hooting and chest pounding. That was how the rest of the day went. Pathetic stuff.

I am proud to say we didn't descend to their level. We went a little lower. They'd go down to the sea to cool off and displace a lot of water with their big hammy muscles. We'd soak their towels and loungers in iced water.

Retaliation would be merciless. We'd go for a mosey around the other day-beds to see if we knew anyone, and we'd come back to find our clothes strewn all over the place.

Classic move and countermove stuff.

Then things got silly. We came back from talking to some girls at the bar and found our glasses had been filled up with piss.

'What's your fucking problem?' I asked.

'What? What you going on about?' came the reply.

This is typical of beefcakes. They don't really want to fight. Neither did any of us, for that matter. Nobody wants to fight gymsexual gorilla types when they are on holiday, for fuck's sake.

I remember when I was about twelve or thirteen and my dad was teaching me how to box by smacking me in the face to stress the importance of 'getting your fucking guard up'. (That, Dad, is why you can't have a hippie as a pet. Anyway . . .) 'The thing with muscle-bound fighters,' he'd say, 'is that they can't swing their arms to land a punch, so everything is straight.'

'So what are you saying? Dance round the sides and go for the temple?' I'd ask.

'No, son, no. Just kick 'em in the bollocks then knee 'em in the head.'

I'm pretty sure that kind of manoeuvre is frowned upon among the Marquess of Queensbury set, but that wise piece of paternal advice has often risen to the surface, like acid reflux, down through the years.

At that moment in Ibiza the foot-to-the-bollocks, knee-to-the-head combo seemed like a very good idea. The temperature was soaring and so was my temper.

So that's how it was in the Blue Marlin. The stuff they don't tell you on TripAdvisor. Territory was disputed for hours. At one stage the beefcakes set up a little game. They would pitch small stones to land in plastic cups that they had arrayed. Tossing small stones seemed like a waste of the lifetime they'd spent getting buff in the gym, but that wasn't the point. Every time they missed a cup – and they missed like a centre-half volleying from forty yards – the stones would hit our loungers. Our sacred area. It was the sort of behaviour I hadn't seen since the nine-year-old bullies ruled the roost in the school playground.

Fortunately we were footballers. The gymsexuals had asked questions of our masculinity. There would be no questioning our maturity, though . . .

10

In Ibiza we had rented an amazing villa. Well, that is to say we were renting the villa of a Real Madrid player who had bought the place once upon a time for ever ago when he was madly in love with his girlfriend, a successful DJ. But even galácticos get their hearts broken and we had stepped in to pick up the villa at a 'bargain basement' price for one week. Which was good for him and for us.

Frankly, the DJ must have been mad. I would have married him. You can walk out on a superstar but not a villa like this. This was one incredible place. We should really have invited the owner along to cheer him up with champagne and yoghurt raisins, but the thought hadn't occurred to us as we boarded the twelve-seater Citation private jet at Luton Airport.

I know Luton Airport doesn't seem like the appropriate take-off point for swanky private jets, but we weren't actual galácticos. There would come a time in all our lives when private jets and expensive villas would be only memories. In the meantime, we'd just be sensible and live like fucking mad kings.

I was always a bit ambivalent about private jets, but I actually miss them now. The pros are that you can load them with crates of champagne, beer, etc. There is no limit so long as you can drink it. And you can also get up to anything you like with any girl travelling with you, provided you don't mind an audience. Footballers love an audience.

Also, you can skip the queues for customs and security and have all that dealt with privately at airside as you pull right up to the plane in your limo – classy. And the same applies when you land. In fact I've landed at various places in the world where there have been absolutely no checks and a car has simply whisked us out of the airport, no questions from anybody. It gets you thinking dangerous thoughts.

In hindsight, OK, not so ambivalent. I love private aeroplanes. And I'm socialist enough to wish that everybody else should have them too. Until then, just me.

On these trips I am basically a passenger in every sense. I don't volunteer to take charge of much of the itinerary or the accommodation when we go away. I just let myself end up wherever the bossy types lead me. Then I write about it.

I do, however, have a very good friend who is now a commercial pilot for British Airways. Back when I was playing football, he was getting his hours up by flying private jets. He is very, very handy to know. And a mate. For life. Obviously.

I made what might have been a fatal mistake. I mentioned my pilot mate to the alpha males in the travelling party. These guys weren't going to Ibiza to study the influence of the Carthaginians and the Romans. They just wanted to party to the point where future generations mired in austerity and poxed by Brexit would think that they were all mad. Historically mad.

Landmarks of madness. The high-water mark in the history of decadence and madness.

I don't feel the need to compete with that stuff. When it comes to holidays like this, I go along and enjoy what I can. So I didn't mention the private plane possibility out of any need to big myself up. I mentioned it because their minds were already made up that this year we would fly in a private jet rather than easyJet. I supported this decision wholeheartedly. Plus I happened to know somebody who had a private plane. Or flew one. Same thing.

Initially I wished I had kept my trap shut. I like my mate. I considered the implications of the lads completely taking the piss by loading the little plane with every sort of shit imaginable. I had bad dreams of them trashing the thing. I would be in the aisle shouting at them like a supply teacher out of his depth, then popping up to the cabin to say, 'So sorry about this, mate. I hardly know them.'

I needn't have worried. They did actually take the piss by loading the plane with all sorts of shit and trashing it, but my friend didn't seem to mind. In fact, when we landed and he poked his head out the back, he claimed to have seen far worse. He had expected worse from footballers. He hadn't needed to handcuff any of us, make an emergency landing or bail out with a parachute.

His verdict thrilled me and disappointed the others. He's a good lad because he spills the beans about who has travelled with him. He keeps the little grains of gossip coming. 'Your man from Manchester City flies back to Serbia after every home game to gamble with his mates; I usually have to help the limo driver carry him off the plane and into the car, he's that fucked. Then the other one down at Chelsea, he likes to fly to Madrid to party, but I have to wait for him over the weekend and fly him back on Monday morning for training. Plane stinks when he gets off.'

I try to imagine what he'll say about us. 'Three of them rented the thing one-way. Bloody cheapskates. They didn't even trash it properly. You can see why they're just average Premier League players. They'll be League One and crammed into easyJet within three years, probably headed out to Marbella.'

I got the lads to give him €1,000 as a tip. He's a mate after all. The tip was nowhere near enough apparently. That's what you get when you do a favour for the skinflints of high rolling.

A brand-new white Mercedes was waiting for us on the tarmac. It had blacked-out windows with bulletproof glass. We felt safe from all our enemies.

'We use this when the Prime Minister comes here,' said the driver.

'You mean it's been used before? For fuck's sake.'

'I can put flags on the bonnet if you like?'

We exchanged glances. Did he think he was dealing with kids?

'Yes please,' we said, like characters who had strayed out of an Enid Blyton book.

So the Mercedes drove out of the airport with two Union Jacks flying just above the headlights. He didn't have any North Korean flags. That would have been funnier.

Ibiza is a beautiful jewel in the Mediterranean Sea. The northern part is lush and green, sleepy even. I had stayed in a villa in the

175

north a few years earlier, atop a cliff, overlooking the sea, as cliffs often do. I'd paid £13,000 for the week, but three years later it was purchased by a Russian consortium who literally did nothing new to it whatsoever apart from branding it back in Russia as *the* villa to stay in for oligarchs visiting Ibiza. They bumped up the price to £100,000 a week in the summer months and the place has never been busier.

It's all in the marketing down Ibiza way. I was so disgusted by the shallow greed of the Russian operation that I withdrew my custom. Relations between myself and Russia have been cool ever since.

When I was staying there, Kate Moss was in the villa next door. I don't think she was renting. She'd just broken up with Pete Doherty. I remember taking a stroll outside the gates as the sun was going down and seeing her drive past me in a red convertible Mustang, her hair blown back by the breeze. It looked like a shoot for *Vogue*. I'd like to tell you she waved at me and blew a kiss but she didn't. Maybe she winked at me; she had sunglasses on so it's a possibility. She was definitely playing it cool. That's what I tell people anyway.

Twenty seconds later, I was still waving happily at the rear fender of Kate's Mustang when a white Transit van exploded the serenity of the moment. It was chasing after Kate with what appeared to be at least a dozen paparazzi hanging out of the windows trying to get a shot of her. Or run her off the road. It was hard to tell.

What a life. If I'd had a white horse, I would have galloped after them to save Kate. I was wearing flip-flops though and unprepared for knightly errands.

The eastern side of the island is full of beautiful coves and amazing little beaches with shacks owned by guys who spend their days combing the rocks around the beach looking to spear an unsuspecting octopus. They then hand the poor mollusc (some of them come out of the water with their eight arms up in a gesture of surrender, apparently) over to their chefs to cook for the customers' lunch. Sad, but it's not like the octopus was going to go to college.

In the afternoon, the same guys will skipper their speedboats for the shack's customers who want to relax away from the beach, while drinking champagne and making a lot of noise.

I like the eastern part of Ibiza but the place has a problem. It doesn't have the sunset. A major planning oversight. The sunset is a big attraction for all kinds of people visiting Ibiza. Sunsets are like catnip for stoned hippies.

The honour of hosting the sunset falls to the west. The west always seems to win the bidding wars for hosting sunsets, except on Venus. But in Ibiza the west has a problem too. San Antonio.

San Antonio is to Ibiza what the Elephant Man is to a Gucci photoshoot.

Like three distinguished diplomats recently arrived in friendly territory, we made our way to the plush villa that we'd rented in the hills of Cala Bassa, to the south of San Antonio. It was just expensive enough to be affordable and to ward away the chavs, while also offering some of the best sunset views anywhere in the world. It was a popular choice.

We piled into the villa. It was stunning. The sort of place I have always wanted to build in Ibiza. I've always wanted to have a holiday home on the island, but the prices have exploded in the last five years and today the sort of villa I used to have my eye on, which would have set me back about £1.5 million at the time, now goes for somewhere around £6 million. My timing in football has always been spot on. In property it has always been fucking disastrous.

So I rent villas instead. But even the rental fees have floated up, along with Ibiza's popularity. When I started renting beautiful villas in Ibiza, it was possible to get one for £5,000 for the week. Today those villas start at £20,000, and you can pay up to whatever you like. Forty, fifty grand a week and so on – £100,000 even, if you're from Russia.

I was born ten years too early. My career should be peaking now, just as the crazy TV money is kicking in. Thanks, parents.

Our villa was by no means a favour. I mean, it was a favour that we were able to book it directly, and for slightly less than you'd normally pay because we knew the player. But it still cost us £27,000 for the week. I'm told it was supposed to cost £30,000 but they probably tell everybody that.

This is a guy who earned £100,000 a week for years. I felt that he should be reaching out to lesser footballers a little more charitably. Then again, if you had a villa that you could rent out for £30,000 a week, why the fuck would you be doing freebies?

The villa was a statement. Villas in Ibiza, or anywhere, are about the views. The views across the bay were breathtaking. The perfect blue waters were dotted with flocks of muted sunseekers ambling about below. The infinity pool gently spilled over the blue tiles and down the side of a sheer wall. The outdoor speakers pushed chill-out music down the rocks towards the sea, and the chef we'd hired was busily preparing the BBQ for lunch. Big prawns, steaks, and a beautiful mint salad that I've never quite been able to replicate back home. I think it's missing the sunshine.

The bullshit really falls away at those moments; even footballers, whose sole purpose on earth is to sleep with as many women as possible, are able to savour the simple pleasure of squeezing a freshly picked lemon over a beautifully grilled prawn.

I live for those moments. I'm rarely happier than in those fleeting seconds when people so obviously immersed in one way of life forget themselves. Deep inside them there is the soul of a micro-closet culture vulture. It may be a brief revelation, but it's incredibly fulfilling and profound to me. Even footballers can revive a man's bruised faith in humanity. How about that?

'I should definitely have had a wank before I came,' said Matty, ripping the head off a prawn.

'That's a contradiction in terms, isn't it?' I asked.

'Don't give me all your fucking big words. Ceri rang back, she's sorted the table at Pacha tonight, can't wait! CANNOT FUCKING WAAAAAAAIT!!!'

The echo around the cliff subsided along with the laughter around the table. Matty is a funny fucker. He hasn't got a mean bone in his body and he lives for living his life. On his terms. If he gives footballers a bad name, that's because you don't know him properly. I think we've all got mates like that. You have to know them, and until you do, you'll always be dubious and err on the side of caution-cum-twat.

'Should we hire a helicopter?'

That's Matty being a twat.

From Cala Bassa, Pacha, the local edition of the nightclub franchise, is around half an hour in a cab. Plenty of time to have a beer en route. No rush. The trouble is that everything is a rush for footballers when there's a night out at stake. Matty would happily have left the villa there and then. And the club didn't open for another eight hours. And even then it'd be quiet. Midnight is the time to arrive at a club. If you're going to do it properly, anyway.

So we agreed to go to the Blue Marlin that afternoon, to work on our tans, do damage to our livers through alcohol intake and inflict further suffering on our bank balances.

The helicopter picked us up in Cala Bassa at ten p.m. It dropped us off again at a jetty at 10.06. A more time-efficient waste of money you will never see.

By this time we had inflicted more damage on ourselves than we had intended. We'd left the Blue Marlin many euros poorer and with a giant fly in the ointment of our holiday, so we were in sour mood as we made our way up to Pacha. We still had unfinished business with the beefcake set but we'd try to revive our spirits at the table we had paid through the nose for.

Pacha!

My first thoughts on Pacha were like that moment in adulthood when it suddenly dawns on you that your dad didn't really take the family dog to the farm after all. He'd actually had him put down at the vets. And Grandma wasn't quirky, she was a family embarrassment. Your first time wasn't a rite of passage, it was the talk of the town among the girls at school, for all the wrong reasons. Shorter than a helicopter flight from the Blue Marlin to Pacha, and way less exciting.

I'm never really sure what I expect of nightclubs. Or what they expect of me. I used to be a massive clubber in my late teens, but that was a different person entirely. He doesn't exist now. Before I arrive, I know that the aesthetic of the place will offend the eye. Gaudí himself would struggle to add anything pleasing to the architecture of a club inside and out, not least because he's dead. The outside usually features a doorway with shitty lamps either side of it producing flaccid flames which just about light up the grim mugs of the bouncers and one stunning woman – it's always a stunning woman – wearing an *ushanka* (a Russian hat) and holding a clipboard.

And that is the Pacha set-up all over the world.

Plus one other small detail.

The stunning woman is a bitch. She's always a Grade A, industrial-strength bitch. I think they battery-farm them somewhere.

I don't care if you're Robert De Niro, Calvin Harris, Leonardo DiCaprio or Lionel Messi. Her goal is to impress upon you as a man that she, as a woman, is in control of everything. She holds the key to the door. If you don't lick her thigh-high boots, then you don't get in. It's as simple as that. She has the power to embarrass you beyond normal levels of embarrassment. Tail-between-the-legs, bollock-naked, cock-shrivelled embarrassment.

And she underpins her power with the nuclear armoury of a woman who knows that there isn't a man on earth who doesn't

181

want to sleep with her. She has no intention of sleeping with anyone, of course. As men, we're all beneath her, but not in the way we'd like. That's just the way she likes it.

Her mood darkens when I tell her I've already booked a table. People who have booked tables can't be asked to grovel in order to actually get to the table. Without laughing at her for not smiling and for appearing so miserable and for wearing a big furry hat in the Ibiza heat, you couldn't crush her feelings any harder.

Once in, you walk past a cloakroom, where a woman never quite pretty enough to hold down the job of chief *ushanka*-wearer takes the jackets with the look of a woman wondering if this is the best that life has to offer. I always tip these girls. Then, while an equal measure of trepidation and excitement washes around your stomach, another very pretty woman who clearly has a lot going on upstairs takes you to the table you've booked for €2,000.

And do you know what that table is? It is not fit for purpose for the Knights of the Round Table, even when most of them are away questing. It is not a table that you can sit around for Christmas dinner. It's not even the little table that you sit the kids around next to the big table for Christmas dinner. It is a table roughly the size of a starter plate. It has the dimensions of a normal table only if you happen to be looking at it from very far away. Like, say, Cyprus. And this is your table for the evening. It's a space just big enough to accommodate an ice bucket stuffed to the brim with Red Bull and vodka, so long as you make no sudden movements that might send the whole lot cascading to the floor.

You then order champagne because, well, you just do. And you stand around your little table like you did when you were kids standing around the coats heaped on the floor at your first school disco. Except you've paid two grand for this dance.

I always feel very stiff when I walk into a place like this. Figuratively, not literally. I don't like standing up and being on view. Call me old-fashioned, but I do like a seat, and I also like being able to hear what someone is screaming into my ear. It always seems to be something urgent.

Standing there like a dick is the very moment when you realize that the excitement derived from somebody saying 'Hey! Let's book a table at Pacha' is vastly different from actually being in Pacha with a table. It's the *Stand By Me* dog all over again. What we'd done here was to pay €2,000 to stand among equally stupid people who were now staring trance-like at a DJ hovering above them in a booth. They were watching him as if he was a meteor that would, at some point, crash on to the dancefloor below.

As the night went on, our personal space was confiscated, as if personal space had been made illegal. The place turned into a mushroom field of these little tables. More and more sprouting up until we literally couldn't move. We just stood there like idiots. Everybody did. The only people having any kind of a good time were the regular punters on the dancefloor. They were the only ones in touch with their true selves. Or the only ones filled with Ecstasy.

Now I'm not a prude about drugs, though I have strong views on the subject. But as a footballer, Premier League or otherwise, it just isn't on the radar for me. That is by no means the case for other footballers. Cocaine is a popular recreational choice among footballers of all levels out of season. I've even witnessed players taking Ecstasy in season. That's just crazy to me. Many of the elite players who get caught have the whole thing hushed over. A lingering injury problem is always good. A phantom back problem that won't go away. Nobody can argue with a back injury. Even the world's foremost experts in the subject don't really know a fucking thing about it.

These super Ibiza clubs aren't like clubs in Las Vegas. They remain loyal to the clubber. Vegas wants your money and it is shameless about it. As such, Vegas prices out regular punters. But in Ibiza a club without regular punters doesn't work. Ibiza clubs are very different beasts. They have a wider and more diverse commercial business to consider. They mix albums to sell and create club music to break to the masses and so on. They are far larger entities than simply the star DJ who is playing in the booth on any given weekend.

I used to go clubbing all the time before I became a footballer: Ministry of Sound, Gatecrasher, Cream, Godskitchen, you name it, I was there. But these clubs aren't the place to be as you get older and, let's face it, snobbier. That night I hated it and felt aggrieved about being charged so much for something that was delivering so little. Revenge would be taken on Pacha.

I looked around. In all honesty, I was bored. I saw two beautiful girls dancing up on a podium. Dancers for Pacha, with legs up to here and smiles out to there. They were holding the attention of almost every sober man in the building.

One was Spanish. And she was fucking beautiful.

In football we have players who fall in love easily. They are usually members of the youth team on their first away trip. They are part of a football team and as such they sidestep the ritual rejections inflicted on most mortal men. They get in the door off the back of being associated with a professional club, and they think they are gods.

I myself have never fallen in love abroad. Apart from at that moment in Pacha.

For a while I looked back on that moment and thought that I must have been looking for something to fill my night. I was out. A Premier League footballer. And I wasn't having a good time. That's not on. I had paid through the nose for a good time.

And then it happened.

I spied a bunch of lads on the dancefloor. Muscle-bound twats, bumping into everybody in their tight white V-neck T-shirts, skinny jeans and flip-flops. Fucking flip-flops? In a club? Cutting-edge naff. They had the worrying glow of a group who'd had too much sun but would probably be enviably brown by the following morning.

Now, Your Honour, please take into account that I was tired and emotional and angry and my radar had narrowed to locked-on mode.

Vanity knows no bounds for some people. I know a player who puts a tampon up his bum when he goes on a night out, just in case he soils his favourite pair of white D&G briefs and embarrasses himself when he strips off alongside whatever woman has agreed to come back to his apartment. Great villa, shitty knickers is a dangerously mixed message.

One of my team-mates came back from the toilet and I pointed out the pricks to him. My hunch was right. They were the same gymsexual, beefcake, roided-up pricks we'd had run-ins with on the beach that day.

Clearly my friend had snorted half of Ibiza during his most recent trip to the bathroom. He just didn't care. 'Don't worry about it,' he said. 'Here, have some of this instead.' And he reached inside his pocket, pulled out a small bag and gave it to me.

He had a point. I took the bag, stuffed it into my pocket and walked off to the toilets.

The bright lights of the bathroom woke me up. I actually felt alive and awake. I saw clarity. I had a clear sense of what the night called for.

I took out the bag and did what had to be done.

I tipped the bathroom attendant €20. I've always done this. They love you for it. You will go to the bathroom countless times during a night at a club and they are always rammed and hostile. One payment of €20 on your first visit will ensure that from that moment on you jump the queue, use all the after-shaves, and are generally looked after like a god. It's well worth it, trust me.

I stumbled out of the bathroom, found our table again and poured myself two vodka and Red Bulls.

The music had hit one of those repetitive troughs where the beat doesn't change for about fifteen minutes. A friend of mine who owned the Ministry of Sound back in Blighty once told me that DJs do this in order to allow the clubbers to dissipate their energy from the initial taking of drugs. Apparently there are times in a night when it is obvious that the dancefloor has emptied. The DJ then has to wait an appropriate amount of time for the drugs to kick in, as people make their way back to the dancefloor, before he plays his big tunes. Otherwise the biggest tunes are wasted. It's a science.

Anybody who regularly goes to clubs recognizes this low point in the evening. I did. And so did the two dancers.

Podium dancers are, to me, a strange and unexplained phenomenon. No man ever thinks he has a chance with a podium dancer. So no man ever approaches the dancers up on the podium to offer them a drink. They'll approach them for photos and to leer from close up, but never with the offer of a drink.

Usually I'm one of those men. But only because the phenomenon interests me.

I bided my time now. The night was still in a lull, but the music was slowly picking up again. People were 'coming up', as they say in the drug-taking business. The mood needle was getting back to good time happy on the dial. The lights returning like an epileptic's nightmare; the beat picking up with its hypnotic thrum; people beginning to move again. Within minutes the place was starting to bounce like it was experiencing a series of small earthquakes. People were getting hot.

The two dancers continued to milk the break, sliding up and down the pole in lieu of doing any real dancing. I was able to appreciate their squatting from a purely gym-based perspective. I've squatted more weights than Swampy has squatted in spinneys up and down the country. For the briefest of moments I was able to appreciate the perfect muscle definition brought about by those squats. And the hot pants. I appreciated those too. But all that could wait. I had a drink to deliver.

I picked up the two glasses of vodka and Red Bull and walked over to the platform where this extremely hot Spanish dancer was doing her thing. We hadn't met, but I had decided that I was in love with her.

'Hey,' I said. Always a good in. It's my smoothest line.

She looked down on me, and at that point it was fifty-fifty whether I would get a smile or a stiletto through the eye. But she popped a flashbulb of a smile that suggested that she either couldn't believe somebody could be so stupid as to talk to one of the dancers, or that nobody had ever dared to speak to her before while she was working.

She may have been grateful. She might turn me into an hilarious anecdote to tell her friends. I honestly didn't know. Top clubs take their dancers very seriously and I didn't want to upset her.

'Hey,' she said back. The art of conversation. See, we were different to the pack, she and I.

All hugely encouraging.

Spanish women do something to me. They are so fiery. They look at you with a face somewhere between disdain and casual wonderment. And that is so fucking sexy.

They are the matador. I am the bull. Sure, they'll leave me dead and bleeding in the dust, but the thrill of charging at that red cape . . . Magic.

'You look hot,' I said. I had brought my A game.

I handed her one of the vodka Red Bulls. She took the drink and sipped through the straw. She shouted down to me, quite tenderly I thought, 'Thanks, you look hot too.'

Please don't hand back the drink, I thought. With conversation like this, why would you hand back the drink?

Carmen, as I'd decided she was called, bent down and roared what I rated as a massively sexual 'thank you' into my ear. Her long legs began to push the rest of her perfect frame skyward. I reached out and grabbed her hand to steady her. You're not supposed to do that but she had called me hot. I think. Maybe she had said 'you look not too hot'. That would have been sexy too though.

'Listen,' I said, 'now that we're best friends, can you do me a favour?'

She flashed that confusing look of disdain and wonderment that could end up with a kiss on the lips, a slap on the face or a kick in the groin.

Now this may come as an enormous shock for you, having read the above exchange. But, as I think I've said before, I'm actually not very good with women. I am an observer. I like talking to women if they talk to me first, but it's all pretty forced, unless it's blatantly obvious that a woman likes me. And even then it's touch and go. I'd rather they committed something to paper that was legally binding, that stated their intentions categorically.

My Achilles heel is that I adore Spanish women. Still, I hadn't studied them closely enough to know what to expect when they flashed that look. I was suddenly so nervous that I wished I had a tampon up my bum.

But she took the bait.

'What would you like from me, Mr Vodka Red Bull?'

I'd have married her there and then. That is what I would have liked. I still love Carmen.

'Listen,' I said, 'it's my friend's birthday. He's the one on the

189

dancefloor in the white V-neck T-shirt. Too much sun. Flip-flops. See him?'

'I can see him,' said Carmen.

'Well, that's my best friend. He's twenty-one today, and I just want to do something a little crazy for him and make him feel special. I'm thinking maybe you can help?'

And with that I pulled out the small bag I had in my pocket and gave it to her. Then I explained what I wanted her to do.

She agreed.

The music duly went down and the big spotlights went up and at that moment Mr Muscle became the King of Pacha for about a minute, as the whole club turned to look at this beef-bound idiot on the dancefloor who was jumping around with his mouth open as he tried to gobble up the yoghurt raisins being thrown to him from one of the Pacha podiums by the hottest woman in all of Ibiza. And from our shitty €2,000 table we watched the whole thing unfold.

I'd discreetly shared an important detail with my travelling companions. Every single one of those yoghurt raisins had been up my arsehole in the Pacha bathroom about five minutes earlier.

The crowd cheered and counted all twenty-one raisins as they looped from the podium and into the beefcake's mouth.

'Happy Birthday!' they all shouted when the final one went in.

Happy Fucking Birthday!

I still have the pictures. Somewhere. I'm keeping them to show my grandchildren how men settled things in the wild east of Ibiza back in the old days.

PART FIVE

Welcome to Las Vegas

11

So you have made it. Well done. Your face is on football stickers and young men who are selling very expensive cars want to shake your hand and pretend to be your best friend.

It all happens so fast that even if it happens, as it did to me, a little later in life, you still feel as if somebody has put a hood over your head, bundled you into a limo and dumped you into some world with no rules and no limits.

You know those people who say that if they won the lottery, they wouldn't change a thing? They'd still go and work in the factory and live on the terrace and sup watery ale in the local? Miserable bastards should be barred from even playing the lottery.

What is the point in handing over a huge fun-size cheque to somebody who thinks that their regular life is as much fun as they can handle?

I can trace my career, the financial side of it (and therefore the football side too), through the holidays we took and the things we bought. It's a line that runs parallel to the growth of the Premier League. From the days when everybody went to Marbella and footballers just lorded it over those who had been saving all year to get there, to the world of private villas in Miami or Dubai where the entire point is to keep the rest of the world out. That's one way of telling the financial life story of the Premier League.

When Deloitte brought out their report for the 2015/16 season, the first time that Premier League wages had passed the £2 billion mark, they topped the piece with one incredible statistic. 'By half-time of the second Premier League game that is televised domestically in 2016/17, more broadcast revenue will have been generated than by all the First Division matches combined 25 years ago.'

That is the context of this book. The Premier League is one gigantic, out-of-control money machine. It defies all laws of economics. The same product just keeps on getting more and more valuable. Last season, when Spurs lost to Newcastle on the last day of the season, they dropped from second place to third. That single place cost £1,236,083. Four years previously, the drop would have cost just £755,062.

As no Spurs fan will need reminding, Arsenal stole that second-place slot. They were the biggest Premier League earners for the season, having topped up their second-place reward of £23.7 million by appearing on TV some twenty-seven times, bringing them income of £101 million before tickets (the most expensive seats in the league), sponsors, merchandise, exhibition games and so on. If they repeat the trick precisely and come second in 2016/17 and appear on television the same number of times, they will get a cheque for £152 million.

That is the extent of the madness. If players get a huge cut

194

of the profits, that is because players put bums on seats and satellite dishes on gable ends. Top players who grind to stay fit, and who struggle through injuries, and who work on their game relentlessly, now make maybe half as much as a mid-ranking Hollywood star. Jennifer Lawrence made $52 million in 2014 and complained rightly that if she was a man she would have made a lot more. Nobody tells Jennifer Lawrence that her earnings are obscene. Footballers hear it all the time.

We have caught some of the madness. We didn't create it, but it's contagious. So champagne wars and luxury villas and private planes? If you had the money, if you won the lottery, wouldn't you?

At my peak earnings – and it's strange to think that people now say, yeah well, that was before the money got silly – I earned a basic wage of over £30,000 a week. Sometimes I would try to be sensible and say to myself that there would only be a few years of this, and if I spread all those £30Ks out over a lifetime, they wouldn't go that far.

Then I would remember all the other stuff.

When I moved from my first pro club to my second pro club, I was introduced to something novel and lovely. The appearance fee.

By then I was not just getting paid a lot of money to be a footballer, but if I actually *played* on Saturday, I got a bonus of £2,000. That's right. The one thing in the whole world that I had ever wanted to do, and would have done for just about nothing, I was getting paid well for, *and* I was getting a bonus for actually doing it, when I would have given £2,000 a week of my wage back just to be in the first team.

When I moved on from there to my next club, the appearance fee went up to £3,000 a game. I had assimilated the concept of appearance fees into my lifestyle by then. I got taught a lesson though. They call them bonuses because that is what they are. When the manager wants to punish you, he takes you off the bonus drip feed. In a month where there are eight games and you have been relegated to the stand for all eight of them, you are down £24K. In a ten-month season, if you continue to go nose to nose with the gaffer, you are paying the best part of a quarter of a million for the privilege of staying in the fight.

And of course your manager knows that you are more than likely mortgaged to the limit of your basic wage, and that all the bonuses pay for the extras, the madness, the froth. So he squeezes you till your bank screams. It takes very little pressure to make those bastards scream.

When you aren't playing, you miss out on so many little bonuses the general punter never considers. Bonuses are the fuel of excess. A quick guide:

Win bonuses first. Yes, the whole point of the game is to win. We all know that. But in case footballers forget to win, there is a bonus for getting three points.

If you start the match then you get a full win bonus. If you start on the bench but you get on the field at some stage, you get a half win bonus. If you start on the bench and you stay there for ninety minutes, you get nothing.

Ever wonder why so few players mind being thrown into a match with two minutes left when the team are 3-0 up? It seems like tokenism putting a player on for a couple of minutes just to break the momentum of the game. Well, tokenism doesn't

196

show up in your account at the end of the month. A half win fee does.

What I have just been talking about are personal win bonuses. They are set in your own personal contract. Depending on what sort of agent you have, you might be on a pretty hefty win bonus, or the agent, as mine used to do, would have the bonus built into the wage.

For instance, the club would say, 'We're giving him so much a week but with this win bonus, if they win twenty-five games a year, well, just look at what he will earn.'

Will they win twenty-five games a year? Of course they will. It's a lock.

'OK then, we'll just build that money into the basic wage in that case. Seeing as how you are certain you will be spending it anyway.'

Clubs are wary of that approach. They want you to be incentivized. They don't want you going on to the pitch without a financial incentive. So if you play hardball, you will get a better basic, and you may well still get the bonuses on top.

But when you scale it up you hit the big boys: Agüero, Rooney, Hazard, etc. These are the guys who aren't really that fussed by win bonuses in a league game. They have their bonuses pegged to winning trophies.

Roughly speaking, the win bonuses for a player winning a trophy at a Premier League club would be the following:

The Premier League: £500,000
The FA Cup: £100,000
The League Cup: £50,000

The Champions League: £750,000–£1 million pro rata

That's a whole lot of Marbella right there.

But here's where it gets more complicated.

You also have a squad bonus. The names of twenty players are submitted to the FA at the start of the Premier League season. Your captain will generally take the club's offer of a 'pot of money' at the start of the season and see that it gets split pro rata. That means that the youth team players who play at the end of the season, when relegation or promotion is certain, will receive a few grand. That pot is whatever you can negotiate. The most I've had a cut of is £2.5 million. Those of us who played in almost every game got £125,000. Each. More on that shortly.

The problem with negotiating the pot for the following season is that you are all away on holiday when the bargaining is done. Footballers aren't big on planning. Shortly after you get back with your tan and your stories, some idiot pipes up, 'Well, what are the bonuses this year?' And everybody looks at each other. Has nobody looked after the bonus? For fuck's sake.

The club has now got you by what are known in the trade as the balls. The bonus sheets have to be handed in to the FA for the purposes of fair play rules. They have to be scrutinized. It has to be done soon. If not, there will be no bonuses at all.

By the time a group of players get their act together on bonuses, the club will happily have let the clock run down on the deadline for submitting the list. No club chairman ever sticks his head into the dressing room and says, 'Well chaps, high time we all sat around the table and negotiated what sort of bonuses you would like.' So quite often players just sign their names and agree to whatever the bonus pot was the previous season. Every few years, somebody will say, 'How come the club has got richer and richer, but the bonus pot has stayed the same?' And then a negotiation will get done.

I heard, incidentally, that the Leicester players were initially stiffed on their Premier League win bonuses, but as the tidal wave of goodwill grew, the club made good and paid what was earned and well-deserved at the end of the season.

Now, keep paying attention.

You have your personal win bonus. You have your club win bonus. But one or both bonuses can be pegged to your club's league position. Chief executives are not stupid. Honestly. It roughly works like this – but keep in mind there are big clubs and small clubs, even in the Premier League. So let's take an average Premier League club.

Position 1–3: £10,000 per win (after the first month. You have to allow for alphabetical ordering in the opening week's league tables. As I said, chief executives aren't naive.)

Position 4–6: £7,000 a win

Position 7–10: £5,000 a win

Position 11–17: £3,000 a win

Position 18–20: £2,000 a win

When I signed for my first professional football club, I had a win bonus of £200. There was no clean-sheet bonus. No goal bonus. No assist bonus. Actually, assist bonuses have largely died out. Fuck it, just stick it on the bottom line if you would.

The bonuses went up though. When I signed for my next club it was £1,500 a win. Then it went up incrementally to £3,000 a win, and then the Premier League rules took over and bonuses began to be pegged to league position. It ended up that eleventh in the Premier League was worth less than top six in the Championship. Chance of going up. Chance of going down. That bloody chief executive.

What else? Well, we have what are called cumulative bonuses. So after maybe ten games, you'll get a £20,000 payment. Then after another ten games, you'll get the same again. This is pegged to what we call a loyalty bonus.

If you negotiate a big loyalty bonus, you'll get it spread out in this manner. Otherwise you might get, say, £50,000 after forty games.

These are always the first payments to be struck off when clubs are getting rid of a player. Legally they owe you every penny, so long as you haven't asked to leave the club, but those situations are as stressful as divorces. Everybody knows that the player will probably take a financial hit for the sake of a clean break.

You always start from the point where you ask for everything, every penny of what is due to you, and the club always starts from the point where they've immediately taken out your loyalty bonus and halved your basic salary as their first offer.

Loyalty bonuses are a bit of a misnomer, to be honest. When it gets to the divorce stage, there is no loyalty.

Then we have the common-or-garden bonuses. Goal bonuses for strikers. Clean-sheet bonuses for defenders and keepers. Midfielders claim a bit of credit at both ends, and as I said, in the old days there were assist bonuses too. Nowadays a good midfielder will largely forgo those bonuses to shove up his basic wage. The ability of an Özil or a Coutinho to deliver a large number of assists will be built into his basic wage, with smaller bonuses for scoring goals.

Paul Pogba's reported wage for signing with Manchester United is £13 million a year net, plus £7 million for image rights. His agent, Mino Raiola, a man who seldom misses a trick or leaves a penny on the table, won't have done much faffing about over bonuses.

I think that goal bonuses are the only bonuses you can sometimes see on the pitch. Most strikers will lay off a pass to somebody in a better position if they want to keep getting picked, but penalties are a different matter. You will see the occasional little squabble as players stand over the ball when a penalty is given. Nobody is arguing for the right to run over to the fans and kiss the badge and be a hero for thirty seconds. Well, just a little bit. But mainly what it is about is the goal bonus. Not necessarily this year's goal bonus, but the negotiation of next year's. I played with a winger who campaigned like a rat in heat for the right to take penalties and free-kicks. At the end of the season he could say, 'I played out on the left wing and I scored ten goals. SHOW ME THE MONEY!'

An old pro once said to me: 'TSF, get on everything.'

He remembered Dean Saunders scoring about twenty-three goals in a season once and twelve of them were penalties. At the end of the season there was no asterisk after Saunders' name concerning the number of penalties he had scored. He was a twenty-three-goal striker. Dean got a big move for the next season.

Get on everything. Good advice.

12

We grow older. We grow richer. We change. We are footballers, so we don't mature as such. We just change. We get bored more easily. We crave pastures new.

When I started playing football, every summer we all flew like great flocks of migrating birds to Marbella. Every chance we got, we took off. The whole known world as far as we were concerned was in Marbella. And we footballers would land there and strut around the blue pools and strobed clubs knowing that we had more exotic feathers than all the other poor, sad wading birds.

And then a few intrepid and well-minted souls expanded our idea of the universe. If you went further than Marbella, you didn't fall over the edge of credibility. So we tried out Ibiza and nothing bad happened to us. If you kept going, it was rumoured that eventually you got to some kind of Shangri-La. Eventually you would end up in the place now known in dressing-room myth and legend as Las Fucking Vegas.

Early explorers returned to their respective clubs for pre-season training and told tales of tanned girls, mucho bling, easy cocaine and never-ending parties. Within days, we'd all heard the stories. There was a brave new world out there. A new frontier of debauchery and excess. We would boldly go and we would boldly blow more than any football men had blown before.

That's where the hustle lies. It's in the never-ending search for locations around the world that the camera can't see. The places where the tabloid expense accounts can't reach. Get it right, and you can bend more rules than the Catholic Church in its prime.

When the big money made its way down from the board-room and gushed into the pockets of the players, everything changed. For one thing, the entire Premier League decamped from Marbella to Las Vegas, every fucking summer. Marbella was as yesterday as Butlin's. The season was dead and so was Marbella. Jetting off to the Costa del Crime had been a tradition as old as apprentices cleaning boots. Ibiza had had its time too. The island still has its followers but they don't boast about it as much. Even with the revival. Now with the money flooding football, even the apprentices had the cash to get to Sin City, Nevada, if they wanted to.

When Paul Pogba was about to sign for Manchester United, for twenty-five times more money than was sensible, where was he photographed? In the swimming pool at Wet Republic in Las Vegas, surrounded by lovelies who wanted to talk to him about the geopolitical implications of the recent Turkish coup. Meanwhile Pogba's agent was negotiating fees of £20 million just for himself.

There was only one thing we needed to understand before

we flew off. And I'm sure it was the same for Pogba. Vegas is a bottle of smoke.

Deep within the Venetian Hotel on the main drag lies a nightclub, a nightclub like no other. Tao Club is where dreams come true. Forget about the fake canals and the phoney gondoliers up in the lobby. This is primo fantasy land for grown-ups. Not fun for all the family.

Tao is 60,000 square feet of the high life spread out over multiple levels. Models in bathtubs full of petals welcome you as you arrive. Fine cuisine and clubbing at night. A beach, Tao Beach, by day.

Of course there are multiple levels to everything. Especially romance, love and sex. All of which Tao provides.

Petals, beautiful models, a fake beach. Vegas has the whitest and brightest of smiles as it slips its hand into your bulging pocket. Welcome, friends. Welcome.

Bottle of smoke.

Brace yourself for this news flash, citizens of Earth. There are girls who just want to sleep with us footballers because of what we do, what we earn and the attention we attract.

To be honest, I don't really know what that's all about, outside of the fact that they just enjoy having sex with attractive young men. There is perhaps only the remote possibility that the player may fall in love with the girl in the quiet moments after the act. But probably love is not the point. The reality is that usually the player is trying to remember which door he came in through. And, shit, what her name is. And how long it's been since his last drink. And whether or not it would be

OK to find the car and drive home. And when exactly he last saw his mates.

After a while – OK, after a very long while for some footballers – casual sex with women who just want to bed somebody rich or famous or both gets stale. Then there is the next level: girlfriend potential. Girls who look the part but who have more to them than looking the part. They expect you to notice that there is more to them. They even expect there to be more to you.

They won't sleep with just anybody; they're more choosey, which makes you feel good if you are one of the chosen. OK, sometimes there's a touch of Chelsea FC about them. They'll cherry-pick the best-looking players and they'll expect all that goes with that once you start to go steady.

Some of them are 'dicks', as we gallantly say. They are only interested in 'the life', and when they aren't staring at themselves in a mirror, their heads are lodged firmly up their own arses.

'Have you met John's new missus?'

'Nah, what's she like?'

'Yeah, she's OK actually.'

'Really? She's not a dick?'

This is good for John. Seeing a friend dating a dick can be like watching him living in denial about a serious illness he has developed. He'll come out the other end shaken and weakened and in serious cases having been surgically removed from half of everything he has ever earned by a divorce lawyer with a scalpel.

The longer you are in football, the more depressed you get

about human nature. But if John's new squeeze does turn out to be a genuinely nice girl and you get on with John, the two of them might become a couple you and your wife will begin to go out with for dinner. Like in the real world.

Finally, there are the 'worldys'. In football, the word 'worldy' refers to anything that is amazing and that fills us with awe. For us the Seven Wonders of the World are really the Seven Worldys of the World.

Vegas is full of worldys. Many of them have had their breasts surgically enlarged. They are worldys with two deeply tanned worlds hanging out of their dresses. These girls are something everybody should see once in their lifetime.

When I was something of a Vegas novice, my friend Kyle was the man to go to Vegas with. He was my Tonto, and I knew he'd look after the Lone Ranger. He'd ridden these happy trails before and he knew what to look for.

Kyle is good-looking and also a very wealthy footballer. Which in his case means he has slept with at least four hundred women, although he doesn't put that stat on his Facebook page. Five of them were worldys, he reckons.

One night in the Tao Club we had reserved a booth through a fixer whom Kyle knew. Even if you are riding with Tonto, a fixer makes life in Vegas a million times easier. We had secured a front-row booth. He was very good at his job, this fixer. One of the world's greatest DJs was sharing his record collection. Our fixer arranged that this world-famous DJ would send a bottle of very good champagne to our front-row table.

That's a timeless Vegas folk tradition from the days of the elders. Sinatra and Elvis would have bottles delivered to tables of mobsters who had come to see them perform. Back then it was a sign of respect. Today it's a sign that we have the money to pay the fixer to pay the world's best DJ to pretend to pay for a bottle of champagne and to have it delivered to us in the least discreet way possible. To make us look like guys everybody should recognize. Really, only the people at the neighbouring two dozen or so tables need to notice. We feel famous and connected. We bow towards the DJ booth to acknowledge the generosity of our mate, the world-famous DJ, and as soon as we raise our glasses we forget entirely that we actually paid for the whole business ourselves.

Of course, we had more than one bottle to deal with. On our table we had an ice bucket large enough to wash a Shetland pony in. Should we have chosen to order a Shetland pony. Or have the DJ appear to send us a Shetland pony. Either way, we just had to ask our fixer.

Our ice bucket was actually filled with $2,000 bottles of Grey Goose and bottles of Jack Daniel's, flavoured with cinnamon and honey for health reasons. The bottles were surrounded by floating cans of Red Bull. You've never seen so much Red Bull. An entire mountain range in the north west must have given its life in bauxite just to make the cans on our table.

Kyle loved this scene. Music. Alcohol. Beautiful women. Worldys everywhere.

And Kyle. People knowing that whoever the fuck he was, he was somebody.

With the music and alcohol components of the evening having been taken care of, Kyle shifted his attention to the women. He is no fool. These places are filled with women who are miracles of modern science. They transfuse your money into profit for the house. And you feel no pain. They help you spend; they let you haemorrhage your money. They encourage you to drink faster and longer and more expensively and more manfully.

And they are all beautiful.

Watching them work is an education. A beautiful woman is sliding past a young guy who is brandishing a jeroboam of Château In Your Face which cost him more than his dad ever earned in six months.

'Oh, wow, champagne,' says the girl. 'It's been so long since I've had a glass of champagne; the bubbles go straight to my head.'

What can the player do? 'Well, try this,' he says, like Sir Walter Raleigh throwing his cape over a puddle.

She takes a sip. 'Wow. That is *so* nice. You must know champagne. You stay right here. I am going to go find my friend and come straight back to you. Actually, can I take a glass for her as well?'

She vanishes for five minutes, a full glass in each manicured fist. She tosses one full glass into a bin, followed by half the contents of the next.

She returns. 'Aw. She's talking to some guy but she loved the champagne too. She said thank you so much. Can I join you?'

And for the next couple of hours she will sit and be absorbed in the wonder of the player.

'Wow, really? A team called Crewe Alexandra? That is *so* funny.'

He feels like the fucking worldy now. And he hasn't even mentioned Accrington Stanley.

He knows that these professional girls exist, but this one is different. She cares. She really does. She is engaged. And now that she has the hang of it, she drinks like a fish. She's chasing down the champagne with swigs of beer and gulps of Red Bull. She seems to be getting tipsier and tipsier. As she does, she gets even more attractive, and the player realizes that he is becoming even more interesting.

In fact, all she is doing is taking slugs of champagne and spitting them back into the beer bottles and Red Bull cans. The player is the one getting drunk. Gloriously, expensively drunk. She is just helping.

Kyle and myself. We needed that sort of company. Top-of-the-line illusion. Our fixer vanished in search of the owner.

Soon there was quite literally a parade of stunningly beautiful women discreetly walking past our table, auditioning for the thrill of sitting with us. They wanted so badly to hear the story about the League Cup replay in the sleet at Hull.

At the table behind us were three World Cup winners from Brazil. That would have been a celebrity mismatch anywhere but Vegas. In the Church of Vegas, though, all soccerballers are equal in the eyes of the house. As long as you can pay, you'll be treated equally. And if none of you can pay, you'll all be shot just as equally. No favourites. Our indecision about the girls was crippling us. The Brazilians were helping us decide on the basis that they assumed they had better taste and more experience in everything.

Finally our fixer arrived back, sidling along with quite literally the most beautiful woman I had ever seen in my life. She wasn't dressed like the other girls; she looked elegant in a style that whispered that she didn't have to try as hard as the others. Her hair was long and brunette, and her complexion was perfect from every angle.

Being absolute gentlemen, the footballers at both tables, drawn as we were from many diverse cultures, stood as one and roared, 'That one!'

I think at that moment all the other women in the club can never have loved 'that one' more.

Next, there was an unseemly battle, like two wealthy clubs vying for Messi's signature. The Brazilians wanted this girl's company too. In the end Kyle promised our fixer a large amount of money, which I assumed he had previously earmarked as a charitable donation to solve the problems of three under-developed nations.

It was done.

She flowed to our table and sat down beside Kyle. She had a liquid grace about everything she did. Instead of the customary kiss on the cheek and hug, she offered us her hand and we each shook it gently. Nothing impressed her overly.

We got into a champagne war with the Brazilians. A pissing contest, where you send the most expensive champagnes known to man to each other's tables, until somebody breaks down and cries. The war escalated quickly. Single bottles were followed by entire cases of Cristal, which were met with the atomic bomb response of an entire case and twelve shots of tequila. This ended with Kyle flying a bottle of champagne with sparklers hanging out of it over the entire club on a zip wire. It was crazy. It was unheard of. It was victory.

It was the mother of all bills, and it was coming our way.

The fixer had that look on his face. The look I would come to associate with a doctor frowning just before he says, 'Yeah, I think it might be an STD.' And he is thinking, 'Oh mate, but you've got bigger problems than an STD.'

'Guys,' the fixer said, 'the house wants you to take a look at the bill. It's $130,000.'

We took a look at the bill. Yes, it was $130,000. He was right.

Kyle: Tell him to just stick it on the main bill.

Fixer: They're not gonna do that, you're gonna have to pay some now, guys.

Which was about the moment when Kyle realized that this lovely girl sitting beside him was entirely unimpressed.

'I really don't care about any of this stuff; when are you going to get to know me?' she said. Her green eyes looked into Kyle's bleary eyes and asked the question. There is more to me. Is there more to you?

They talked. Had he seen the Picassos in the Wynn? She planned to travel to Paris and Rome and wanted to study literature in Barcelona. She wanted to see the world on her terms. She was very interested in the study of people and how they behave.

Kyle was behaving well. The fact that somebody was interested in him as a real person and not as a wealthy footballer had sobered him up considerably. As had the bill.

This woman was half-Iranian. Her skin was olive perfection. Her back story was fascinating. She hated this work. She could never feel at home in America, let alone Las Vegas. She sipped her champagne and seemingly appreciated its subtleties.

She loved the Grand Canyon. It had filled her with awe and humility. Vegas was a monument to man. The Grand Canyon put man in his place.

Kyle told her that he'd won $60,000 at roulette in Caesars Palace. Instantly he regretted saying it.

'I don't like gambling,' she said. 'It seems to be such a waste of life to be indoors and losing money while you do so.'

Kyle remembered just then that he thought that too. Exactly that.

There was a sadness about her, a poignant twist to her beauty. She wanted simple things, a life of the mind and the heart, and she had ended up here in Las Vegas.

Kyle looked into these green eyes and fell in love. Not lust. Love. He cared for her and her life. Already.

'Do you know what?' he said. 'I'm pretty hungry; I didn't have anything to eat before I came out. I bet my fixer could get us a table at the Picasso restaurant . . . if you want to, obviously.'

She fed him black salmon. They talked more. They drank good wine. His mind wandered. How was he going to tell his wife? Just say 'Look, I found somebody else'? Try the old 'it's not you, it's me'? Pretend he had a disease and was going away to see the world alone and to reconcile himself with the life he had led? Who said there must be fifty ways to leave your missus?

One thing Kyle knew. He would pass through this life just once. And this was the woman whose hand he wanted to hold as he did so. If she wanted to live in the outback with Aborigines, he would follow her. If she wanted an igloo in the Arctic

213

Circle, he would build it. If she wanted the Taj Mahal, it would be hers. She shared his soul. She would share his life.

The famous fountains of the Bellagio Hotel were halfway through their evening ballet as they walked afterwards. She led him to a spot away from the tourists.

'I come here a lot to watch the fountains,' she said, 'but I've never been into the Bellagio itself.'

Perfect.

'Follow me,' said Kyle, and he held her hand and led her inside towards a penthouse suite.

By the time the elevator stopped at the right floor, Annalise, for that was her name, had taken her shoes off. She walked down the hall to the door like a child of nature.

Kyle covered every inch of her in kisses. Showed her the full range of his moves. He had never felt so nervous before.

When he awoke, fuzzy-headed and happy, the sun was bleaching the room. First day of the rest of my life, he said to himself, and got up to see what part of the penthouse she was exploring.

I found him hours later sitting on a banquette looking out over Vegas as if that mad city held all the mysteries of the earth and he had just solved the hardest one.

'Well, mate,' I said. 'Good night?'

'She fucked us,' Kyle said.

Dr Sanchez down at the hospital was a lovely man, especially considering that he was coming off a seventeen-hour rotation.

We were leaving for the UK that afternoon and Kyle needed a once-over. He wasn't wearing any shoes. Just the free pair of slippers that the hotel stuffs into the socks and pants drawer.

His shoes were with his soulmate – staring at the humbling awesomeness of the Grand Canyon perhaps.

'Sure,' said Dr Sanchez.

He checked Kyle's blood pressure and his temperature and other vitals. Then he said that he wanted to take a blood sample. Kyle asked if he could just piss into a cup instead; it's quicker, after all: we know that from being drug-tested during the season. Alas, Dr Sanchez explained that blood samples are more accurate and that if we didn't mind waiting he'd have the results in an hour.

Fast-forward two hours. Dr Sanchez's shift had yet to finish. He sat down with us holding a clipboard. He was surrounded by some student medics and a handful of nurses.

'Now,' he said gently. And everybody smiled softly at Kyle. 'Good news. No sign of an STD.'

'Aw, thank fuck. Cheers, Doc.'

'One more thing,' said Dr Sanchez. 'Kyle, do you know what benzodiazepines are?'

Kyle didn't know. Me neither.

'Well, Kyle, it's a class of drugs which we call benzos for short. Benzos can be used to treat a few things.' Dr Sanchez paused. 'But around here it's most commonly found in Rohypnol.'

Kyle was bemused and confused. 'But I haven't taken Rohypnol. Why would I take it? It knocks you out.'

Dr Sanchez leaned back in his chair. 'I know, Kyle. And if you prefer not to, you don't have to answer this next question. Did you perform oral sex on this woman you met?'

Dr Sanchez had our full and undivided attention now.

'I think I did, yeah.'

The students and nurses were grinning now.

'Well, Kyle, this is what has happened, buddy, so far as we can tell. You took the woman back to your room. You got down to business, and at some point you performed the oral sex act on her. Unfortunately, and we see this every now and again, these women who operate here are going to the bathroom just before and putting liquid Rohypnol on their . . . you know . . . their private parts. When the guy performs oral sex, he laps up the drug like a kitten at a saucer of milk. Then pretty soon he's out of it. My guess is that if your safe was locked, you probably gave her the code without even knowing you did it.'

It all made sense. That was how Kyle's 60K had left the room, along with everything we had intended leaving Vegas with, including a couple of watches worth a combined total of over $100K. One of them was mine, which made it not very funny at all.

The medical staff were almost doubled over now. Dr Sanchez was having to compose himself before starting each sentence. Thank fuck they didn't know about the champagne war with the Brazilians.

'Kyle,' said Dr Sanchez, 'do you feel OK now? Is there anything else that doesn't feel right? Do you feel nauseous, headaches?'

Kyle was still trying to take in what he had just been told. 'Well,' he began. 'I'm OK. It's just that I've had this taste of salmon in my mouth ever since I woke up.'

That was it. That did it. The medical staff were holding clipboards up to their faces and their shoulders were bouncing up and down so hard that I thought they were going to have to be sedated themselves.

That is what makes the city so thrilling. Do you remember the bit in the Disney film *Pinocchio* where the children are allowed to go aboard a boat and do all the things that kids want to do behind their parents' backs? They drink, smoke and gamble and one by one they begin turning into donkeys. It's a deal made with the devil. You can have it all, everything that you've ever dreamed of, just so long as you remember that you hand over your soul the moment you drive past that world-famous sign that says 'Welcome to Fabulous Las Vegas'.

You arrive as a king in waiting, but you leave like a donkey. That is Las Vegas, baby.

13

For us, the previous ten months had been a long trench war against relegation. We were part of the Premier League landscape but we were a designated Glamour Free Zone. We had all the perks except mass popularity. So we performed that way. Heartless and artless.

I'd played my part in the great Premier League survival campaign without pulling up any trees. In fact, in that particular team it was hard to pull up a daisy, let alone a tree. We were ruled by the need for absolute togetherness and we had draconian laws outlawing mavericks. We had to. Or else we'd find ourselves tumbling arse over tit back to the Championship barrio.

It had worked. It hadn't been fun, it hadn't been pretty. It wasn't supposed to be. War is hell, and so was watching us play, but we survived. We knew that the scraps of fun we'd stolen during the season, both at the training ground and when turning up the odd victory on a big matchday, were irrelevant. It was all about survival.

There had been notable wins though, against Tottenham,

Arsenal and Manchester City, but those triumphs had been achieved through bloody attrition, not style or humour. Those days were anything but enjoyable. We counted the casualties afterwards and headed home. It usually felt to me as if somebody had crawled into my lungs and slowly begun to fold them up over the course of ninety minutes. It was as if the rental agreement for my lungs had expired and the repo men were taking them away. Those traitorous bastard lungs obligingly shrunk themselves like month-old party balloons. I can still remember the burning sensation, like a hot knife in my chest, as we defended for our lives in the last ten minutes. No fun.

When the campaign ended, there was no question about it. We had earned Vegas. The trouble was, our egos led us to believe that Vegas had earned us. And being the hustling town that it is, Vegas was happy to play along with the idea that it had earned us too.

In the immediate aftermath of the match that had bought us another year in the Premier League, survival had meant only one thing to us. One glorious thing.

Pride? No.

Professionalism? No?

Job satisfaction? No.

Sating the loyal fans? No.

It meant a pro rata split of the bonus pot that had been agreed at the start of the season between the players and the chief executive. The pot held £2.5 million.

When squads have secured promotion or dodged relegation before the end of the season, they are said in the game to be 'on the beach'. The only thing a team on the beach can be

219

relied upon to do is roll over in their remaining matches. From the moment we saved our Premier League lives, we were on the beach, waiting for somebody to oil our backs and bring the drinks. (To combat the on-the-beach effect, clubs began pegging bonuses to league positions, but back then nobody had yet had the foresight to do so. Simple, better times.)

Those of us who had played more games than we'd missed knew what our efforts meant. A one-off payment that would be hitting our accounts immediately for a sum in the pleasant £125,000 area. A person can go a long way on £125,000, even a footballer. Especially if he is only going for a week.

It had been decided way back in January, between myself and three other players, that every single penny of our take would be coming with us to Las Vegas. That is the sort of thing that killed Marbella. You could buy Marbella with a good win bonus. You could barely leave a trace in Vegas having staved off relegation. That's why Vegas was deemed good value.

You see, not leaving a trace is what makes our excess a success. There was a brief, golden window in time when there were no greaseball paparazzi in Vegas, no snooping laptop jockeys from the tabloids hiding in dark corners. At least not the sort who knew what Premier League footballers looked like. The people whose business it was to splash us and our sins on the front pages of English tabloid newspapers had no idea that we were even in Vegas. The poor dopes were still camped on shitty old boats with telescopic lenses in the harbour of Puerto Banus. Wondering where everybody was. Three things tabloid hacks are untroubled by: brains, conscience and an adult's grasp of grammar. And when they did find out where we were, they'd have needed the Hubble telescope with X-ray attachments to see what we were up to.

For a Premier League footballer, spending wildly on debauchery but leaving no trace means not having to endure any of the plagues of modern life. You know. Stuff like regret at not having created a steel-reinforced pre-nup agreement. The irritation of having your father-in-law geld you with garden shears. Those scandalously expensive super-injunctions that people on Twitter don't understand. Getting sacked with a large pay-off by the filthy hypocrites who run your club.

Vegas was uncharted territory, and it was a paradise because nobody in the city had ever heard of us. Some of the locals knew that there was a strange and foreign place called the English Premier League, but when it boiled down to it, they didn't actually give a fuck. Unless it is followed by the word 'cash', the word 'foreign' puts Vegas residents off anything new.

'What is that? Like soccerball? Oh, OK,' girls would say, without ever breaking the intense concentration they needed to see which sort of credit card we were using to buy their cocktails.

We were young, fit, rich and famous in another country. It was a licence to do anything we wanted. And we did. We made the Wolf of Wall Street look like a guide dog.

We arrived just when Las Vegas was getting out of the family game. Bob and Myrtle and their three-point-five kids, all wearing braces and all openly obese, used to come for a week in Vegas and try to do it cheap. They dropped some quarters in the slots and grazed like cattle for the rest of the day at the all-you-can-eat buffet. Bob and Myrtle were no longer the big prize. Bob and Myrtle were small potatoes with big asses.

221

There was an explosion in spending by the billionaire owners of the hotels, who wanted to bring young money into Vegas. Wads of young money with owners who weren't sentimentally attached to those wads. Vegas wanted people who would throw those wads of money into the air like confetti, just for the fun of it. Just to see what the fuck happened when all the money landed.

That's precisely when we arrived. We didn't necessarily want to gamble or to endure the cruel and unusual punishment of Celine Fucking Dion. We wanted to part with large sums of money in nightclubs which didn't attract the riff-raff. We wanted private pool parties and personal fixers. We wanted to enjoy debauchery in a city that understood debauchery.

We were footballers. We had fucking earned it.

Vegas is a competitive business. Footballers are competitive people. We might look like a band of brothers when we have just won some tin cup and we are all bouncing up and down singing 'Campioni, Campioni' with stunning originality. But . . .

I'm talking out of school here so I have to be careful.

But some of us have egos. In fact, almost all of us have egos. Some of us have egos you should need planning permission for. Others have egos that loom like the MGM Grand. I mean egos you can see with the naked eye from the moon.

So, together, on holiday, with our wads and our fixers and expensive immunity from the tabloids, we compete to draw attention to ourselves within the group. There is a culture of topping what any player did before you. So each crazy story is sequelled straight away by something similar but more outrageous.

More money.

More drinks.

More drugs.

More women.

Legend 2!!! The ICU Years.

It starts at Gatwick Airport. Home, as you know, to Virgin Atlantic Clubhouse.

In the real world, it is thought that a British Airways first-class flight might be an appropriate and upmarket spending experience for the Premier League player. Wrong. Outdated thinking. It isn't what you're doing, it's the way you're doing it. Return first-class flights on BA, coming in at around £10,000, don't impress anybody. That's a drop in the ocean. And when you are flying across the Atlantic Ocean, you want distraction. Not elegance and class.

You don't have to be David Attenborough to know that Virgin air hostesses are statistically far more likely to disappear with you for days on end. It is a distinguishing trait of the species.

Back when I was playing, there seemed to be a certain corporate tolerance towards the issue of missing air hostesses, because their absences guaranteed that the footballers who had briefly abducted them would be coming back as repeat customers. That may just have been our imaginations of course. Did I mention that we have egos? Our one tragic flaw.

Here's a secret. There are four Virgin air hostesses that almost every single Premier League footballer knows of. They are the Messi, Suárez, Neymar and Ronaldo of their trade. One of them is married to my friend, but I happen to know that at least two other Premier League players are currently sleeping with her. And so does her husband, for that matter. Word is that, unlike her husband, she is good in any position.

And that's just how it is. That's life in the Premier League. Sure, you can sleep with whomsoever you want, but you'll be on the front page of the *Sun* the next morning if you're not careful, or lucky. If you're going to do that sort of thing – and, fuck it, who isn't going to do it? – then better sleep with the she-devil you know than the one you don't. As your dear old mum told you years ago, if you are tempted to sleep with outsiders, it's easy but dangerous.

Easy? Yep. Amazingly so. Depressingly so. Dangerous? Sadly, a lot of young men who can play football learn about this the hard way. They think that all a Premier League footballer has to do is announce that, yes indeed, he is a Premier League footballer and it's open sesame.

Wrong. Wrong. Wrong.

You wake up in the wrong bed staring at the wrong ceiling while the aspiring model is in the loo texting her agent to get a few paps outside the front door quickly before the moment is lost.

And anyway, it's so shallow.

Aim higher.

Some relationship advice. Safe sex for a footballer is sex with no chance of being caught, photographed, tweeted about or blackmailed. Or having to remind yourself that the woman is married to your brother. The other stuff – awkward rashes and babies – can all be dealt with.

So. You show. You don't tell.

You show what you are wearing on your wrist. You show

those shoes. You show the bank card with the credit limit of infinity and beyond. You show everything about you that screams money. You kill all the regular Joe shit you use when the TV people interview you. Right now, you are clearly 'a somebody'. You are so confident about being 'a somebody' that you don't need to explain any of it.

Really, the less anybody knows about the precise someone you are, the better. And, look, when the sun comes up in the morning, you can still convince yourself that she really liked your personality.

I have been in bars and overheard lads telling girls that they are footballers. That's how you spot somebody who isn't a footballer. Never, ever say that you are a footballer. What you are is a somebody. And because you can back that up, that is enough. She will tell her friends that you were a somebody they would have heard of. Somebody in Wall Street, or maybe some guy who discovered the cure to cancer, or a winner of *The Voice*. Recognizable, but somehow your exact name and the nature of what you do frustratingly eludes her.

Anyway. As I said, it all begins at Gatwick Airport where two American women called Kristin and Nicole agree to abandon their trip to Atlanta where they were going to visit their family. Instead they opt to come with us to Las Vegas for five days.

Without passing judgement on their folks or Atlanta, I wasn't the least bit surprised. We are footballers on holiday. We are the cowboys. Women are the Indians. The first-class departure lounge is The Pass.

It's the ambush. I've seen it done countless times. Footballers quite literally meeting women in first-class or business lounges

225

at airports all over the world, and just buying them a ticket to come fly with me. An entire squad I played with once kidnapped two air hostesses on a private plane that we'd chartered from the UK to Dublin. The plane was grounded for two days and all it meant was that some douchebag in the south of France couldn't get back to the UK for some business meeting he was having. Cry me a river. There were no other consequences.

In other words the tabloids didn't find out, so the football club didn't care.

Virgin Upper appeals to footballers on a number of levels. Mostly lower levels. The bar at the back is a winner and the air hostesses are flirtatious in a really very good way.

On our flight were two of the four air hostesses known and admired by Premier League footballers up and down the country. We have their photos stuck in our Panini albums of footballers' favourite air hostesses. We have their numbers listed beside fake names on our mobile phones. These women were the very reason my three team-mates and I were on that flight. Until BA make a splash in the transfer market, they will never compete. We knew why we were there and the air hostesses knew it. This was the time to just be a footballer.

The moment the plane took off, the cabin was filled with the clanging of seatbelt buckles being impatiently opened and jettisoned. We'd been tied down for too long. The overhead light and the captain's velvet voice ordered us to keep our seatbelts fastened, we hadn't yet achieved a cruising altitude of blah, blah, blah, but if you know the upper-class attendants on more than a passing basis, you are hardly likely to be told to sit down.

Anyway, it's not anarchy. There is a race to be won. Hidden away in the staff quarters are three specially made single beds for the staff to rest on. There are four of us. It's a contest among the players to grab one of those beds.

On a night flight it's all really easy. It isn't Tuesday night at Stoke. It's pre-season friendly stuff. The girls finish attending to the other passengers before turning down the cabin lights and retreating to the staff quarters where they will find . . . us.

We'll be there, tanked with champagne and cocktails, reposing like life models on the little single beds. We haven't won the first prize in life. We *are* the first prize in life. You get the idea.

It is customary to go through a few bottles of champagne before getting better acquainted with the girls. This can be clichéd and a bit pathetic, but fun at the same time. That's the best most people can hope for anyway, isn't it? One of the champagne bottles will be used to play spin the bottle, and as the game goes on, the sexual acts will inevitably become more explicit. We will pretend to be as surprised by this as the stewardesses are pretending to be.

And sometimes we *are* surprised.

I once saw a player open a bottle of champagne inside one of the girls. As talents go, I'm not sure how useful that was, or how expertly it was done, but like the dog walking on its hind legs, it's not that it is done well, it's that it is done at all.

I asked the player who served up this amuse-douche where

he had got the idea from. He'd been in a relationship with an IT girl. No. Not the sort of IT girl who comes down from the fifth floor to fix your desktop, you plebs. You know the sort, the ones that aren't famous for anything but for some reason everybody knows who they are. There are magazines full of them if you need further information.

Anyway, he had been at a party for *Loaded* magazine (you were expecting that he had been at a convention for sommeliers?) and at the end of the night he'd ended up lying on a bed while one of *Loaded*'s front-page girls kindly stripped for him. In a surprise turn of events, guilt got the better of him and he repeatedly spurned the subtle advances of the *Loaded* girl. She stormed out and caught a cab to the nearest nunnery.

It had taken huge amounts of willpower, but the following morning the player went to training with the feeling that the world owed him something. He had been a model of virtue with a naked *Loaded* girl. But really, what is the point of charity or virtue if nobody gets to hear about it?

His only reward was a very tearful phone call from his IT girl. She had been meaning to tell him that she'd been having an affair with one of his team-mates. For over a year. Yeah, all through last season. He thanks you for your assists.

The player just didn't see the funny side of it. He experienced a sudden conversion. Like the guy on the road out of Damascus instead of the road to it. His faith in the quality of IT girls had been destroyed. He decided to make the most of his position as a young, attractive man with money to burn. He could take his pick of women, and for the next few years he decided that the female population of the planet would be to him as the pick 'n' mix in Woolworths is to a fat boy from Feltham.

And that's what he did. The following week at a party, at which I was present but not crucial, he pulled a singer from one of the world's biggest UK girl groups (yes, that one), and as you've probably guessed, it was she who asked him to perform the opening of the champagne bottle in that special way. His first uncorking took place in a room at the Sanderson Hotel in London. The entrance to the room is signified now by a blue plaque placed on the corridor wall by the Heritage Foundation. The champagne houses of Reims have daily meetings to discuss adding the manoeuvre to future marketing plans. Turning moments into memories . . .

Meanwhile, back on board in the staff quarters, things were in full swing. A stewardess and a close friend of mine were in the top bunk, clocking up the air miles. Footballers wake up looking at many strange and unfamiliar ceilings in the course of a career. There are none as disconcerting as the ceiling inches above you on the top bunk in the staff quarters of a Virgin aeroplane, when you have a flailing stewardess giving you a private demonstration of the entrances, exits and emergency passageways. It is like coupling in a coffin. Houdini might be able to pull off something special. Cruyff might fit in one of his turns. The rest of us just settle for a six out of ten performance.

Unless . . .

Somebody or something was tickling my buddy's toes.

He checks the limbs and digits of the stewardess. All where they are supposed to be, unless you are her husband.

Something still tickling those toes.

He risks compressing some discs in his spine in order to

229

turn his head around. A camp steward who moved with a song in his heart when he was pushing the drinks trolley earlier was tickling my friend's toes with his free hand. With the other he was, well, uncorking himself.

There are places (I have played in some of them) where three is a crowd. Right here, three was a crowd.

'Was he putting you off your game, mate?' I asked sympathetically afterwards.

My mate is generally sensitive to another man's needs.

'Fuck off,' he said to the steward.

'Tsk, don't worry about him,' said the stewardess, and grabbed him by the hair.

He tried to concentrate. I will draw the line at tickling, he told himself. But if he starts sucking my toes or licking my ankles, that's it. Red card.

The engine noise was really noticeable now. The steward began tickling my mate even more flamboyantly.

'Listen, fuck off.'

She put her hand over his mouth and kept it there till the three of them landed safely. Then my mate squeezed himself out of the place like a man secretly trying to escape an MRI machine. The steward was zipping up his flotation device as my mate made his way through the darkened cabin back to his seat. He was wearing an expression I'd seen on his face before, when he'd scored a comical own goal.

What the fuck, I thought to myself after he'd told me of his woes, and pressed the button for full recline. Coaches always told him that he needed to be a bit more versatile. There were barren years for him when that would have counted as a pull!

The sexual tension had dissipated and the footballing contingent had made their way back to the seats, which were now horizontal. I drifted off, remembering the last time I was on this flight. It was shortly after the PFA awards. The UK's foremost glamour model (yes, the one you are thinking of) was on the same flight. She'd been driven down to London in the back of a limousine with two footballers I knew. Word was already out that they had double-teamed the model. Backs and forwards style. That story was part of football folklore for a while, but the world moved on, and now it seems quaint and old-timey.

'Morning, sleepy head,' came the call from the steward, followed by a cheeky tickle to the arch of my mate's foot.

Before my mate could register anything by way of response he was gone, doling out the coffee and croissants to the business passengers, who must have wished that Vegas meant the same to them as it did to us.

Everybody has their own private Las Vegas, the Vegas they go to and think to themselves that they are being bad boys and girls. But everybody suspects there is another Las Vegas where there are richer people who are being even badder boys and girls.

They're right. That's the Las Vegas we go to.

I pulled up the window blind, and there below us was the red dirt of the Nevada desert, as much a sign of Vegas pending as the first glimpse of the sea of neon.

Mustang Sally touched down a little after one p.m. local time.

From that moment on, we were on the clock. A very expensive clock. We made the most of every second. We sidestepped the concierge awaiting our arrival on the safe side of 'nothing to declare' and made a beeline for the limousine that had been pre-booked about three months earlier, when Premier League survival had started to look on.

The limo was suitably tacky. Not the sort of tacky where you have to wipe your feet getting out. Just tacky. Limos sound like a great idea until you are in a town full of limos stuck in limo gridlock and you realize that you look like just another arsehole in a limo. Some Joe Blow from the sticks who thought hiring a limo would be a bit different.

Still, Kristin and Nicole were suitably impressed, as were the two all-star air stewardesses, who managed to sink two bottles of champagne in the twenty-five minutes that it took to migrate from the airport to the Bellagio Hotel.

The Bellagio is, to be blunt, the bollocks.

Not the dog's bollocks. We're talking the winner of the top pedigree dog at Crufts. Three years in a row. In the Best Bollocks in Show category. His bollocks. Yes. That mutt's nuts. That hound's rounds. That bow-wow's pow-wows.

So, if you are staying in, say, Circus Circus, a quick word.

Sorry.

If only you'd had pace, touch and a good agent.

Like so much of Vegas, the world of the Bellagio gets better with every extra dollar you spend. It was built for $1.6 billion and the opening ceremony alone cost close to $100 million. And that's the point of Vegas.

Steve Wynn, who built the Bellagio, is the guy who once

232

put his elbow through the canvas of a $139 million Picasso he owned while showing it to some guests. He had been about to sell the painting. Wynn shrugged and said to the group, 'Well, I'm glad none of *you* did that.' He got the picture repaired, sued his insurance company over their revised estimate of its worth, and then a few years later sold the painting to the same guy for $155 million. It was now the Picasso that Steve Wynn put his elbow through. Of course it was worth more. The insurance company dweebs just didn't understand Vegas.

The Bellagio is where a fight broke out when a guy tried to join a game of blackjack in the middle of an epic losing streak by a Texas oil tycoon seated at the table. Being a Texan, long on money and short on manners, the tycoon offered the man a wad of money to go away. He wanted to continue his miserable losing streak on his own at the table.

'You must be worth a lot of money,' said the guy.

'Sure. Over a hundred mill. Now get lost.'

'Tell you what,' said the guy, 'I'll flip you for the whole hundred million.'

The guy had been reserve left-back for Leeds in the Peter Ridsdale days. Not really. He was an Australian media tycoon worth so close to $2 billion that nobody quibbled when he rounded the number up.

That's the Bellagio.

And that is the hard soul of Las Vegas.

When I hear people boast that they're travelling thirteen hours in economy and restricting themselves to $400 a day, I just think, what's the point? Now, that isn't to denigrate anybody who doesn't earn a fortune, but you're going to have more bang for your buck in the Costa del Sol on $400 a day than you ever are in Vegas. You'll get nowhere in Vegas.

In order to enjoy the place in the way nature intended you have to be prepared to spend money in the knowledge that you'll have nothing to show for it but the memories when it's all gone. And the dressing gown you nicked from the Bellagio. And the matching flip-flops. A gift for Mrs TSF in the absence of hitting the number seven straight up with my last $20.

If spending the money causes you pain, you're in the wrong city, having the wrong holiday.

Vegas understands that point. Americans say that if you can fake sincerity, you've got it made. In Vegas, if you can fake sincerity with people who have it made, you are well on your way too.

The hotel manager of the Bellagio comes from around the counter to hug us when we're in town. It's like that programme where Davina McCall reunites long-separated families. He is very moved to be reunited with our credit cards again. You can almost feel your wallet being lifted as the hug takes hold.

It may be as fake as a Kardashian smile, but at the same time I'd be most put out if he didn't make the gesture. Louis is a good guy. Knows when to talk and when to look the other way. He is right on it whenever it is time to pay any bill, but all the time in between he is adept at looking the other way – and never more so than when we shared our room with two air hostesses and two strange American girls who were meant to be in Atlanta. Louis was his usual confident, half-blind self.

The don't ask, don't tell policy has served both ourselves and Louis well over the years; in fact, it's probably an apt metaphor for Las Vegas itself. In the Bellagio, what goes on tour, stays on tour. Back in the Marbella days, what went on tour often developed an embarrassing rash later.

'Guys, guys, guys. Great to see you again. How was your trip?'

'You got the limo I sent for you, right?'

'This is my personal cell number.'

'José will show you to the villa.'

'Anything you need guys, OK? Twenty-four/seven.'

Nobody does service like the Americans. You can sit in a bar anywhere in the UK and not be offered a drink or any conversation for hours. We Brits would rather starve with dignity than provide polite service to each other. In Vegas, every bartender is your best friend. Within ten minutes he will have managed to ask whether you are in the market for a beer, a bang or a snort, without opening himself up to any comeback. It's an American art form.

José opened the door. 'Yentlemen,' he said in a blend of cracked Mexican English, 'da garden villya.'

I've stayed in hotels all over the world. You name it, I've stayed in it. From the seven-star Burj Al Arab in Dubai with its £100 cocktails to a room the size of a shoebox, and with the scent of an old shoe, in forty-degree heat in Malia. No frills. No air conditioning. No hope. On the whole, hotel rooms are all awful, universally awful. But the garden villas at the Bellagio Hotel in Las Vegas singlehandedly go some way towards redressing the balance. When the revolution happens, it would be wrong for the proletariat to destroy the villas in a fit of resentment. They should aspire that some day every citizen

235

will get a short stay in one of them. Until then, Premier League footballers are prepared to do their bit to keep the residences financially viable.

Strictly speaking, they are not hotel rooms but houses set within the grounds of the hotel, and at $6,000 a night they are worth every cent. But regardless of how much money you have, guests can only book a villa once they've been through a fairly extensive email exchange and vetting process with a member of the booking staff. In short, the hotel wants to know how much you are likely to spend in their casino. They want to know who you are, what your job is, how much you earn, and they want testimonies as to the good character of your credit cards. It's like opening a bank account where you lose your cash every time you make a deposit. If you're not rolling high enough, you're not getting a garden villa.

The beauty is that Vegas does sucking up so well that the city actually makes you feel that you vetted it rather than the other way round. Thank you so much for choosing to spend your $6,000 a night with us.

José walked us around, explaining in his capacity as our official butler that the villa has eleven telephones, 'so you're never more than a few metres away from anything you want'.

Well said, José. We are Premier League footballers. We have panic attacks if we are ever more than a few metres away from anything we want.

The room was frightening. Nou Camp frightening.

There was a bar. I don't mean a minibar or a couple of token bottles with lipstick-smudged glasses that haven't been dried properly. I'm talking about a full-on bar, with every major drinks brand seductively hung upside down, ready to be dispensed into a pristine crystal-cut tumbler. There were smoking jackets and silk-lined slippers. The private lounge had a nine-ball table and the air was laced with trouble. Good trouble.

It was like the opening scenes of one of those American spring break movies. Except classy. Vegas classy. Which costs more.

Despite José's best attempts, nobody could work out how to lock and unlock the safe. It was almost as if they didn't want us leaving our cash behind when we went out.

I opened the back doors to what I thought would be a corridor leading to the casino because, well, why wouldn't it? Instead I was confronted with a beautiful swimming pool and a hot tub that just screamed depravity. It was hard to believe that the infamous Vegas Strip was only a throw of a crumpled-up hundred-dollar bill away, but we were spared even that short journey. The depravity could come to us.

The only problem with the villa was that the interior décor contract seemed to have been won by my nan. She has muscle in Vegas. Bless.

Two things Americans cannot do: upscale kitchens and soft furnishings.

And silence. Three things.

In Vegas, the world centre of distraction, you have to stay a little bit focused, or else hire somebody to be focused for you, as you are making your way through your £125,000 bonus. You need a fixer. That's why the next thing we had to do was call Jesse.

Jesse was the fixer in Las Vegas and there was nothing he

couldn't get. He knew all of the concierges. Ditto the hotel owners, the managers, the brokers, the dealers and so on. If you wanted to buy a watch or some diamonds while you were there, Jesse would have half a dozen dealers flown in and queueing outside your hotel room with cases full of stuff to show you. If you wanted to be on show while purchasing – and there are many that do – then he could arrange for you to be on the best table in any nightspot in Vegas while the same people opened up their cases surrounded by bodyguards and people taking pictures of you.

I have seen it done on many occasions. Personally, I felt that was a step too far for players who had merely avoided relegation. If we had won the Premier League, well, maybe.

If you wanted front-row tickets and the chance to walk to the ring with a boxing champion at a fight at the MGM, Jesse was your man. If you wanted to go to the hottest private aftershow parties in Vegas, Jesse could get you in. If you wanted to dance with Rihanna or Beyoncé, then Jesse could make it happen, although he needed notice for that. If they wanted to dance with you? Same thing. Who they gonna call? Jesse. And again, it will take a few days, girls.

When you see footballers hanging out with top American A-listers, I can almost guarantee you that the players have clubbed together to pay anything from £100,000 to £250,000 for the pleasure of schmoozing and selfies. It happens all the time. Jesse could even have you spin a tune behind the decks at any venue, so long as you paid. When Guetta or Aoki are playing, you'll regularly see people who have paid an awful lot of money to be there, patiently standing behind them, waiting to spin a tune so that they can pretend to be a world-famous DJ for three minutes.

There is nothing you can't have in Vegas, so long as you know Jesse and Jesse pays the right person. That's what Vegas is all about, and everybody knows it. If you can pay somebody enough money, they'll get you anything you can think of, and even their bosses won't complain, because their bosses are doing it too.

It's the ultimate service industry. Proof of how far mankind has evolved from the animals.

We had Jesse playing for us. Proof of how far we had evolved from Marbella.

So. Listen and learn. We're going to say this just once more.

If you're coming to Vegas to spend serious money on the right things, you need a fixer. Don't do it on the cheap and decide to give some kid from the youth team on the Strip his big break as a fixer. You'll think you're getting a Marcus Rashford, but you'll end up with some busted flush who should still be playing Conference football and learning the moves.

Spend the money. Get yourself a gnarled bastard with a few scars but a good plastic surgeon and a really smooth manner. A fixer who knows every mover and shaker in the city and has the run of every joint in town. A guy who can get you anything from top-line tickets in the evening to bail and a lawyer in the morning. A guy who doesn't just know the concierge at every hotel worth going into, but who is owed favours by every one of those concierges. Ditto every restaurant, every pool party and every show. He'll fix VIP tables, VIP show tickets, VIP hotel rooms, VIP poker games, VIP women and VIP drugs. Queues?

He won't even understand the concept. There is *nothing* a good fixer can't fix for you in Vegas.

And our fixer for the week was the aforementioned Jesse. The fixer's fixer. He lives to make things happen for wealthy clients. He truly gives the impression that money isn't the issue. He would do it just for the love of us.

You see spoiled rich bastards. Jesse sees tormented, unfulfilled souls. So shame on you people.

14

After working out who was sleeping where and with whom, we were told that the limo was waiting outside. José had put an envelope on the table and I ripped it open and tipped the contents on to the table. It was stuffed with tickets to all the shows we'd asked for and also a stack of complimentary chips for the casino to get the ball rolling.

But the casino could wait; there was a more pressing cultural engagement that required our immediate attention. Also lying on the table were a bunch of wristbands for Wet Republic, a huge pool party at the MGM Grand. A quick check of our unfeasibly expensive watches told us that the pool party had been up and running for approximately seventeen minutes now. They would be starting to worry about where we were.

We had rented a bungalow overlooking the main pool across at the MGM. $15,000 a day. Because we are worth it.

If you don't know the Wet Republic Pool Party held in and around the 53,000-square-foot Ultra Pool (an American football field is 57,564 square feet, but less fun) then, Bob and Myrtle, that is why Vegas never calls you any more.

Fifteen grand seems like a lot of money but it was an 'Event Saturday' and you are talking 18 per cent auto gratuity, 4 per cent service charge and 8.1 per cent tax, so it's the common-sense choice. If you don't want to spend that brass, you can rent anything from a deluxe cabana down to a day-bed (if you want to show that you play in League One or lower, or that you come from Yorkshire).

And anyway, a bungalow was also the safe and sensible option just in case we found ourselves unable for some reason to get the limo back from the MGM Grand to the Bellagio across the road. So stop being so judgey.

The lads and I, plus the air hostesses and Kristin and Nicole, were led to our bungalow. It was beautiful. The sort of thing you'd build as part of your own private villa in the best quarter of your mega-bollox villa in Ibiza – perhaps overlooking the Med, which is just nature's Ultra Pool. The bungalow had a fridge, sofas, ceiling fan – very important – TV and private pool. Right up my street. If life was fair I would have been raised in a bungalow like this.

Now, I know this may sound like a strange thing for a Premier League footballer at a Wet Republic Pool Party to say, but I don't like big crowds. I know that for fifteen years I played in front of tens of thousands of people twice a week, but that was different. They were scenery. All those faces blended into the surroundings. They were part of the architecture of the stadium. It was spookier if the stadium was empty. With a full house, you couldn't distinguish individuals. The crowd was just a single organism moving and chanting in unison, and far less scary for it.

No, it's crowds of individuals that scare me. I don't like lots of people moving around me. Myself and the Queen are very alike that way. So she says. Shopping malls, busy train stations and crowded supermarkets are no-go areas.

On the face of it, Wet Republic looked like my worst nightmare, but down these mean streets a Premier League footballer must go. Worse, many of the individuals larking near the daybeds were drunken young American lads. Historically we have never seen eye to eye with their tribe. They have never been able to hold their beer, for starters. And to be fair, why would they be able to hold it? Most of it is piss.

Anyway, I'm easily wound up by idiots and, not to be judgemental, most American college boys you run into appear to have chosen Idiocy as their major. With Loudness as a fall-back subject.

However, thanks to the discreet upmarket location of our bungalow at Wet Republic, set back from the main pool, we had a haven not infested by idiots, rodents or other pests. The experience was bearable.

Nobody could see me. That's important. I don't mind spending money. I can spend money as stupidly as a sailor on shore leave, only more so. I just don't have the need for people to *see* me spending the money. That adds no value to the experience. But the three players I had come to Vegas with spent money for the pleasure of having people watch them spend it. Exhibitionist spending. At Wet Republic, they were in danger of attracting idiots to the bungalow.

I had just become aware of this danger when there was a loud cry of 'Oi-Oi!' That's when you know it's English people.

The same distinctive call also tells you they are friendly English people, because no English man ever shouts 'Oi-Oi!' unless he's having a good time. No football hooligans ever pillage a foreign town shouting 'Oi-Oi!' as they charge down the natives.

I've bumped into fans all over the world and it hasn't always been good news. Because of the distance between certain clubs, it is necessary to stop at service stations for fifteen minutes on the way back home from some away games to allow the driver to take his break. Unfortunately there are no private bungalows at motorway service stations. We often ran into fans, and usually they were pissed. If you'd won, then no problem. If you had lost? Stay on the bus and piss into a bottle. If they were fans of the team you had just beaten, then tell the bus driver not to be such a selfish bastard and to just drive on. Those fans will hate you. They will worry you like a dog worries sheep. Nice cuddly Premier League sheep.

There were a few clubs whose fans hated me in a special way. Once, we pulled into Cherwell Valley Services on the M40 and met two busloads of fans from one of those clubs. Rough sorts, all of them. Not the prawn-sandwich-eaters of Old Trafford.

All hell broke loose. They boarded our bus and came looking for me. At the time I was actually round the back of the services building, having a piss against some crates, because I needed to call Mrs TSF with an ETA and I couldn't get a signal in the building itself. Courageously, I kept the lads waiting for an hour until the two coachloads of angry fans pulled out of the services and continued their journey without taking my limbs with them as trophies. And they would have hurt me badly. There was no doubt about that.

The point is that none of those fans shouted 'Oi-Oi!' when they saw our bus or our frightened faces. These guys by the pool were Watford fans on a stag party. And actually they were as friendly as they came. They asked for pictures and autographs, which presumably were ruined the moment they were inserted into the wet pockets of their swimming trunks, but that wasn't my problem.

Kristin looked at me. 'Um, who the fuck are you guys?' she asked.

'We're nobody – don't worry about it,' I replied.

'Yeah right,' said Kristin. 'I just want you to know that even if you are somebody, I don't really care. I just like hanging out.'

Now that is the best thing any girl can say to you, so long as she means it. I mean, that's marriage and kids material right there. If she means it.

Kristin seemed sincere, but she needed a little test.

'Cool,' I said. 'I just want *you* to know that I'm making do with you until something better comes along, OK?'

Kristin laughed and called me a 'giant asshole'. Test passed. And that is how to tell a good girl from a girl who will put you squarely on the front page of Monday morning's *Sun*. She will forget all about her family in Atlanta and come with you to Vegas at the drop of a credit card and she doesn't even care who you are.

I've learned from the best in our business when it comes to women. I have a former team-mate whose belt can be used for abseiling over cliffs. It has to be that long because it has over a thousand notches in it. Ironically, he never abseils over cliffs. He just runs off the edge and keeps running like

245

a cartoon character until the music stops and he falls. But like a cartoon character, he is basically indestructible. And invariably overdrawn.

I asked him the key question on a bus to an away game against Manchester United. He conceded that only a small percentage of those women had left him feeling happy or fulfilled. How small a percentage? Well, just three of them to be precise. Three out of a thousand.

I wish he could have met Kristin.

Not really.

You may think that what I'm about to say is nuts, but I spent the next couple of hours of that day with Kristin pouring me strawberry daiquiris while I read a book.

Kinky? C'est moi.

I was reading *Kitchen Confidential* by Anthony Bourdain. It's about Anthony's life as a New York chef who fights his way to the top. Along the way he tells you all about how the world of the top-level chef really works. He reveals the tricks of the trade, who is an arsehole, who isn't. He tells you what the trick to becoming a three-Michelin-star chef is. He blabs about the copious amounts of butter that deceive the palate, and argues that to become a chef, all you need is one big knife. It's a classic.

I was good warm, good drunk, and feeling good. I was so happy in my own little world at that moment, despite all the carnage going off around us, that an idea popped into my head, seeded by Anthony's book. I made a quick note on my phone: 'idea for a book about a Secret Footballer'.

(The entrance to that bungalow now has a blue plaque placed

246

on the wall by the Heritage Foundation. They get about, the Heritage Foundation.)

The reading-room tranquillity with optional daiquiris couldn't last though. Now, our bungalow came with a private pool so we wouldn't have to risk getting verrucas in the 53K-square-footer. But if you have a private pool, it stands to reason that it won't stay private, because the nature of having something nobody else has means that those people will inevitably want it. Capeesh?

Nothing attracts girls like ripped sportsmen peacocking in a private pool while all the paunched douchebags in the cheap seats and day-beds stare and think murderous thoughts about those sportsmen.

I made my way out of the bungalow towards the pool and was confronted by the sight of my mate Steve hugging a girl I'd never seen before while they rested against the edge of the pool, both staring out at the chaos of the main pool. They appeared to be slowly grooving to the music. At least that's how it would have looked from the main pool. If you were standing behind them, as I was, you'd have known that Steve was dirty dancing.

Footballers are an extrovert breed. Well, all footballers except me. Footballers don't mind nudity. They don't mind being the centre of attention. They get changed in front of thirty other blokes every day, they take a shit with the door open looking out into the dressing room, they fuck girls in the bed next to you when you're rooming together before an away match, they'll often whack you on the side of the head with their cock when the physio is massaging you on the treatment table. None of it is a big deal, and nobody knows how to stop. Casually pleasuring a girl in front of hundreds of people is nothing. The risk of being recognized by Watford fans (Oi-Oi!) or, worse, being captured on camera-phone never enters a footballer's head.

Or at least it didn't then. Unfortunately, as is almost always the case, the same girl turned out to be quite popular and attracted her girlfriends towards our pool, and they in turn attracted a large group of American lads vacationing from the Advanced Idiocy Studies Faculty at Moron State University.

Now American girls can be pretty cool. I mean, some of them can wreck your head, but most of them just want to have fun. But the guys – and stop me if I have said this before – the guys are fucking idiots. They make you feel sorry for the girls. It must be like living under the fundamentalist regime of the Taliban of Idiocy.

The Premier League has its share of characters who can't do joined-up thinking, but they are intellectuals compared to these guys. These are guys who dress like retired golfers and who high-five each other when they successfully manage to order an orange juice. These are guys whose range of expression runs from Awesome to Totally Awesome. If Trump ever builds his stupid wall, the deal should be that these people are kept on his side of it.

They don't even travel well in their own country. I've read that 60 per cent of Americans don't have a passport. That group includes those who don't understand that there is anywhere else they could travel to. It includes white collar, blue collar, trailer trash and hillbillies. A diverse range of American whiteys who all share the same basic traits. Loud, ugly and proud. There should be a season when they can be culled by hunters. Maybe clubbed like baby seals with learning difficulties.

The specimens that had sidled up to our private pool, looking to win their girls back, were the perfect example of the Americans the world loves to loathe. Except that now they were annoying me personally. Really fucking annoying me. I wanted to complain that I had been having a nice afternoon reading, but I knew that many of them came from states where marrying your cousin was legal but owning a book wasn't.

I lay down next to Kristin and tried to win my peace back by burying my head in some imaginary sand. It was no good. The constant yelping and cries of 'Woo!' every time one of them downed an apple juice without dribbling half of it made me shake inside.

Kristin kept telling me that Steve Aoki was doing amazing things on the stage with two turntables and a microphone, but by that point she'd poured so much strawberry daiquiri into me that she could have told me Liberace was duetting with Elvis and the Rat Pack and my nan was DJing afterwards and I still wouldn't have been able to appreciate it. Aoki could have been playing a cassette of old glam rock covers for all I knew.

Kristin could see that I was becoming agitated. I was going to blow like the volcano outside the Mirage. My face had tightened and my answers were in shorthand. Drunk shorthand, which is more difficult to read.

'Do you want to cool off?' she asked.

The thought of jumping into a private pool that had become a Petri dish for Steve's private fluids didn't really appeal. Getting in among the hundreds of revellers with their verrucas in the main pool was less attractive. On the other hand, it was so hot.

The noise level kept ratcheting up. The place had really booted off. Aoki was now spraying the crowd with champagne as if he was a Premier League footballer on holiday. Fluids were everywhere in the Wet Republic. Being sprayed, being swum in, being fornicated in.

In the big pool, a boat appeared with two lads rowing in between their fellow partiers as if they were picking up survivors from the *Titanic*. They were dragging girls on board as they went. True humanitarians. And in fairness, it was decent banter, which I appreciated very much. Dusk had fallen and the $600-a-pop champagne bottles being delivered to cabanas and bungalows now had sparklers sticking out of them. Mankind's creative ingenuity never ceases to amaze.

At one point I swear I saw a monkey. Given that A Monkey never appeared on the bill, however, perhaps it was a hallucination.

The American lads had moved back to the centre of the main pool, having finally sussed what Steve was still doing to one of the girls they had followed to our private watering hole. They had decided to see Steve's good loving as a 'fuck you' to the American nation, a gob on the crust of Mom's apple pie. They were preserving their national honour by throwing empty plastic cups our way. Each of them landed like Scuds in our pool and splashed the girls as they sunbathed.

Where is the War on Terror when it is really needed?

I should have tried to stand up and shout that somebody might get hurt, but then I thought that when you have just recently developed opposable thumbs, throwing shit must be quite a novelty.

Then the music stopped dead and some cool-looking official, who was perhaps Minister for Equality in the Wet Republic, announced that there was going to be a bikini contest for any girl who wanted to enter. The champion stood to win $250,000. Which was fucking nuts. I mean, we only got £125,000 for staying up in the Premier League. This was outrageous!

Naturally, Steve did the only thing he could do. He waited for the event to get going, swapped costumes with Nicole, and walked as bold as brass on to the stage. He looked like he'd crammed a full English breakfast into his bikini bottoms. He needed a few full English breakfasts to fill out the top. The place went crazy; people were whooping and wolf-whistling, and even the DJs in the booth were doubled over.

It was very good from Steve, and the moment has gone down in football folklore. The only people pulling against the tide of hysterical popular acclaim for my friend were the American lads from Moron State. They threw enough cups at Steve to force him from the stage. Fucking philistines. Otherwise, Steve exited to applause.

The bikini girls kept hustling for the fat cheque. Quite a few of them didn't seem to have been taken by surprise by the announcement of the competition. They were like Rihannas who had turned up for a karaoke night in Marbella because there was a good prize on offer.

Finally a girl called Annalise (no, not that one) won the contest. She posed with her cheque for $250,000. Shortly afterwards, Steve Aoki came over to our bungalow with a bottle of champagne by way of a wooden spoon prize for Steve. It was a nice gesture, but there was a motive behind it, as I would discover later.

I was still irritable. Seeing a mate in a bikini contest only does so much for me. I wanted a cigarette, even though I knew I wouldn't enjoy it. The high-fiving idiots who had just discovered throwing would try to knock it out of my mouth with a beer bottle. I closed my eyes and prayed for a tornado in their trailer park.

'Any cigarettes?' I asked Kristin.

'No, but that's Nicole's bag there. She might have some. Take a quick peek.'

The nearest thing Nicole had to cigarettes was a packet of tampons. My craving was so bad that I considered it for a split second.

'Let's just go inside,' said Kristin.

'It's OK,' I said. 'Pass me the strawberry daiquiri can you?'

I was primed with the drink. I was still pissed off. I had an idea.

'You wanna have some fun?' I asked Kristin.

She looked puzzled. Then she realized. 'Oh my God,' she said. 'Oh. My. Freaking. God. Please don't, you're fucking crazy!'

And with that I took the tampons from Nicole's bag. Peeled them. Soaked them in the strawberry daiquiri and hurled them high into the air at the dozen American loudmouths, who were now busy splashing water in the face of any girl who came near them.

Time stopped. The fattened tampons hung in the evening sky like things of odd beauty and then began the arc down towards their target area. A shoal of a dozen or so back-to-front baseball caps.

The fin of a great white shark cutting through the Wet Republic's Ultra Pool wouldn't have sparked a quicker evacuation. Suddenly 53,000 square feet of pool just wasn't enough. The American guys screamed like schoolgirls.

My aim was poor. I was drunk, and basic science tells us that strawberry-daiquiri-soaked tampons are not aerodynamic. So the bombs rained down fairly indiscriminately. This was an unexpected bonus. Nobody had noticed the drunk near the bungalow launching the things. It was dusk. Everybody had noticed the loudmouths who had been causing trouble all day long. If there were strawberry-daiquiri-soaked tampons in the airspace above those idiots, then it stood to reason that they had put them there, and now they were acting as if they had just lost their testicles as a way of hiding their guilt.

Quite rightly, people were horrified. The small but feared army of the Wet Republic was mobilized. Four of them, but beefy enough to displace most of the water from the Ultra Pool. There was a brief skirmish. There weren't enough brains underneath the baseball caps to work out that resistance was futile and likely to cause injury.

Management looked on. People stood dripping and excited. What was the Wet Republic's legislative stance on the death penalty? I stood in the evening shade of the bungalow, watching as the miscreants were extradited to some place beyond the borders of the Wet Republic. And peace returned to that blue and horny land.

I lit a cigarette and the flame briefly highlighted a face

plastered with the smuggest grin since the winner of the Smug Grin competition at the Tory Party Conference remembered that of course he had bet a lot of money on himself to win the contest.

I took a step towards our private pool. Either the alcohol would give me immunity from Steve's leakages, or they would have died by now. For 15K a day, you expect a filter system. I had the weird sensation when my feet planted themselves on the floor of the pool of there being some sort of matter wrapping itself around my ankle. Surely not a condom of Steve's that was now attacking me? For fuck's sake.

I bent down and fished out what turned out to be a piece of paper. The handwriting on it was soaked but still legible.

'To the Watford Massive, best wishes, Steve'.

Class is permanent.

I stood in those warm and exorbitantly priced waters and drew on my cigarette. A sense of calm came over me. I was moved to consider the fate of people in those countries who always expect war. Some of us elsewhere in the world (like us peaceable Englanders) do not. Some people appear to draw their self-esteem from conflict. They glory in the war without worrying about the outcome. Like Wimbledon back in the eighties.

I've always wanted an easy life. War is hell. I thrive when peace flutters about my person. I've also come to realize that life is about creating your own peace, and that in order to achieve it you must occasionally start a riot. And if tampons and strawberry daiquiris are all you have to hand, then so be it. The Molotov cocktail was born out of the same desperation.

*

At the end of the night I called our man Jesse at the Bellagio and he sent the limo to the MGM. Before long it was loaded up with four footballers, two air hostesses, two American girls miles from home, and two strippers who had been sunbathing at Wet Republic and were due to perform that night at Palomino Gentlemen's Club in downtown Las Vegas.

Nicole asked if we could stop at a corner store on the way back. She needed cigarettes. We told the limo to go ahead as the main entrance to the Bellagio was just around the corner and the short walk might, by some miracle, help with the alcohol poisoning most of us were experiencing.

If you've been to the Bellagio, then you'll know that on the left-hand side as you look at the hotel there is a walkway flanked by a glass balustrade. As we strolled along the walkway to the pagoda that adjoins the right angle towards the main entrance, a black guy jumped out in front of us.

The dialogue ran as follows.

Black guy: Hey man, look it here.

TSF: No thanks, pal.

Black guy: No, no, look, man, I got two rings, diamond rings I gotta get rid of right now. I got 'em yesterday but I gotta leave town tonight.

Steve: You stole them.

Black guy: They liberated, check it.

Jinky: They're nice.

TSF: They're fake, you fucking idiot. Jesus, as if he's knocked off two diamond rings with the sales tags still attached to them, you knob.

255

Black guy: Hey bro, they real yo.

At first I thought that the two strippers had set us up. Fairly low-level scam. I was disappointed in them, rather than angry. I was pretty rude to the guy with the mobile diamond store. I asked him to prove the worth of his shit. He duly took the rings out, turned on the light on his iPhone and shone it at the diamonds. The light accelerated towards the ceiling of the pagoda we were standing under and lit the place up as if a seventies disco ball had just been hit with the laser from the Large Hadron Collider.

Holy fuck. Still, I'm not an idiot.

TSF: That doesn't mean anything. Glass does that. If they're real diamonds, then they'd be able to put a scratch in this glass from one end to the other.

So he took one of the diamond rings, pushed it into the glass balustrade, and dragged it from one side to the other. When he'd finished, the glass was scratched to fuck, but the ring was completely untouched.

Oh.

Jinky: What do you want for them?

Black guy: Five hundred both. Then I gotta leave Vegas.

TSF: They're not real, you fucking clown. Is he gonna go to all the trouble of spending ten years inside for five hundred dollars? And where's he travelling to on five hundred dollars, the end of the fucking street?

Jinky: It's five hundred for fuck's sake. You spent more than that buying her more tampons and cigarettes.

Nicole: Huh?

Black guy: Huh?

TSF: All right, fuck it, here's the money. Jesus Christ, let's just get to the fucking villa can we?

15

I'm not a big connoisseur of strippers. I really don't know much about them. I don't even know what I like. The rest of the male species seem to be fans, however, and maybe that is what puts me off. I have some friends who are turned on only by strippers. It's not my style, but horses for courses and all that.

However, I have to admit that when you arrive back at a more intimate location, such as your villa at the Bellagio, and there are two professional strippers in your pool, topless – because why wouldn't they be? – and they are downing tequila shots and licking salt off each other's tits, well, my petty snobbery evaporates.

There is a life lesson in there somewhere.

Things were going off, and I was dozing off. This is where I'm at my best. I can relax. Once I know that girls are willing to come back and have fun and there is no competition around, I chill. Soon the air hostesses and Nicole and Kristin were as bare-chested as the strippers. I was on a sun-lounger looking at the sky and the moon above, but the conversation was keeping me awake. The women were comparing their breasts.

I was drifting in and out like a man fighting the effects of a general anaesthetic. I was missing lines of the conversation, but basically the strippers were wishing that they could go back to having natural breasts, but because of their job they couldn't, and the air hostesses wanted enhancements, but because of their job they couldn't. The grass is always greener.

The last thing I remember is raising my head with one final gargantuan effort and slowly opening my right eye to see half a dozen women standing in a circle touching and squeezing each other's breasts. They were like a tribe from a picture in an old *National Geographic*, but with way more hair product. Then I was gone. I drifted off hoping I would wake up and find the girls frozen in time, still dripping and naked.

Indeed, I awoke a short while later. Steve was filming himself teabagging me; damn air steward must have told him I was game for anything. Actually it was Steve's laughter that woke me. I'm told the footage of him in action above me still exists. Steve is the footballer who lost his phone in the back of a cab, only for it to be found and sold to a national newspaper. The box-office stuff was Steve in action with some unknown girl. So I should be worried. Yet for some reason I'm not. I think the world will be on my side if that film ever turns up.

'Come on, you prick,' said Steve tenderly, 'we're going to the casino.'

I don't come from a normal family. We are working class but we weren't like anybody else in the street. The other kids were all taught to survive. We were taught to escape. Think long term, not short term.

So one thing I missed out on was gambling. The bookie's was like some foreign embassy to me. I didn't know what went down in there. Same with the slots. The dogs. Bare-knuckle fighting and drinking in the park.

I don't know how to play poker and I don't want to know. On team coaches travelling to away games in the Premier League, I've watched guys who think they know how to play poker lose £30,000, £40,000 or £50,000 to guys who do know how to play poker. That could often be on a short twenty-minute trip from hotel to stadium. The worst I ever saw was a guy who laid his diamond earrings down as part payment, only to be met with the response 'Fine, where's the rest?'

At a different Premier League club I played with, I would wake up in the middle of the night before a match to see my room-mate sitting in the glow of his laptop checking the scores from minor league baseball in America. Now, I don't know about you, but I don't know the first thing about the New York Yankees, let alone the teams they send to the bush leagues. But this guy thought he did. So he'd come to us off the back of a threat from some very heavy people in the capital who had given him his final notice.

The transfer generated a signing-on fee that was handed over in part payment of the outstanding debt. It's all glamour and fairytales in the Premier League, you know.

The floor of the Bellagio casino is much the same as any other floor at any other Las Vegas casino. I have to say that I prefer Caesars Palace, but that's only because when it comes to losing my money, size matters to me. I like being able to hole up in a corner away from other gamblers and play the slots, with waitresses bringing me free pina coladas in exchange for a $1 tip. They call the real high-rollers 'whales'. When they see my $1 tip, they know they are dealing with an average-sized sardine. What they don't know at the outset is that I hold an unofficial world record for the most pina coladas in a single seating. So $25 worth in tips is pretty good going from one customer, I'd say.

I'm very good in my own company and I don't like people seeing how much I'm losing or how much I can drink. The casino floor of the Bellagio is smaller, and when you're with a bunch of strippers, a load of other girls and a group of guys who are clearly 'somebodies', you're really at the mercy of the crowd. Some people ride the bets of others; I ride the fact that I'm part of the group that's holding court in a town where that means something. And pretty soon a crowd gathered around our craps table.

Like many of the games in the casinos of Las Vegas, I don't know a fucking thing about craps. I'm not convinced that any of my team-mates did either. But we did know how to attract a crowd. Vegas crowds like to watch people winning big. But watching people losing big is pretty interesting too.

Just the act of watching integrates rubberneck tourists into the Vegas vibe. For craps to become a decent show, however, it requires the right character to be holding the dice, somebody who just loves to be the centre of attention, somebody incredibly over the top, win or lose. An over-caffeinated 'American' when they lose. Accentuate the positive, dude. Loudly.

Steve ticked all the boxes. Duly elected. I settled in to watch him lose.

Craps is won and lost on the roll of a pair of dice, and Steve was in his element with this uncomplicated process. 'What are we going for, people?' he'd shout. The answers came back to him in languages that were incomprehensible and from all over the world. It didn't matter to Steve. 'Fucking love it!' he'd shout. 'Let's go with my man from Japan, seven!'

And, bang, seven would come in.

I've been in casinos all over the world and one thing holds true: luck has an expiry date. Generally about fifteen minutes after it starts being luck. Fifteen minutes of lucky dice and the cold front of reality sets in.

Except for a long while, Steve didn't lose. He couldn't lose. He was up $20,000 by the time I wandered off to the slot machines. I chatted to a couple of girls. Well, they had spoken to me first. Had a pina colada. Looked in on the roulette table for a bit, in case they were struggling for custom. And then I headed back to the craps table, which should by then have been as quiet as a church and reeking with the stench of defeat. I didn't want to see Steve kicked in the rocks by Vegas odds.

But when I got back to the craps table, Steve was up $50,000.

Unbefuckinglievable.

Louis himself had appeared at the side of the table, pretending to be happy for us, but alarmed that Steve was winning it all off the back of the hotel's complimentary chips. Security were there too, and the overhead cameras were focused on Steve, as men in hidden offices tried to work out if this was a scam artist, a good gambler or an idiot surfing his drunken luck. The crowd that had gathered an hour earlier had been swollen by a busload of Americans desperate for the cheap Vegas experience of watching somebody win big.

I ordered another pina colada. Not knowing what the fuck to do next, I persuaded the two air hostesses to walk around the hotel floor with me, each of them taking an arm as if I were a wealthy courtly gentleman. Which I am. Or at least I was. The air hostesses were beautiful, and as I walked through the lobby I felt like a king, a boulevardier of the continents. If you didn't know anything about the girls, you'd marry one given the chance, like my friend had a year earlier, but you'd probably regret it in the morning.

Even so, I couldn't help but feel a sense of 'what might be' as I walked through the hotel with the air hostesses. So I was like putty in their hands when they suggested that we go back to the villa and cool off in the pool. As I sat by the pool, the girls staged the best Vegas show since Sinatra first hit town back in '51.

We were completely and utterly high and drunk by the time it occurred to us to check back in on Steve. I was prepared to comfort him and give him my little homily on luck and how you only got a short-term lease on it. But there were fifty people at least still gathered around the table. The house had switched dealers twice. They do that to throw your rhythm off and give you pause to think. At that moment you should get up and walk away. Steve was still there but the tide was going out.

Half an hour earlier he'd been up by $100,000. Now he was at $50,000 and falling. Yeah, like that cartoon character who runs off the cliff. That was it. I don't know why, but it made me so angry. The way I saw it, Steve had won $50,000. The way

Steve saw it, he'd lost $50,000 in the last half hour. The way the house saw it, he owed them $50,000. Not legally, but because that's how it works. I'd seen this before. Before you know what's happening, you aren't winning any more and the casino is asking you to show proof of funds to cover your losses.

The tourists were starting to look deflated. Jesse was hovering for a while and looking less worried about being taken out to the middle of the Nevada desert and buried. (Not by the Bellagio. Obviously.) The dealer looked smug. The math was kicking in. It would all be OK.

The dealer didn't count me into the equation though. Nor did Steve. The break from the floor had done me good.

Steve was in the thick of it. He had the stare of kids I have seen on team buses on their way to play for the first time in places like Old Trafford or the Emirates or St James' Park. Rollercoaster eyes. I tried to talk him round. No go. He was convinced that he was on a roll, even though that roll was in the direction of the gutter now.

I placed a hand on Steve's shoulder. The dealer told me not to interact with a player at the table. A surefire sign that it was time to go. When a player is winning, you could make him piggyback you around the table as you shouted 'Yee-haa!' and mimed lassoing a steer for all the house would care. Losing requires respect though.

Steve had the dice and was ready to roll again, so I did the only sensible thing I could think of and grabbed him around the neck and pulled him off the stool he was sitting on, just as he flicked the dice out of his hand.

All fucking hell broke loose.

264

The dealer went into a fit, hollering about house rules. The tourists woke up and began booing like a herd of stereotypical Americans. Security came sprinting down through the aisle between the slot machines.

Shit, I wondered, maybe this is something even Jesse might not be able to fix.

Where the fuck is he?

I hung tough. Security were keen to throw me out in old-fashioned arse-bouncing style on to the pavement of The Strip. We were obliged to point out that all of us were staying in one of the villas. We had a sort of sucker immunity.

Steve was ungrateful. He was disorientated from lack of sleep. Vegas casinos allow no suggestion of what time or season it actually is. You float through time till you land with a bump.

'Hard seven,' said the dealer.

The fracas stopped. Everybody looked at the bath-shaped table, and there, at the plug end, were two dice that were showing a three and a four. It was a ten-thousand-dollar freak of a throw.

'I'm on a fucking roll, baby!' shouted Steve.

The herd mooed joyously.

At that moment our fixer Jesse came jogging down the concourse. He looked as if he'd just remembered something crucial. In fact, he had. We had booked a table at Tao Club. If we were thinking about getting our arses over there any time soon, then we'd better hurry as the club wanted to sell our table again.

Steve saw sense. It was wise for him to have a varied and balanced diet of vices. It was time for drugs. Hard drugs. Jesse

265

had reappeared just in time. He was beside himself. Even fixers like to look good sometimes.

It's easy to forget the golden rule of gambling in Vegas, or gambling anywhere for that matter: bet with your head, not over it. When he'd calmed down and set his mind on the idea of sampling some Las Vegas snow in the privacy of his own villa, Steve took his chips to the cashier. He cashed out to the tune of $60,000. Back in the villa, the girls took pictures of themselves on the double bed with bills thrown all over them. I still have a couple of those pictures. Steve has none of the bills.

We opened the safe that nobody knew how to close and chucked the money in, before showering, changing into our best gear, and heading out to Tao feeling like the kings of Las Vegas.

Just four Premier League athletes at rest with friends.

16

Tao. Remember Tao? Yes, we will always have Tao.

The club. The beach. The memories of old champagne wars fought by proud veterans.

Was it day or night? We weren't sure. Should we be eating or swimming? Who cares.

I'm having flashbacks. A previous visit to Vegas is running through my head like a fucking Tarantino movie as we enter Tao.

Matty: What's that dance?

Della: Na, that's coke.

TSF: Fuck sake, grab her legs . . . get out the fucking way . . . open the door!

We move outside. No limo. Fucking Third World.

TSF: TAXI!

Cut to hospital.

Della: She's gonna fucking die, she's choking!

Matty: No she's not. Look. Keep slapping her face. Be cool. HELP! SOMEBODY FUCKING HELP! You've got to relax.

Doctor: Right here, guys. OK, what has she taken?

Della: Cocaine, I think.

Matty: You think?

Doctor: OK, and what's her name? CAN I GET A CART HERE, PLEASE? Come on, man. Her name, what's her name?

Trolley arrives and the girl is taken away.

Matty: Why don't you know her fucking name, Della?

Della: Why would I?

Matty: You were dancing with her!

Della: No I wasn't!

Matty: You said she'd taken cocaine.

Della: I said I *thought* she had. I don't fucking know, do I?

Matty: Then . . . who is she?

Slow realization that nobody knows who the girl is.

Della: She's just some girl that he picked up off the fucking floor!

TSF: She needed help.

Matty: Ah for fuck's sake, you fucking idiot! Now the police are gonna talk to us, you twat. They're gonna want to know who gave her the coke, and what are we gonna say?

Della: Who did give her the coke?

TSF: I don't fucking know, do I? What shall we do? Let's just do a runner back to the hotel room.

Della: Yeah!

Matty: And then she dies? And the doctor tells the police three fucking English lads came in with her at three a.m.?

TSF: And the CCTV has probably clocked us coming in with her to be fair. I probably shouldn't have grabbed her legs in hindsight.

Della: NO, BUT THAT'S YOU, ISN'T IT? YOU DON'T FUCKING THINK!

Big brawl between the players in the hospital lobby. Well, a brawl, but a trying-not-to-draw-too-much-attention brawl.

Two hours later. Players sitting down in the lobby. Concerned but falling asleep.

Doctor: OK, who wants to take this young lady home?

TSF: What?

Doctor: You guys did the right thing bringing her in. You see this bracelet right here? It's for epilepsy.

TSF: Epilepsy?

Matty: She doesn't look paraplegic.

Doctor: Uh . . . no, epilepsy. It's when the brain suddenly becomes overloaded and the body goes into a seizure.

Blank stares.

Doctor: Anyway, good job, guys. Look after her, and if she

269

has a relapse call me using the number on this card, OK?

Turning to girl.

Doctor: And keep drinking lots of water, OK? And maybe take a day or two off from the partying, huh?
Girl: OK.

Doctor walks away.

Girl: Soooo . . . who are you guys?
Della: Hi, I'm Della. I pulled you out of the club and got you to the hospital.
TSF: Really?
Girl: Thanks so much. So, where are we going now?

Let's not kid ourselves. We come to Vegas to commit as much debauchery as possible, away from our WAGs, in a place where the cameras can't follow and where the saying 'what happens in Vegas, stays in Vegas' is a mantra that is followed so rigidly that two players I know have those very words tattooed on their inner bicep. They both go to Dubai now anyway. Good luck on that honeymoon.

But this incident didn't stay in Vegas. At least, the girl didn't stay in Vegas. Six months later, Della took her from the bright lights of The Strip, where the girl worked as a party girl, back to the dim lights of Wigan, where he married her without a welcoming line of girls in petal-filled bathtubs. She lived the dream backwards.

I think of her as we enter Tao. How is Wigan today?

History lesson (because this book is basically an academic work of social history).

Of all the champagne wars fought in this sprawling club, there has to be a redeeming moral. When somebody disses you to start a champagne war, you can either take it on the chin, or you can give as good as you get. And if you were like us back in the heyday of the Premier League, in a Neverland where nobody knows you, with your looks tended and your ego rampant, then, my friend, you were gonna get a fucking war.

Now think fast shots of girls frantically ferrying champagne bottles back and forth with sparklers in the tops. Making your point is messy . . . and expensive. People have suggested that a fizzy water war might have less devastating effects on the participants. But devastation is the point. It must be inflicted. Widespread devastation.

Now think exhausted girls lying on the floor. Smoke of battle clearing. Tell-tale $1 tips from TSF lying about their persons.

But a point? There is none. In Vegas that *is* the fucking point. That is the Tao of Vegas.

(And this book is nothing if not a primer on important philosophies of the world.)

So when we enter Tao, and once I'd finished thinking of Wigan, I scoped the place to check that there was no fucker in there who would engage us in a champagne war. At huge personal risk, but with the mind of a military strategist, I had just saved Steve $60K. It would seem a pity to lose it now buying champagne for somebody we didn't rate.

In fact it would be immature.

271

I was thinking sensibly. It would soon be time to get out of town.

Any time you leave Las Vegas without a criminal record, and with most of the belongings you came with, is a good time.

Money will come to you again. And if it won't, well, you shouldn't have gone to Vegas in the first place.

We packed the bags, left tips for the maids. Checked the place for anything we might have forgotten. And anything worth having. I could vaguely recall buying a diamond bracelet for my wife. But there was no diamond bracelet. Maybe I had imagined it.

There were two diamond rings lying in our fruit bowl, though.

Fuck me! Boys, we nearly forgot our $500 rings.

At McCarran Airport we saw a familiar face. A manager nobody in the game particularly likes. This man had been responsible, as we saw it, for the systematic bullying of many of our friends and fellow players. He was a dinosaur, a man who would pull out all of the stops to get his way at a player's expense. When a manager wants to get rid of a player there are two ways to do it. The right way and this guy's way.

The right way is to keep integrating the player and treat him with the same respect as the other players so that he doesn't cause any problems and comes to understand naturally that he isn't playing in the team and should probably move on.

The other way, the wrong way, is to arrange friendlies at the other end of the country on a Tuesday night and send the player travelling with the youth team by Transit van. Then to have him in on Sundays to do absolutely nothing. Just to bugger up his day and his family life and generally make him feel as excluded and alienated as possible.

This manager had done that to many of our friends.

One of the lads suggested he call in a bomb scare on the manager's plane. But after five seconds of intense deliberation, it was decided that nobody fancied playing in the distinctive orange kit of Atlético Guantánamo. But apparently, after the plane had taken off, the police got word that there was a man smuggling drugs in his stomach, who would be bringing his cargo in on flight BA117 from Las Vegas.

If you were flying in or out of Heathrow on that particular day, you may remember that there were widespread delays. It makes me smile every single day to think of a rubber glove with a copper's stout finger in it vainly exploring the arsehole of that most masculine of men.

I had my own shit to get through anyway. Penance for a start. Inhaling a box of paracetamol made me feel halfway to recovery. It was as if I had more than one hangover though. They were stacked in holding patterns above my head. One would land. I would deal with it. The next one would start its descent.

Never again, I said. And right then I really meant it.

I made the drive out to Birmingham's jewellery quarter to visit a Jewish guy I knew called Hash. Hash was one of the smartest people I'd ever met. He had an incredible business supplying jewellery to any footballer who wanted it. Rolex watches? Go to Hash. Engagement and wedding rings? Talk to Hash. Birthday bracelets and necklaces for your WAG's birthday? Hash was your man. Even the black players, who like to have specially made-up unique pieces such as diamond crucifixes (while they live lives devoid of virtue), went to Hash.

For four or five years, Hash cleaned up. He never asked where anything came from and, crucially, he never fleeced you on the price.

That's what I mean by smart.

That day I went to see if Hash could rip off a Tiffany eternity ring my wife had had her eye on for a while, and which would now go some way towards appeasing her in the light of my Vegas trip. The diamond bracelet I had bought her had been stolen, or had got lost, or had never existed. She knew what went on during these kinds of trips, but this one was going to be a particularly hard sell.

Hash didn't have a shop; he had an office above one. There was no name on the door, and the room was sparse, just a horrible fake walnut tabletop perched upon cold metal legs, with two swivel chairs finishing off the look. It was all set up for a quick escape.

Hash showed me the rings he currently had available and steered me towards the one he wanted me to buy, as all good salesmen do. A beautiful eternity ring.

We agreed a price, and as we shook hands on the deal he spotted a glint from my wedding finger and asked me what I was doing walking around sporting a woman's engagement ring in full view of the world.

I could only vaguely recall what the ring was doing there. Oh yeah. It was easier to wear it coming through customs than to explain its presence in my luggage. I was about to tell him where it had come from, but as I opened my mouth to talk, I was immediately shot down.

'No, no, no,' said Hash, 'I don't want to bloody know where it came from. Can you get it off?'

With some gentle persuasion, the ring came off and I handed it to Hash, who put it towards the eye he'd covered with a jeweller's loupe, which he used to read small marks on silver items and to check the clarity of diamonds.

Hash examined the ring for about a minute before lowering the loupe and looking me dead in the eye.

'Do you know what this is?' he asked.

I didn't, but the next time you visit the Bellagio Hotel in Las Vegas, remember to check out the scratch on the glass partition on the walkway to the entrance. It was made by a three-carat diamond ring. One of a pair bought for $500 in a moment of drunken impatience from a black guy who had to leave Vegas immediately. So he said.

Turns out they were the real deal. One hundred per cent genuine.

Hash opened the briefcase that never left his side, delved inside, and handed me £23,000 in cash.

'What about the eternity ring?' I asked.

Hash just grinned at me. 'It's a gift for your wife,' he said.

I never saw him again.

Aside from wondering down the years whether or not I was now a bona fide international diamond smuggler, I also sometimes wondered what exactly happened to Hash. He had such a fantastic business and was fair to us players when most people looking to sell us things were intent on ripping us off.

About a year ago I was with another group of footballers I'd once played with when Hash's name came up. 'Terrible what happened to him, pal,' said one of the players. Apparently he had been in a hotel room in the UAE, selling watches to two men posing as footballers from the Middle East, when at some point in the proceedings they stabbed him to death, before making off with his briefcase.

Anyway, that was Hash while he still had his health.

And that was us while we still had Vegas.

PART SIX

Dubai or Bust

17

I played in the Premier League, a business that has given employment to footballers from over 105 different countries around the world. That's as diverse as it gets. Not that we were interested. We weren't there for the diversity and the cultural exchanges.

People find it amusing how lacking in curiosity footballers are. People generally feel free to be condescending about it. The fact is, we are bred that way. You went to all these amazing places and you didn't see the tower of this and the palace of that? You didn't try the puffin kiev or the cat dumplings? My word.

No. Professional football is about eliminating surprises. It's about keeping players in the same environment no matter where they are. The world is training ground, dressing room, physio room, pitch and not much else. We are thrown into that world to do a job. While we are there, we pretend that the bond between us is unbreakable. That night we lost 2–1 to a couple of goals in injury time that made us family, and so on . . .

When it's over, though, and we are bounced back into the real world, we all just go our own way.

I was relegated once. Relegation is like being in a hospice, but a hospice where everybody believes in reincarnation. Everybody knows what is going to happen soon but nobody really wants to talk about it. Nobody wants to talk about what might happen. And nobody wants to talk about it when it does happen. We came back from the crucial game on the team bus and nobody spoke. We were a relegated team. Nobody said a word. Why would we? At last we didn't have to bother about geeing ourselves up for the next game. We didn't have to go through the motions of all those same old inspirational speeches and doomsday warnings. It was over and done with.

Finally I said, 'If you watch the hedges by the side of the motorway closely, you can see loads of deer.' I'd noticed them on my way into training through the course of the season. By the end of the trip everybody was on the left-hand side of the bus, trying to spot deer. The sheer excitement of some of the players when they spotted one was incredible. All those times up and down that road and nobody had ever noticed the deer.

We didn't have to talk about relegation, we just spotted deer instead. Then we got back to the stadium, got into our cars and drove home. A lot of us never saw each other again. Five years of living in each other's pockets came to an end spotting deer on the side of the road from the team bus after being relegated.

But what are you supposed to do when you get relegated? Nobody knows. Life goes on. There are still deer to be spotted but there are careers to be finished out. Spotting deer and being curious will have to wait.

We're not curious and we are not supposed to be. It's a lovely picture, isn't it, when you see a team which has just won a trophy and they've got their arms around each other, and they're bouncing up and down singing the Campioni song about themselves, and you look and you think, this guy here is from Africa, and these two guys are Asian, he's a Russian and he's French, and that guy there is from Iceland. Isn't football a beautiful thing the way it brings people together from such diverse cultures?

Bad news. In every dressing room I've been in, the ethnic and racial groups have stuck with themselves. The black guys socialized with the black guys, the black French guys socialized with each other, the white English guys stuck together; the Irish, the Welsh and the Scots were co-opted into that group but had their own private groups as well. The other foreign players? Well, it depended on where you were from. An American seemed less foreign than a Croatian, for instance, so the American might land with the Anglo group. The Croatian would be left to fend for himself. Then there were the goalies. Separate study to be done on goalies.

I don't know how the black guys referred to the white guys, but I know that the white guys often referred to the black group as the tribe. Is that racist? No. I don't think so. It's the sort of humour that makes life in the dressing room tolerable for people from so many different backgrounds. Yes, everybody could have pretended we were some football version of Up With People, but we weren't. We were little caucuses filled with people just trying to be comfortable in their own skin. We stuck with what was familiar because it was easiest and

281

it allowed more time to focus on football. It didn't mean we didn't like or respect each other. It meant that we were there to win football matches, not to have workshops where we spoke about our feelings.

You believe all the guff when you're a young pro. One for all and all for one. Once, when I was still basically a kid in football terms, we were playing a team in the latter stages of the LDV Trophy. (I should have issued a glamour alert warning at the start of this story – apologies.) During the season we had drawn with the opposition home and away. I was sure we would take them this time. We were on our way to the big time, to Wembley.

We got hammered. It didn't make any sense to me.

What went wrong, Gary?

Well, the night before, a disproportionate number of, ahem, northern women had infiltrated the team hotel and banged on doors until they found where the players were. Then they'd kept them up all night. The players laugh about it to this day. I can't. I know that a knock came on our door and when it was opened there was a white girl standing in the corridor who looked like a Vegas hooker who stayed indoors a lot. Pale. The black guy I was rooming with kicked me into the corridor and dragged the woman inside.

I had to bang on doors in my pants until I found a room that had a youth team player in it. His room was deemed off limits to the hookers. It gave off an air of sanctity. He had a Bible out; we said a prayer. Straight up. To this day he is the most God-fearing player you'll ever meet. Sadly, as I said, neither the player nor God did anything for us. We got stuffed. But nobody really gave a shit. Everybody just wanted to be comfortable and successful. We lived on football's terms. The LDV Trophy was a joke. I just wasn't in on the joke.

The same with foreign players. Were they good or were they bad was the only question. We never really wondered how it was that every foreign player seemed to either have good English when he arrived or picked it up pretty quickly, whereas none of us was comfortable with any other language. Where did they go on holiday? Back home, we supposed. What did they do there? What was home like? How were they seen there? Did they intend to go back there after football? Really? But there's no M&S over there, is there?

Nobody cared about the cultures of others.

I played with a great Nigerian player for a while at one of my clubs. Nobody ever asked him what life was like in Nigeria. Just like we never asked anything of the South African player who grew up in a township that suffered a famous massacre during the apartheid years, or never said much to the Zimbabwean except to make jokes along the lines of 'fuck off, mate, you people are still putting machetes through people's heads'.

And so on . . .

Not bothering to find out anything about different cultures allowed us to fall back on stereotypes when we needed to abuse somebody. Dressing rooms are beehives of abuse and slagging.

I had a good chat with my Nigerian team-mate one day. We called him King. 'Listen, King, serious question. Am I the best player you've ever played with?'

He looked as if he had been shot. 'No! What?'

283

'Well who the fuck is better than me that you've played with?'

That was a way of getting him to talk about his career, because he was quite modest and most of us were too cool to come straight out and say, tell us about the famous players you have played with.

So he named a name: 'Number one would be —'

And I'd feign outrage and say, 'What the fuck could possibly make *him* better than me?'

Then we'd get some little titbit of information that we could store away. Before long everybody had gathered round and he'd be talking about the De Boers, Finidi George and so on. I think we got through about sixty players before my name started coming in for any consideration, but we'd all learned what we wanted to. What the big guys were like.

We learned little things by accident almost. One guy used to send a good chunk of his wages home to his village in South America to build schools and libraries and to pay for irrigation. He was just another guy in the dressing room to us. At home he was a legend, with over a hundred caps and a political career waiting for him. I played with an American who put a lot of money into affordable housing. He was smart. He had his wages paid into a US bank account and cleaned up on the exchange rate. Another guy bought every house on the street he grew up on in the north-east. Did them up and revived the street, which was dying on its feet.

Some guys just saw what was coming at the end and prepared. Danny Spiller is a good example. He had an undistinguished career, the highlight of which was two spells at Gillingham. But in the summer of 2016, when his house burned down, it turned out to be a £1.5 million mansion, and luckily his £200,000 Ferrari Spider was spared the inferno. He'd started secondary selling for Herbalife towards the end of his career after reading that Messi used the stuff. By the time of the fire he had a distribution team of five thousand people. He was still only thirty-four and mucking about with non-league football.

In the dressing room, though, we seldom talked about these things – guys' backgrounds, business plans, etc. We talked about cars and women and other players and other clubs. That was the common language.

One of my best friends, funnily enough, was Icelandic. Honestly, he was the best footballer I ever played with. Not technically, not inspirationally, but in terms of being super smart and knowing what was happening at any given moment. He knew the politics of football. If a player had a problem and went to this guy, the problem was solved. He was a benign godfather who held the squad together, and everybody respected him. He should really have been our captain because he was definitely our leader.

I visited him in Iceland when we were both done with football. We drove down and got the ferry across to Vestmannaeyjar to see David James play for the local team. We took a quick tour of the island, which is basically a volcano. It last erupted in 1973, and even if it was a natural disaster, the island got lucky. The wind was blowing the right way and the fishing fleet was in. Everybody who needed to be evacuated got off the island quickly. When everybody came back, the island was covered in ash and one third of the buildings were gone. They got down to the clean-up with amazing resilience. The lava, when it cooled, had extended the area of the island by two kilometres and provided additional protection for the harbour. The heat from the lava was directed to heat the town.

Today you can drive up the volcano and see houses that were engulfed in the lava. They've been chiselled out of the rock. You look through the rock and see the metal remains of bunk beds and kitchens, completely frozen in time. It was just another Icelandic story. They got on with life as they have always done.

Later, with another former player and his wife in tow, we drove the car off the ferry and headed up towards Reykjavik. This other Icelandic player was the life and soul of every fucking party. A complete bombscare. He did not give one solitary fuck what anybody thought. Once, in America, he decided to do chin-ups with a bottle of Corona in his mouth. He knocked his two front teeth out when he banged the Corona bottle against the pipe he was doing the chin-ups on. When we found his teeth and gave them to him, he swallowed them, 'for safe keeping'. Whenever a new round of drinks was bought he would toast it with a proper old Viking toast; it went 'Oh yay, oh yay, oh yay . . .' There was more stuff all about the Vikings invading various parts of Europe and, hey, lock up your daughters, and so on. Some of the lads remembered the toast and did it with him. I felt that was so they could look like they were Vikings. Being a Viking in America was deemed to be exotic by the natives. I missed that one.

We drove on, me with these two unique men in their homeland, past incredible waterfalls and glaciers and geysers. Just incredible. Steam belching out of the earth at random moments

286

by the side of the road. None of the Icelanders batted an eyelid, but imagine driving along and the side of the road just suddenly erupting!

It wasn't the time to tell my mates that things had been interesting on our estate too, you know.

When we played together, my mate was always clear that when football was finished, he was heading back to Iceland. His heart was set on this, despite my putting to him precise and cogent arguments like 'Why the fuck do you want to go back?' He lived in a beautiful house, his kids went to a great school, his missus was happy. He was famous and well liked.

He was ahead of me in his thinking, I realized. He knew that when football ends, it just ends. No credits. Just start again with whatever resources you have.

He is very loyal and very political. He hadn't liked what happened to his country in the economic downturn. As far as 2008 is concerned, Iceland was hit hardest. There is no doubt about that. They reacted smartest though. They just let the country's three biggest banks collapse. They didn't torment themselves trying to save institutions which had failed them so badly. It was the third largest bankruptcy in history and it happened on this little island. It was an economic volcano, and when it was done they just set about clearing the dust and rock as usual. The country reinvented itself, reminded itself what banks were for – namely to serve. And they stopped being beguiled by easy foreign money. It's working. Jobless rates are down, IMF loans are being paid off well ahead of schedule, output levels are on a steady increase.

My mate went home during all of this. Like much of the

planet, parts of Iceland had been bought by the Chinese when the prices were low. My mate has had offers for his business but he won't sell. Not because he doesn't need the money, but because he, like many in Iceland, is desperate to show the world that they can do it on their own again. The Chinese want to build a hotel at the fjord near where he lives. He's not having any of it.

If he isn't prime minister of Iceland some day, I will assume that the country has an unbelievable array of political talent with integrity to choose from. And if he is prime minister, a lot of us who shared a dressing room with him for years will wonder how we missed the fact that we were playing with maybe the smartest footballer in the world. Or, one of the smartest people in the world who just happened to be good at football.

But that's football. He spoke such perfect English, made such English jokes, he could drink like he was English, and he had such a grasp of day-to-day footballer problems that to us he *was* English. I saw him as English. Everybody did. He was one of us. That helped him and everybody else. He understood perfectly what was required.

I'm talking about him here because this is a book about footballers travelling. If you are looking for thoughtful critiques of foreign cultures, you have bought the wrong book. This is a book about footballer culture. A culture not greatly admired and not held up as a model for society as a whole. But it's the culture that makes football tick. It's the business of making the world generic and homogenous so we can just play football with each other and stop wondering about what's out there.

We were bred that way. I came late and escaped a lot of the

conditioning, and as such I was often like a foreigner myself in dressing rooms. But most of the lads had been with clubs since their early teens, and had grown up being told again and again and again 'Don't worry about that, just focus on your football'. They did. Nobody ever tells a footballer to take a gap year and go and see the world. Together we saw the world, but only after the world had been made to feel as much like home as possible.

Regrets? Not really. Football finishes while you are still young. The world is still there, old and waiting. And, like a mate with whom you shared a dressing room for years, there's plenty of time to learn about differences and what makes things tick. The world is out there, just like the deer were still there the evening we got relegated.

We have it all to look forward to. And we have some weird memories to look back on, even from the latter years of our glorious careers.

18

Listen. Mrs TSF and I got married in Barbados. Bought out the whole first-class section at the pointy end of the plane and flew the family and friends out. We had the Cuban Brothers playing. We had a crazy big villa. A beach. Ice sculptors flown in. Top champagne flown in. The works. It was the dog's bollocks of weddings.

Could it all have been done cheaper?

Oh yeah. See your point.

Would I sometimes like to have all that money back?

Definitely.

Would I like to have it back at the cost of never having had those mad few days getting hitched to the woman I love, and having so many people we love sharing the mad novelty of the whole thing with us?

Nah, keep the money. Deal is off. Something always turns up. You can't go back and fetch it from the past. Don't take it all too seriously. We sure as hell didn't.

It's funny how people love to tut-tut about what footballers earn and how they spend it. It's as if football money is being prised from the hands of the sick and starving.

When I signed for my first club I would have happily played for a fraction of the money they paid me. And that money didn't amount to a whole hillock of Heinz. All through my career I would have played for less than I got, and when the end was nigh, I did play for less than I ever imagined I would. It was football. I loved it. In my head, I had been a footballer for all of my life. I just never realized that being a footballer wouldn't actually last all of my life.

And you love football too. Most of you. That's the point. The money we get paid is just a by-product of the world we live in. It's a world that gets off on football. You pay for season tickets and sports channel subscriptions because you love football. You buy replica jerseys and football duvets and football lunch boxes because you love football. And Sky and BT and the rest spend billions on rights orgies because they know that, yes, you love football, and when football is on the telly, that is a really great time for advertisers to show you all the other things they think you might love.

Religion used to be the opium of the people. Now it's football. And we are your dealers, your growers, your suppliers. If there is a problem, it's your problem. Get help. Have your family make an intervention. Go cold turkey. Wean yourself off football and into opera. We'll still be playing football when you come crawling back.

Where did you want your money to go? If you wanted to help the sick and the needy, you would have sent them a cheque instead of buying a season ticket. Did you want the fat chairman and the Chianti-swilling shareholders to become more bloated on your wedge? Like they used to in the bad old days?

More than most industries, the money in football goes to the people who do the work and spill the sweat and bleed the blood and make the magic.

Us!!!!!

As Marx said, to each player according to his ability, from each fan according to his weakness. Now go back to your *Guardian* and stop worrying.

The money goes to the players. Get over it. Move on. Write to Jennifer Lawrence and tell her she gets paid way too much for pretending to be other people, and tell her while you're about it that she hasn't done that very well since she made *Winter's Bone.*

To most of us footballers, when the money starts falling on to our shoulders and into our pockets, it's as strange and novel as a blizzard of snow on a hot summer's day. We don't sit down and fret about the poor fucked-up environment. We play. We go a little bit mad. We make snowmen on the beach. Because we can.

Since we were kids of eleven or twelve, we have dreamed of being footballers. And now that we are footballers, it turns out that there's a pile of money available to us also. Sorry if we don't behave like chartered accountants or risk assessors when that happens.

The fact is, football takes so much of you along the way that you aren't fully formed when the money hits you. People say 'you're so lucky to be a footballer', as if you had applied for a job as a quarryman and ended up playing at Old Trafford due to a clerical mistake.

We are lucky, but we are dogged and resilient too. On the way up you get more knock-backs than you get pats on the back. You see mates who are better than you being cut from teams, from squads, from clubs, and they disappear off into that shit scary place you call the real world. You get coaches who don't understand you, and coaches who understand you perfectly but just don't like you.

And you learn two things. One, be a hard, resilient little bastard. And two, always back yourself.

Remember when your teachers and your worried parents and your sensible friends all said the same thing? 'Football? Get some sense. Get yourself a job, an education to fall back on. Then you can have your daydreams.' When they said all that, you backed yourself. You took the risk that you would be coming home with your tail between your legs, listening to the 'I told you so' chorus, and wondering if everybody else would be two years ahead of you in their careers and their mortgages, all the way to the grave.

Because we are hard and resilient and we always back ourselves, very few of us make any plans for tomorrow. We take our seasons one match at a time and we tackle our problems only when they are about to tackle us. We don't prepare for a future we can't even imagine. Fuck it, we are living in a present few people can imagine. That's enough. We don't hedge bets. We don't make contingencies.

If you were on a white-water ride with your friends, just hanging on but laughing your head off and feeling so free of worry, so full of thrilling abandon, would you think to yourself 'Hmm, I must check what the interest rate on my savings account is'?

Really?

Andrés Iniesta makes the point in his book, *The Artist*. 'People see footballers as different beings, as if we're untouchable, as if nothing ever happens to us, but we're people. Of course we're privileged, but in the tangibles we're the same.'

We are. We are the same. Only richer.

In the end, if you despair of young footballers having any common sense, and you hope that a beauty queen might actually bring peace to the earth one day, there is good news for you. The joke is on us. No matter where we go in the world, no matter how much we pay, whether we go three-star, five-star or seven-star, we keep coming up against walls. This far and no further, boys.

The real wealth in the world, the obscene wealth, the old wealth, the globalized wealth, the hidden wealth, is out there running the universe. Badly. Malignly. That money takes its holidays in places we have never heard of. That money flows through caverns and corridors we will never see.

To that silent money we are all just non-league plebs. In the grand scheme of things, we don't matter. If you want to be disgusted by wealth and what truly rich people do to each other and to everybody else, get yourself into that world if you can, and have a look around. That's the money you need to be complaining about.

In that world, the money is measured by its age as well as by its oceanic volume. For us footballers, on the other hand, the money just runs out, usually while it is still fresh. We just wake up one day with no job to go to. No sense of who we are. And we wonder why we bought such a big house, because this morning, with no job and no income, we realize that mortgage is going to eat its way through the savings like a python snacking on a jack rabbit.

Most of us end up with the same money worries as everybody else. Except the damn numbers are bigger, which means the bastards at the bank who once massaged your balls and your ego any time you showed up now act as if they've been ripped off by a particularly cunning form of leper. If there is one thing banks cannot abide, it is dishonesty.

So there you have it. Forgive the cliché, but most footballers I know come from humble beginnings. And the few that don't had to back themselves twice as heavily and put up with twice as much shit in dressing rooms.

So we have this brief, dramatic life where we play like gods (sometimes) and we live like kings? Fuck it, we are kings who have had no preparation for palace life. And then it goes away. Poof! How'd they do that? Your number is up. Please give back your jersey. Your ermine. Your pearls. No more free boots.

Oh, and your wife just said that she doesn't know when things became so distant, but she doesn't feel compatible with your bank account any more.

Yesterday it was, 'Fuck, isn't that TSF who plays for—'

Today it's, 'Do you remember him? I think that's the guy who used to play for—'

Tomorrow it will be, 'I think he used to be a footballer or something. Poor bastard.'

But as Iniesta says, 'We're not martyrs. Lots of people would swap with us. Every job has its difficulties. Every time my dad, a builder, went up on the scaffolding, he could have fallen. But

295

he accepts that risk; he had to. Or the lorry driver, or any job . . . the footballer knows; he grows up with pressure, criticism, having to be strong. I'm convinced there are many who wouldn't make it.'

He's quite smart, Iniesta. That's the consolation when you are arse over tit in debt and depression: not many got this far!

There are so many forgotten ones who just didn't make it and many more faceless ones who do far more important jobs, but none of them ever made fifty thousand people happy all at once. He shoots. He scores. Fifty thousand people on their feet and screaming with joy on a cold Saturday afternoon. We did that while being young and heedless and happy, in our prime.

Look, I don't know where footballers go when they die. Hell probably. Scunthorpe maybe. But I do know where they go when they begin to get old.

Dubai.

As I said, at the end the joke is on us.

So, you're wondering: Dubai? What's the deal with Dubai, big shot? You can't debauch at the top level any more without pulling a hamstring, can you? It takes Viagra, not yoghurt-covered raisins, to get through a week in Ibiza these days, doesn't it?

Stop. Stop. Stop. There comes an age in a man's life when it is improper to talk about such things. We reached that point a few pages back.

Dubai. Here's the pitch.

Dubai is the ultimate family holiday destination for foot-ballers. Footballers with real money. And money always feels real until it's all gone. You take a family of four to any one of the five-star Jumeirah hotels, and after you've tossed your spending money, you're easily looking at being £15,000 down for a week with flights included. When you played, that was probably less than half a week's wages.

And what do you get for that money? Well, the opposite of what we used to crave. You see, nobody really knows us in Dubai. You don't sit by the pool and wait for the first stretched-to-the-point-of-distress replica shirt to approach you carrying three lagers while shouting 'Oi-Oi!' We used to love all that shit. We really did. For about five minutes. Among our people, shouting 'loadsamoney' and necking champagne. Just after you get old, though, that scene gets old too. Very old.

In Dubai there are lots of Italians, Germans, Russians, a few Americans, and a few natives. Nobody really knows who we are. We don't like being recognized any more, but we *do* like the idea of people looking at us and thinking, 'Well, he's young, and handsome in a bit-of-rough sort of way. It costs a lot of money to be here. I wonder what his story is? Tech billionaire?'

You see, we evolve. We become more sophisticated. Once we liked being recognized. Now it's enough to be seen. Our little pleasures are more discreet.

Plus there's shitloads of sunshine. Even if you go there in May and June before it gets mobbed, you are guaranteed enough blue sky to make you forget relegation and the obviously rigged Player of the Year business which saw you pickpocketed yet again.

So Dubai is where Championship and Premier League footballers go with their kids and where footballing couples

297

go together. It's a very well-appointed waiting room for those about to be middle-aged. I haven't yet seen herds of carousing footballing mates there. It's not that kind of place just now. To paraphrase Groucho Marx, it's like being a member of a club that wouldn't usually have you as a member.

There are nightclubs. Tighten your girdles, things are about to get glamorous. I have gallivanted with a few West Brom players in Dubai. Me and the leading galácticos of the West Midlands. We had a night out in the top-floor club at the Jumeirah Beach Hotel. I hated it, but that's just me.

The Mall is the worst place in Dubai. The great leveller. Everybody goes to the Mall to be shaken down and treated like shit. The Mall is as big as the estate I grew up on. Emirates Mall, I think it's called. I assume they paid a consultancy firm millions of dollars to come up with that name. It's a mall and it's in the Emirates. Do you see how it works? Simple and elegant. We love it. Our creatives are really pleased.

The Mall is a jungle crammed with every label you can think of, and more people than should be allowed on the planet under government law.

The EU would never allow this many people in a single mall.

At the entrance to every door of every boutique is a stunning-looking local woman, immaculately turned out and aiming a huge suggestive smile at you. I've seen them lure footballers in with just that smile. These women then set about performing open-wallet surgery on you. Footballers (me included) come out of there with bags of shit they never knew they needed and, amazingly, bags of shit they already don't really like.

But they stop at the girl at the door and say, 'Actually, I'm staying at this hotel, why don't you come down after work, have a drink, some food, blah blah . . .'

And the woman says, 'Oooh that sounds very tempting, I may just do that.'

But you can hear them thinking, 'Oh yeah, because I've been waiting all my life for you, haven't I? As if I'm going to some hotel to meet a westerner, especially one who'd buy that crap.'

It's sort of a tit-for-tat deal where all anybody gets is the tat.

It makes me so nostalgic for the strippers in Vegas, it's sad. They cosy up to us, but really they pity us.

As I said, at the end the joke is on us.

People who don't go to Dubai don't get Dubai. It's simple. If you want a night out at La Scala, you go to fucking Milan, not Vegas. If you want to potter about in the Louvre, you go to Paris, not Ibiza. If your bag is taking selfies outside dainty Roman follies, well, guess where the best place to find them is? Clue: not Dubai.

I go to Dubai for the culture. Every place has culture, it's just that it doesn't all make the Sunday arts supplements. And if it doesn't, we don't really know what we should think about it, do we?

The culture of Dubai is money. Money is what the present period of our civilization will be remembered for. Money and a handful of the goals that I scored.

The culture of Dubai is surprisingly a bit like the culture of Vegas. There was nothing in either place except sand before they created cities designed purely for the purpose of extracting money from rubes. Neither Vegas nor Dubai evolved from living communities. They are workplaces. Clip joints with star ratings.

If there is a difference between Vegas and Dubai (other than that the latter is suitable for holidays with the wife and kids), it is that Dubai likes to think that there is a difference. Vegas knows she is an old whore. Dubai thinks she's a twenty-first-century courtesan.

In Dubai we footballers have finally found a family-friendly destination that doesn't have any cap on our spending. If you want to pay £30,000 a day for a hotel room in Dubai, go ahead. If you want to pay £25,000 for first-class flights in a suite on an A380, and take a shower a mile up in the air with some female company while everybody else is asleep, then you can. If you hand over £500 every time you drink a glass of some whisky-based cocktail in the Burj, they'll keep them coming till you run out of money or consciousness. If you want to hire a Bugatti Veyron for £20,000 a day, after you've put your £100,000 down for the deposit, there are people fighting for your custom. You can drive it to Abu Dhabi with your eight-year-old son in the front seat, as a footballer friend of mine did. A sensational snub to Ferrari World. I've done some of those things, and have been tempted to do them all, but I don't really like whisky.

Moral of the story? It doesn't bloody matter. There is no moral. The only point is that like nowhere else I know, Dubai separates the Haves from the Have Fucking Lots. The Have Fucking Lots own the place. The Haves pay through the snout to share the same sunshine.

In a deep and meaningful way, Dubai is shallower than

anywhere else on the planet. More expensive. More ruthless. More showy. And we footballers like that. It's catnip to us.

Dubai has its novelty element too. It's the only top-class tourist destination in the world where the locals look down on you. They hate us. You know how the people of West Bromwich East look down on the poor unfortunates of West Bromwich West? Yeah, it's like that, but much worse.

You want culture, well, just do some rubbernecking when the locals have to come to an event in one of Dubai's top hotels. They pull up outside in their Lambos, their Ferraris, their Porsches, their Bugattis, their Koenigseggs, their Paganis, and it's billionaire gridlock. They step out and leave the machines idling, just waiting there to be parked. Sorry, but whatever you have in the driveway back home looks like a pre-owned Lada right now. You know this because you've paid thousands to be here and you are taking pictures of what the locals drive around in.

The poor parking valets, who will always be poor in this culture of no tips, try to stash the gleaming cars away without damaging them and getting sacked and deported before dawn. But they don't know how to use the paddle shift gears so they buck-jump two-million-pound vehicles all over the shop. Which would be the less catastrophic life event: to run over a tourist or to bounce a Koenigsegg Trevita into a Ferrari Spider? The tourist loses every time. It is the writ of Allah.

Dubai opens its arms and says to the world, 'Give me your pampered, your spoiled, your huddled upper classes yearning to breathe free, and the folding refuse of your teeming pockets. Send these shekels, these sponds, these lovely C-notes to me, your smart money, your stupid money, your stash and your cash. There's an ATM beside the golden door as you enter.'

Otherwise it's a pretty classy joint.

19

We have truly arrived in Dubai. Footballers are all over the place. We have infested the place like a plague of locusts.

Footballers of my vintage now have families. Our personalities have become too complex still to be engaging with Virgin stewardesses. Some are still playing, clinging to the dream with arthritic fingers. Others are pundits. Some are coaching. Some just do nothing at all. Many of the foreign lads just went home. Which explained a lot. They weren't ever like us. They were oddballs and they didn't holiday with us. Turns out they had entire lives elsewhere. Who knew?

We straddle two worlds. One foot in retirement, the other foot still in the great lake of money that TV brought to the Premier League. We earned enough so that what's left over will keep us going to Dubai for a few years. As I said before, we're like those cartoon characters, dashing out over the edge of the cliff and continuing to run on nothing but air. Then we plummet, and a few seconds later there's just a cloud of dust. Wile E. Coyote always survives these mishaps and bounces back as game as ever. That gives me hope.

We have to face facts though. We're not princelings any more. We're not vying for the throne. It's over. Players who are younger than us and more shallow than us, and definitely richer than us, run around the palaces now.

We find ourselves shaking our heads and telling people that it's not like it was in our day. It's all gone to shit really. At dinner parties we get put beside the man who knew the Rolling Stones when they had nothing. We can bore each other without bothering anybody else.

Suddenly the memories of what we got up to don't seem so funny. Remove them from the context of a group of well-paid, over-sexed young athletes and it all seems pretty cringey. People had to clean up after us. And make excuses for us. And wake up beside us to realize that we had no clue who they were. And no desire to find out. We were cads and bounders and we had a lot of fun. It's all done now though.

Actually, I spend most of my days with a feeling in the pit of my stomach that there is one hell of a payback coming. Just around the next corner.

I'm convinced that somebody is going to knock on the door one day and flash a laminated card. She will be young and heartless and from the Federal Bureau of Karma. She will speak to me like a female Alex Ferguson.

'Good morning. Mr TSF, isn't it?'

'Maybe. Look, we were both drunk. Anything that happened between you and me—'

'Enough. I'm from the Federal Bureau of Karma. Our mission statement is that there are no menus; you get served what you deserve. I shall be your server for the next few years.'

'OK.'

'Now. You used to be a Premier League footballer?'

'I was. I was. Thank God you recognize me. I was worried there when I couldn't place you. Yes, I was a footballer. There's obviously been a mix-up. Nobody died.'

'I didn't recognize you. It just says that here.'

'OK.'

'And were you paid at certain times in your career tens of thousands of pounds a week?'

'True.'

'And to what morally beneficial purpose did you devote these funds?'

'Well, I had a standing order for that dogs' charity. Not much, but how much does a stray dog eat without losing its figure?'

'Generally speaking, you behaved outrageously and did whatever you wanted to do?'

'That would be one way of putting it.'

'There is another way?'

'You could put down that I was young? Unprepared? Easily led?'

'Noted. Very droll, sir. Anyway, here is your copy of the final bill. Check the details and sign on the dotted line overleaf.'

'OK.'

'Thanking you. OK. Listen carefully, Mr TSF. We've decided to give you cancer. And that will start in 2018 for you. Is 2018 a good time for you to get cancer?'

'No. Fuck no. No way. Lots to do.'

'Perfect. 2018 it is. Any problems, there's a helpline number at the top and an email address just below. You have seven days to appeal, but just so you're aware, no footballer has ever had his case overturned. Shit, almost forgot. Bankruptcy starts next week. I'd forget my head some days, me.'

'Jesus. Nobody told me about all this.'

'Oh stop your whining. Man up. If it's any consolation, you got off lightly. I'm off to see John Terry next. That poor bastard.'

'Ha!'

'Look, I wouldn't normally do this, it's against the rules, but if I were you I'd be looking for a very affordable little one-room flat to rent. Maybe somewhere that allows pets. Things are going to get pretty bleak and lonely when she leaves you. All the best.'

I'm not generally superstitious. I don't have an imaginary friend up in the sky. I don't worry about heaven or hell. But I do suspect that the Bureau of Karma is a real thing and I'm enjoying its deluxe starter package now.

That's how I feel. Every day. Like I'm walking around with a giant anvil hanging by a piece of thread right over my head. I did some good things in my life, but I did some very, very bad things too. The balance sheet doesn't look great when I see it from the Bureau's point of view.

Here's a story. I don't carry credit cards any more. Neither does Mrs TSF. We found that we just couldn't trust credit card companies. They'd come looking for their money at all sorts of inconvenient times and then get all huffy when we told them we'd see them right in a month or two. So we had a conscious uncoupling from credit cards and now we use debit cards. It works for us.

This was all very well until we arrived to check in at a very well-regarded Dubai hotel and slid a debit card confidently across the desk. Fingers were crossed behind our backs that no standing orders or outstanding debts had been taken out since we checked the balance at the airport. We looked confident though.

All the people behind the desk winced. They picked up the debit card using a pair of golden tongs and passed it back before it contaminated anything.

'I'm so sorry, sir, but we need your credit card details.'

'Why so? Amex and I have separated. I offered Amex custody of the kids.'

'Well, just in case you go berserk and pillage the minibar. You look like the type.'

'I wouldn't do that.'

'Well, suppose you get into a drunken fight here in the lobby and you smash something for which we then need to over-charge you?'

We make our case to the front desk. Perhaps they might have told us that they didn't accept debit cards before we arrived there as an exhausted little family who'd flown halfway across the world. Soon we were embroiled in a mass argument. Lots of shouting and finger jabbing. Reinforcements were arriving behind the desk, all to say the same thing. The city of Dubai would dissolve and become mere sand again if they didn't get a credit card number. Pronto.

At the height of the argument, I glanced around the lobby to see if people were enjoying the spectacle. The funny thing was, nobody was paying any attention. There seemed to be better arguments and rows going on all over the place. The noise level was deafening. It was like a royal rumble in the WWE. We were blending in perfectly because most of the other guests appeared to be travellers. (Yes, *Daily Mail* readers, Gypsies! Yikes!) Aha. Now we knew why the place was on edge. The reception actually looked as if we'd interrupted the clean-up operation after a full-scale riot.

Two thoughts occurred:

We all look the same to you Emirati, don't we? You think we are all travellers.

All the travellers have credit cards and we don't? Holy shit.

Life around the pool was interesting. At the end of each day, the area looked like one of those garbage dumps that poor urchins from Rio's favelas spend their days picking through. Thirty adults and sixty kids can make quite a mess when they put their minds to it. The mess looked worse when the plates and glasses and wrappers from the stream of snacks and refreshments were all being chucked about in the pool. Sun-loungers went in too. Chairs went in. The travellers didn't give a fuck. Shit everywhere. No respect for anybody.

Now that I am elderly, I enjoy a book and a beer and a lounger by the pool. Getting to the bar, though, was like trying to push your way to the front to leave some graffiti on the Kaaba during the annual pilgrimage to Mecca. It could not be done. A large number of heavy-set traveller men were thoughtfully protecting the bar from having to deal with infidels. It had become a private bar. The most exclusive in Dubai. The bar didn't complain. They were out of stock by the end of each day and the heavy-set men were all blind drunk and bumping into each other.

If we'd still had silly money, we would have cut our losses by increasing our costs and just flying to some other place. We stayed put, we dug in, we weathered the storm. It was like sitting on a powder keg that never went off.

But here's the rub. What had the boys and I looked like to other people in Marbella, Ibiza, Las Vegas even? Is it possible that people once looked at me this way? I think so. Do I have any right to demand the level of decorum and respect that I expect of others these days just because I don't live that life any more? Maybe not.

It's a jolt when that thought buzzes through your head for the first time. The Bureau of Karma have already started work on my sentence. The next time the doorbell goes, I'll send one of the kids to answer it. The instructions will be brief. Just tell them I died. In great pain. Their work here is done.

Dubai was the venue that gave me a sharp lesson about the grim realities of life in retirement.

The first time I walked into the sea in Dubai, I was still a player. I didn't sink the way you people do. I generally hate the sea (in a romantic way), but I couldn't believe how warm the water was.

In the first house that Mrs TSF bought, we had to boil pots of water on the cooker because the heating tank wasn't big enough to run a full bath. It took for ever. So mainly Mrs TSF came to me with pots as I rested from my labours and she went about the place covered in dirt. In Dubai, you take a swim in the sea and you have to use one of the showers on the beach afterwards just to cool yourself down. You do feel as though you have made it when somebody has ferried that many pots of hot water just so that you can swim.

Anyway, my eldest asked me if he could have a go on one of those rubber rings which get pulled along by a speedboat. I'd just retired and was carefully regrading my physique to something a little less overwhelmingly erotic. I was fine with this new body while I was dressed. I wasn't doing any exercise and was eating and drinking more shit than a fat American family, but my view was that I'd earned it. My son was seven and had a few years to go before he began seeing me as a harmless old fart. So I told him, yep, Dad will sort this out. I clicked my fingers and instantly two guys appeared along with a bloody great speedboat.

I could have sat in the speedboat and supervised, but I felt it would make more of a lasting impression on my son if I demonstrated my residual athletic grace by having a go with him. They hooked us up and took us out. They always chart a course (me hearties!) around the Burj because people like to have photos of themselves being dragged along on tyre tubes with that hotel in the background. In a thousand years' time, archaeologists will wonder if it wasn't some cruel and unusual punishment for low-grade crims.

Anyway, Mrs TSF and my youngest, who was four years old at the time, got into the speedboat with the camera and we headed out to the deep. My son and I were next to each other in these rings and he was absolutely loving it, shouting to the driver to go faster. And as we went faster and faster, he was loving it all the more.

Meanwhile, I was starting to think, 'Hmm . . . can't really

hold on much longer, and if I can't hold on, then the little fella must be really struggling.' I looked over and he was belly-laughing and picking his nose at the same time. Never been prouder.

I had water spraying into my eyes and up my arse now. My arms were shaking. It was like getting a colonic irrigation while inside one of those tins with two colours of paint in it which they shake up using that weird machine at Homebase. I didn't like it.

Suddenly we turned sharply and I was flying through the air for what must have been at least thirty feet. As I was flying, everything was pegged back to slow motion. It's a cliché, but it is true: while I was airborne, an entire life passed before my eyes. However, snob that I am, it was David Beckham's life, not mine. (Tom Cruise has to be led away in an ambulance having witnessed my death.)

I had what was probably either a mild panic attack or a case of the shits as I hit the water. Hopefully the former. That lasted a couple of seconds, and then I really panicked. Where was my boy? If the water could toss me into the air like a slightly out-of-shape ragdoll, what had it done to a seven-year-old with arms like worms and legs like two snots dangling from a clothesline?

I had to find him. If I'd gone thirty feet, then he must have been thrown at least sixty. He was that slight. Jesus, look mate, sorry for all the shit down through the years but fucking help me now and I'll be a good boy in future.

I started swimming up through the bubbles to the surface. I looked around, but couldn't even see the boat. I looked the other way. I still couldn't see the boat. Around again. Still no fucking boat. I started shouting his name. I felt so helpless and disorientated. I didn't even know which direction to swim in to find my son, and possibly the wreckage of the boat too.

Then quietly, with its engine off, the boat just glided up alongside me and this little face peered at me over the edge of a rubber ring and said, 'Dad, that was amazing. Do you want a hand getting back in?'

I told him no, and that if he said anything else he'd be going straight back to the orphanage.

My head was fucked. How did a seven-year-old manage to stay in a bloody rubber ring while I got catapulted in the vague direction of oblivion? I honestly could not have held on any longer if you had offered me an afternoon with Kate Moss in the penthouse suite of the Burj, with her asking me what I'd like her to do now, and me saying that I'd have to sleep, and Kate saying OK, she'd wait, because so far it had all been worth it.

That's when I knew I had to do some exercise, and that I wasn't a footballer or professional sportsman any more.

I was an old fart taking family holidays in expensive places, and there wouldn't be too many more of them.

20

There aren't bad hotels in Dubai, not really, but there are some hotels which are better than others. Most people put the Burj at the top of their list. I don't. You see, I found that if you are a travel snob and you can't afford the Burj, the best thing to do is run the place down. My gripe is that the staff are too servile and too plentiful. They are desperate to please you and keep popping out and ambushing you when you least expect it.

I'm not used to that part of having money. I didn't grow up with money. I didn't go to a flash school. We had no servants. I didn't own a car until I was twenty-four. And even then I had to drive it myself. It was one long nightmare.

The service bothers me because you can't give tips in Dubai. In Vegas, for instance, when a porter greets me like his long-lost brother, I know I'm being hustled, and I'm OK with that. No problem, bro. In Dubai, though, you wonder, are there snipers hidden in the shrubberies waiting to take out staff who don't ingratiate themselves cloyingly enough? It's a bit creepy.

Anyway, I can carry my own luggage to the room. And I can

look around the room and ascertain without being told that those are the curtains and that is the window, and here is the bed and this is a television.

So I don't stay at the Burj for two reasons. First, because I can't stand that level of attention being lavished on me by anybody other than Mrs TSF. And second, because I can't afford it.

Then there is the One&Only, just one of many One&Onlys worldwide. We stayed there, Mrs TSF and I, and spent £20,000 for a villa. Even if I could, I wouldn't be spending that much again, but the place came with a butler. And he came very close to ruining the entire break.

Obviously, as a foreigner, if I had shot the butler, the courts would have come down heavily on me. They don't like foreigners shooting the help. But I did think of getting one of the locals to bust a cap on his ass. It's more culturally acceptable when a local does the cap-busting.

To say that the butler couldn't do enough for us would be an understatement. If he could have breathed air on our behalf, he would have done it. If we had asked him to deal with the louts from the bank, he would have taken the calls. I'd switch the light on and he'd say, 'Please, sir, I must do this for you, please ask. Anything that you want, sir, I am here for you.'

I remember grabbing a Corona out of the fridge, and just before I was going to open it I leaned out of the back doors that led to where Mrs TSF was floating around in the private pool on a lilo. I asked her if she fancied a drink of something. As I poked my head out of the door, with my arm holding the Corona behind me to protect it from the 40ºC heat, I heard a *tssss* noise. By the time I turned around, my Corona had been mugged of its lid and there was now a napkin tied around the neck. 'Please, sir, you must let me get you your drinks. Please. Is very important.'

Two nights in, the butler booked us a table at the beach restaurant. We had oysters and champagne. We still talk about the oysters as if they were some nice people we made friends with on holiday. We loved the Oysters. We'd have had them round to our place back home if we hadn't eaten them.

After the meal, we decided to walk back to our villa via the beach. This was a brave decision, given that the humidity was about a million degrees. Mrs TSF and I are suckers for a night swim in Dubai though, and we thought we might have a little paddle. In the event, we were so full that I piggybacked Mrs TSF down the steps into the main pool and back out the other side. Gravity got cross and forced me to put her back on the ground unceremoniously. You have to pick your battles when you get older, especially when Mrs TSF is chock-full of oysters.

We strolled across the beach down to the water's edge, for no reason other than that's what couples do. Suddenly there was a commotion in the moonlight and staff began spilling out of everywhere. They were agitated and calling our names across the sand, and then a golf buggy sped along the shoreline straight at us.

'Mr Sir, Mr Sir, you come now! You come with me, Mr Sir!'

I thought for a moment that we had been unmasked as global celebrities (that awkward moment again) and there was a code red threat to our safety. I was going to be abducted and Mrs TSF would have to offer up the overdraft as ransom.

315

We were taken to reception on the back of a 'speeding' golf buggy. I noted bitterly to myself that they would almost certainly have helicoptered a proper big shot, say John Terry, to safety.

There was a kerfuffle at reception. My Arabic isn't great, a little rusty, but our butler appeared to be begging for his life. He did some earnest pleading and then he started crying. The hotel had just sacked him on the spot for failing to look after us.

The poor man had been sat outside the restaurant for two hours waiting for us to end our war on the oyster population. We had wanted to walk on the beach, however, so we had cunningly left the restaurant by the door that led in that direction. A different door to the one through which we'd entered the restaurant.

I was appalled. I really was. I told the manager that surely they could just whip him. After lots of argument, and the assistance of a local who translated our lines back and forth, the butler was reinstated. The hotel wasn't happy about it though. They seemed really keen to sack the poor man. They noted me as an uppity foreign undesirable.

There are two lines of dialogue in life you should never really use.

'Do you know who I am?' is the first. If anybody asks you if you know who they are, you are morally obliged to look closely for a second and reply, 'No clue, you're going to have to tell me.'

The second banned line is the one where you threaten to tell all your influential friends. I never use this. Unless I'm under

316

pressure. Once when I was trying to sue Holland & Barrett, I found myself telling them that if they didn't play ball, I was going to tell all the other footballers. In Dubai, I found myself resorting to the telltale technique again.

'If you sack this man, I'll tell all the footballers about this,' I said. 'They'll never come here again.'

Recognizing that nothing prompts the wealthy footballer community into action quicker than news of the sacking of an Indian butler in a foreign country, the hotel backed off.

When I arrived home, I wrote a letter. Sternly worded, as if I were writing to the *Telegraph* about the poor quality of the clotted cream I had endured during an afternoon tea at the Ritz. I complained, reiterating my threat to blow the whistle on labour practices in the UAE. Lo and behold, the line paid off again, and the hotel invited us back the following year to stay in one of their two-roomed sea-view suites. On principle, we accepted.

It wasn't quite the villa from the previous year – that was next door – but this place was amazing too. In a considerate gesture by the hotel, there was no butler this year. So Mrs TSF and I were feeling very pleased with ourselves in our brand-new freebie suite, with its fresh fruit baskets daily and complimentary evening meals in any of the restaurants. (I know this sounds like an advert, but they really couldn't do enough for us. I have to say that just in case they're reading this. We could genuinely use another freebie. It is one of life's great injustices – free shit to the people who can afford to pay and nothing for those who already have nothing. Look, if that butler is still mislaying guests, feel free to sack him. Just send the freebie and nothing will be said.)

In the morning I opened the back doors to glorious views and searing heat. I had a book that I was going to demolish while helping myself periodically to the alcohol in the minibar. Pig in Shit level on the Happyometer.

Sunglasses in the height of the Dubai summer are wasted on those who want to read books. The humidity immediately steams them up, rendering the wearer all but blind. Cool but blind. Stevie Wonder sort of thing. So I took them off, and for a moment I thought I was experiencing a mirage. Wave after wave of Indian workmen were wandering past on the pathway carrying inflatables. It was like *The Generation Game* viewed with the aid of hallucinogens. The waiters were all headed to the same location. Insatiably curious as ever, I got back to reading my book.

Minutes later, I noted that all the Indian workmen were now running around on the grass outside, playing a game of football. All this for me? I thought. What a lovely tribute. Bravo!

Then in the middle of the football game I spotted a pale ghost, a lanky white geezer without a shred of fat anywhere about him. I looked at him. Aha. I gave him the universal footballer's nod. He looked at me and did the same. The silent-movie version of 'Oi-Oi!' Only more chilled.

I see you. You see me. No big deal. I'm over it.

Sometimes, if there is a smile tagged on to the nod, it opens the way for a brief chat which must be limited to polite football gossip, and never more than a couple of questions, which you pretend you know the answers to already.

There was no smile from either of us. It was John Terry. Fucking John Terry. Next door.

318

Which of us would be the first to reception to demand another free stay on the basis of this latest outrage? Seeing as I was on a jolly already, my case was slightly weaker.

(Another rule of football etiquette. It's not done to tell other players that you took a freebie. Even if they interrogate you at gunpoint. Nothing conspicuous ever cost you less than 10K. Tell them you got a freebie to Dubai and they'll mock you, pity you and eventually find out how to get the freebie themselves, while continuing to mock and pity you. They'll claim afterwards that they dropped 25K in Dubai. Just a long weekend. Oh man!)

Anyway, I knew John Terry could embarrass me. He outgunned me. In his armoury was the captaincy of Chelsea, and at the time he was still playing for England, still in his prime. Me? I was mouthy and could easily embarrass him with a sharp word or two launched at the wrong moment. It was like how the USA viewed North Korea. I was odd, pesky and unpredictable.

He finished the football match he had arranged with the staff and walked back to the villa that Mrs TSF and I were staying in last year. He was on his honeymoon. The inflatables were for his private pool. It was a crushing blow. He was dissing us by flaunting his inflatables and our old butler.

We decided to get over the fact that John Terry had spitefully opted to humiliate us by spending his honeymoon in the place next door to our freebie villa, and to just get on with bravely enjoying the freebie. It was like living under Vesuvius – we never knew when we might get covered in spewing lava – but we just got on with our humble daily lives in five-star luxury.

Until one morning, when I awoke to a scream from Mrs TSF.

She had been in the garden sunbathing and reading magazines. Now, though, something was up. Something more worrying to her than a sad story in *Cosmo*. I could hear her coming closer to the bedroom while still shouting something in high alarm. Half-asleep, I lifted my head from the pillow to hear what she was saying. My money was on angry hornets chasing her, or John Terry giving her evils from next door.

Her exact words were, 'He's got his cock out! He's got his cock out!'

As an alarm call, you don't hear that often enough. And language like that is why the kids will be going to posh schools.

She came into the bedroom screeching like a banshee. She jumped on top of me, repeating the news: 'He's got his cock out! He's got his cock out!'

'What the fuck? Who? John Terry?'

'No! Jesus. Him!'

And on cue, he came waltzing into the room. A boiler-suited hotel employee. As had been previously advertised, his maypole was on show.

Quick thought. What's the biggest occupational hazard for a flasher in Dubai? Sunburn or castration? They're funny about their laws over there. I think it is far more acceptable, legally, for an Emirati to flash a foreigner than it is for a foreigner to flash an Emirati.

'We didn't order that, did we?' I asked.

When the flasher saw me, he turned and ran back out into the garden. This was fortunate. Most men wake up in the morning having dreamed somewhere deep in their subconsciousness about fabulous sex. They are aroused. It's the morning glory. The horn of dawn. The rise and shine. You know. Footballers, this happy breed of men, wake up in the morning having dreamed about scoring goals and then having sex. It's a testosterone tsunami down in the regions. We wake up with erections that alter the local weather forecasts, so much shadow do they throw. Erections that send planning department officials into a swoon, even in Dubai. Erections that should have elevators.

Anyway, I had woken up with one of these wonders, and it was the perfect excuse not to give pursuit. Poor flasher wouldn't have known if he was to be arrested or harpooned. And suppose he accused me of flashing him? Would John Terry have stood up in my defence? I'm sure he was watching me as keenly as I had been watching him. One false move, Terry . . .

When Mrs TSF's panic had subsided, in synch with my morning glory, we got dressed and went to reception to complain. Joking aside, having a flasher running around the house can be pretty traumatic at the best of times, but on holiday in a foreign country which prides itself on ring-fencing its guests before pampering them obscenely?

There at the desk was the same manager I'd had to plead with the previous year in order to get the butler his job back. His career was obviously going nowhere. We soon learned why. He didn't believe us. He gave us his best 'yeah, yeah, heard it all before' expression.

Mrs TSF was crying. She had been genuinely shaken by the incident, and had then seen her superhero athlete of a husband paralysed not by fear but by his own priapic prowess. We left that part of the story out though.

The manager looked at Mrs TSF dispassionately, as if he had heard that western women had the ability to weep at will but had never actually seen it done before. He listened to me trying to convey what had happened and the fright it had caused. He heard me ask again and again what was he going to do about it. For his own sake, it seemed like a good idea to take some action, just in case the flasher ran into John Terry's place next. He'd lost a bit of pace, but I'd still have backed him to bring down a nervy flasher in a boiler suit.

The manager looked us up and down and his face betrayed his thinking. 'Well, well, well, here we go again, trying it on. What can you get out of us this time? Maybe we should just make you a present of the villa?'

It was an interesting insight. Foreigners are welcomed and fawned over in Dubai, so long as their pockets are full, they have a credit card, and they don't cause a scene or get upset in the reception area. The whole ordeal was unfortunate. Some genuine concern or interest would have been welcome.

We've never been back, which is a shame, because it really is a great hotel. Being flashed at and suffering the insinuation that you are lying? Well, just two of the sort of things that happen, I suppose.

On the last day Mrs TSF and I were strolling down to the beach when we had to stop for a golf buggy that was coming the other way.

'Mr Sir! How has you bin?'

It was the butler from last year, still at the hotel, still working in the villa. Which meant that he was indeed looking after John Terry.

322

There was only one thing to say. I knew people at Chelsea, and they all said that the first question everybody asks them is the same.

'So, what's John Terry like?'

The butler straightened up. I thought he was about to dish some great shit on the Stamford Bridge stalwart. I leaned forward, trying to suggest through body language that he could trust me to be absolutely discreet – at least until I got to my laptop later on.

'Yes, he is a very nice man, Mr Sir. Thank you for asking.'

You thought he was going to tell me that John Terry was a wanker, didn't you?

You can't handle the truth.

Neither could I. I slunk off and was in a bad mood for most of the day.

21

Reasons why people go to Dubai? Well, to be seen, obviously. But not to be overwhelmed. Yes, we could take an easyJet flight to some place that's hot and cheap, but you'd sit with your knees tucked under your chin listening to people two rows behind wondering what sort of a tight git you were. If they had your money, oh, they'd . . .

What I find interesting is that footballers and members of other professions like market traders or commercial bankers are embarrassed if they have only spent £10,000 on a holiday. So they make things up. They convince you that they were staying in the Burj for £5,000 a night, when they were actually staying in a five-star hotel a stone's throw away at a mere £500 a night instead.

Five-star, by the way. Not seven. Even if there is no such thing as seven stars. A journalist made the seven-star thing up long ago. If you stay at the Burj, you drop the seven-star thing a lot into your conversations. If not, you drop the journalist story.

And the Burj plays on that. It isn't above flogging thousand-dollar replicas of itself in the gift shops for people who just came to rubberneck around the place and decided to buy a souvenir that would back up their claim that the Burj was really just a lovely home from home.

(All hotel shops the world over have tat. It's just differently priced and hard to judge when you have bought the right tat. In Vegas, I once bought my youngest a Caesars Palace gown. He loves it. At Trump's place in the same city I couldn't resist buying a pack of Donald Trump condoms – yes, insert your own 'yuge' jokes. At the right moment I unsheathed the sheaths in front of Mrs TSF. 'Mind if I slip one of these on?' She breathed excitedly. Arched her back. Purred. 'Yeah, whatever.' 'They're all the way from Vegas.' 'OK, fine.' 'Ta da!' 'Eh, wait, what's that picture on them?' 'Well, they're Donald Trump branded johnnies.' 'Ew, yuck! Get the fuck away from me, you sick cunt! Jesus.' As I've said already, the finishing school wasn't great. Wasn't even Swiss. May have been in Essex.)

You go to Dubai for the heat also. Go for the heat, stay for the air conditioning. I'm sure Dubai is rich enough to artificially create a nice cool breeze to ventilate the entire city, but then you would have westerners wandering around all over the place. The locals don't want that. No way. The heat is the sheepdog that keeps us sheep in our five-star pens.

At night it becomes really muggy. The air is thick and claggy. After sixty seconds outdoors you are sweating like a pig sitting in a sauna while his mate tells him about these things called barbecues. But you've paid your money, and you're a trooper, so you head out anyway and plonk yourself on to a seat at the rooftop bar and let puddles of perspiration form at your feet.

On one such evening, Mrs TSF and I were gracing the terrace

bar of the One&Only hotel, sweating our tits off and wondering if it counted as being mugged if you go to stay in a place called the One&Only and discover it's part of a chain of One&Only resorts. It made me and my one and only look again at the wording of our marriage vows.

Of course, there is being seen, and there is being seen while pretending that you don't want to be seen. For that reason the terrace area had two turrets tucked into the corners. The turrets had private tables and were roped off with the sort of thick red velvet cords that separate the popcorn and nachos crowd from the box-office queue at your local cinema.

We sat and waited to see who would go and sit behind the Cineplex ropes. Meanwhile the staff brought around cold wet flannels for the gasping clientele to cool themselves down with. Believe me, you need those flannels. We looked for the flannel people as anxiously as accident victims look for paramedics. Please hurry. In the name of God, hurry.

I can't imagine how amusing it is for the poor flannel wallahs to see the great and good of the western world paying thousands just to flop and sweat and be watered down like thoroughbred warthogs after a long trot.

So we're sat there, sweating between our emergency flannels, and I pick up the menu and think to myself, 'Right, it's a Bellini night tonight. I don't know why, but this place feels to me like a Bellini kind of place.'

So I order a Bellini. I have no idea what a Bellini is. I just like the name and the idea of sitting there drinking a Bellini while I wait to be watered down.

Unfortunately it turns out that I have ordered a Whisky

Bellini, which is the traditional deal with a generous splash of bourbon thrown in. Whisky. You know, the stuff people sip to warm themselves up on chilly evenings. I hate whisky at the best of times. I would have rather ordered warm woollen mittens.

Of course, having confidently ordered an expensive cocktail, a man doesn't want to lose face by saying 'Ooh, it tastes icky' while having his face flannelled. That would be childish. So I take a sip and discreetly ditch the rest of my Bellini over the side of the terrace. It's not like it's a pint of lager, and anyway, it's so hot I'm sure the liquid will evaporate before it hits the gardens below.

Unfortunately, a second later I hear a voice say, 'What the fuck was that?'

I had no idea there was another terrace bar below us. I thought we were in the one and only terrace bar in the One&Only. When I peep over, there's a bloke and his missus down below us. I'd basically caught his back with the cocktail, but, luckily, his woman is soothing him: 'Oh, don't worry, it's only water, you'll be dry in thirty seconds anyway.'

Still, this isn't good. You have to be honourable in situations like this. So when we see a couple of stools free up on the other side of the terrace, we go and sit over there. Hee-hee. Apart from disassociating ourselves from the whisky-throwing louts, we are now right where the cold flannels come out. Winning. We are now among the first to be watered down every time. We don't have to watch everybody else getting their fix first.

Next, there's the possibility of some turret action. The door to the terrace opens and a big black dude strides out and conspicuously checks the area. I have to eyeball a warning to Mrs TSF, because I think she's about to tell him not to worry, the whisky-throwing hooligan element just left.

The guy goes back through the door, and when it opens again a minute later, out comes Nicolas Anelka and one of the three most attractive women ever created. They go and sit right where Mrs TSF and I were sitting when I tossed my drink overboard. Now I'm really hoping that the geezer below will realize that his shirt *is* stained and sticky and smelling of peaches and bourbon, and that he will stride up here and have it out with the Frenchman.

You see, Nicolas Anelka is wearing a black shirt, because heat doesn't worry Nicolas Anelka. And he has aviator sunglasses on, because he refuses to recognize darkness. What a prat, I think, as I wonder what's happening with the flannels. It's been forty-five long seconds. Why don't I have Amnesty on speed dial?

Bingo. The door opens and in walk the couple who were down below getting Whisky Bellini thrown on them a few minutes ago. The victims look over at Anelka and you can see their confusion. They know he can be a difficult man, but why would Nicolas Anelka have thrown a Bellini at them? Why? Why? Why?

Mrs TSF and I are losing further precious body liquids now by peeing ourselves with laughter as we glance from the couple to Anelka and wonder just how long he is going to be able to brazen it out in this situation.

Very soon you can tell that Nicolas feels he has had enough. He's tried sitting with common people and, like so many of his transfers, it hasn't worked out as well as he'd hoped. So the dude who scoped the place for Nicolas is sent to the bar for a discreet word with the barman.

Certainly, sir. The waiter comes over, pulls the red velvet rope back and ushers Nicolas Anelka and his date to the private turret table. There was a chance that Nicolas could have stepped over that rope or walked around it. Thank God the waiter was on hand.

Two minutes later, Nicolas and herself come out of the turret again. Now they are sweating their tits off like normal human beings. Mrs TSF and I lapse into another fit of laughter. So do the couple I threw my drink over.

The fella leans across to me and in a thick northern accent says, 'Ere, sometimes it's just too bloody 'ot ta be cool, int' it?'

I take to him immediately and buy himself and his missus a drink to seal our new alliance. Turning to his missus before I order, I ask if she has tried a Bellini here. 'They're amazing. They go down a treat.'

I'll be honest. Behind my back, of course, there were always people who would give me the look and comment loudly, 'You've got more money than sense, you. Twenty grand on a villa? Are you fucking serious?'

It's important to realize that not all footballers go mad like me. Some are prudent. Or tight.

I played with a guy late in my career who considered himself to be very smart with his money. The rest of us thought of him as the tightest tightwad in the world. The cheapest cheapskate. The Mayor of Miser City.

At the Christmas party, when it was his round, he would go to every player to ask what they wanted. When he came to lads sitting together as a pair, he'd look to see how much they had left in their glasses, and if it amounted to half a pint between them, he'd just buy them a pint to share. He bought me and my mate a Bulmers to share between us because we still had some left when he was ordering the round.

I'm sure he still has his money. I'm sure he still has the first shilling his granny gave him as a kid. I'm sure I wouldn't swap being him for being me.

One thing I always understood was that the life could end at any moment and I wanted to live a little beforehand. It's like those vegans. I don't get it. Starve yourself of meat and dairy your whole life so that you can enjoy those rewarding years that are your nineties? Fittest people in the old folks' home? No thanks. Fuck off.

Last year, we wanted to go to Dubai again. Honestly. I'm an addict for this sort of thing. So somehow I pulled off what I now realize was a bastardized version of a holiday to Dubai. Still nice, but a reality check. Like an addict cutting his fix with something white and powdery from the kitchen.

A friend of mine, a League One player, was going to Dubai. Our kids get on, so we thought, 'Why not?' The reality is that he was my perfect cover for when people remarked, 'Oh, you're staying in that hotel? Everything OK?' I'd be able to bat their callous assumptions about bailiffs, etc., right back at them: 'Yeah, well, I don't really want to but you see that family over there? League One. What can I do?'

Aw, they would say, bless. You have a big heart, TSF.

Also, we had to save face in our local community. A family far richer than us had invited us on holiday with them. We would have had to act as their staff for the week if we were going to be able to afford a good meal right at the end. So going to Dubai with somebody outside the caste was the perfect cover for us being what the French would call *nouveaux pauvres.*

This other friend of mine used to be the captain of Chelsea and he was frequently on at me to stay at the Jumeirah Beach Hotel – you know, 'The Wave', as they call it. I'd never been before, but if an ex-captain of Chelsea tells you a particular hotel is the place to stay, then you listen.

Luckily, this was the very same hotel my League One friend was asking us to come along to. The holiday was three birds with one stone.

One. Can't travel with the Duke and Duchess and their household cavalry, I'm afraid. Prior booking, old chap. Charity thing.

Two. Of course we'll go with you, mate. We don't mind if you're in League One. That's just God's little trick giving you less talent.

Three. Took your recommendation on that hotel in Dubai, mate. Cheers. Like yourself, smaller than I'd imagined from pictures, but cheerful.

The very top players in the world are staying in the Burj, the Royal Mirage or the One&Only. I have to put this from my mind. Dubai is not about showing off on social media, it's about being there. If you're not there, then you're not anywhere. And if you are staying at the Jumeirah Beach Hotel, acceptable though it is, then you are not really in Dubai.

If a tree falls in a forest and no one is around to hear it, does it make a sound? Who gives a shit? If I go to Dubai and nobody sees me there – that matters. That's deep stuff.

I'm sorry. I know you've stayed at the Jumeirah Beach and had a great time and been dazzled by it all. The heat. The newness. The cleanliness. The service. The buffet. All right, all right, the buffet is incredible. Those Japanese dumplings are worth the plane ticket price alone.

(See, it goes full circle. I used to travel for the debauchery. Now I look forward to the dumplings. After years of family holidays with Mum and Dad, I had to break free and go on great drinking and shagging tours with my mates. Now I'm burnt out and back in the real world, nothing sounds better to me than a nice family holiday. Throw in a tasty Japanese dumpling and I'm there.)

Anyway, The Wave. If you are there, you aren't on the crest of anything big. What you realize very quickly after an ex-captain of Chelsea recommends a hotel to you is that things change. Even in football. The buzz moves downstream. The in-crowd are 'in' elsewhere. And you don't even know where that elsewhere is.

So even the stock of an ex-Chelsea captain falls quickly in the social markets after retirement. I feel myself about to trace the sad vapour line he has left behind him. The show has moved on and the residue that is left behind is that of a bunch of ex-footballers stuck in the moment they retired when their earnings and lifestyle fell off the cliff. It's a social Pompeii.

We now stick where before we would certainly have twisted.

332

The house doesn't get a makeover every six months. The car isn't changed every five minutes. And the holidays are in the same hotel, because if we try somewhere new and we don't like it, we simply don't have the money coming in any more to fly somewhere else in the world that same afternoon.

I know current players who do that. In Dubai. When the fabled Atlantis hotel opened on the Palm, a lot of footballers went there, took one look, turned around and flew home. It was like a Man Utd pre-season tour to Beijing. They got there, didn't like the state of the field, and flew straight back to the UK. Came. Saw. Fled.

I have a German friend who stayed for two hours and hated it so much that he used the time to book a cab to the airport, some first-class flights and a villa in Florida. That evening he was sitting around his own private pool knocking back expensive cocktails in the land of the free.

One of those Icelandic players I know did virtually the same thing. He resented the fact that there were so many people in the Atlantis he couldn't even book a table at any of the hotel's restaurants. So he stayed one night and flew back to Iceland via Heathrow the following day. It's never overcrowded in Iceland. And the roast puffin is to die for.

Too many footballers have dissed the Atlantis for me to want to go anywhere near it. Too busy, too American, too impersonal. Not for me, thank you.

So that's two hotels in Dubai spoiled for you. Stick with this! You'll thank me later.

In the end, you realize that there are always other footballers who are better than you and other players who are richer than you.

I remember being in Dubai when Rio Ferdinand was there. His wife, Rebecca, had just passed away, and Rio was staying at the Burj. The beach at the Burj is sealed off from mere mortals. Anybody can book a table for breakfast, lunch or dinner at the hotel, so long as they can pay for it, but the strip of beach back over the bridge to the mainland is reserved exclusively for people staying in one of the 202 suites.

Dubai is usually crawling with footballers. It was that summer too. Everybody wanted to offer their condolences to Rio, but none of us were rich enough to do so. That was a revelation to a few of us, the fact that there was a place that was closed off to us. There was another level we couldn't get to. The guards wouldn't be bribed, the people inside didn't care enough about us to come over and say hello.

Looking back, it makes me smirk ruefully to myself. The one moment when footballers were genuinely offering up their human side, without looking for a pay rise or a PR opportunity, with no alternative agenda whatsoever, and they couldn't do it because they weren't quite wealthy enough.

It was one of their own who in a time of grief just didn't want to know. That put the ironic cherry on top of the humble pie. All the guys with me, bar one, were Premier League players earning well over the average £40,000 a week, and they were most put out.

I had to remind them that Rio had just lost his wife; he was trying to escape what we were trying to give him. On the outside they pretended to understand, but their egos clearly didn't.

One question haunted them. Will we look cheap if we don't grieve for our loved ones in a seven-star environment?

That worry about being left behind is not just for footballers. You can't stop moving. If you do, you lose. There is always another footballer who is richer than you, and even if you are among the richest of the footballing elite, a CR7 or a Pogba, there are always circles of people who will look down on you as a mere footballer. And they can afford to draw the velvet curtains and shut you out.

And as for Dubai itself, it will happen there. In a few years' time there will be somewhere more exclusive where the Premier League set have to be.

It's like death, taxes and Kate Moss's imploring texts to me. Inevitable.

Dubai doesn't have pool parties. Not yet, but that will definitely come. Because the sunburnt masses will be arriving soon. You want a bit of Dubai with which to impress the next-door neighbour? Somebody is going to provide it for you, because there is a demand.

Footballers are probably the brand leaders in the business, but most people like to show off a little bit. I have a mate who goes to Dubai every year. The first picture he bangs up on his Instagram page, every time, is an image of the Burj Al Arab, with the sun going down behind it. He'll add an incredibly thought-provoking caption, like '#I love Dubai'.

He's never stayed in the Burj Al Arab, he can't afford to. But everybody thinks he lives there for a week of the year, at least.

Not everybody can do that just now, but they will. You get into the upmarket tourism trade, there is always going to be a mid-market and a downmarket coming along right behind. The finger in the dyke works for water but never money. If you pile them high and sell them cheap, you just need a lot of people to make it work. Give them sun, sand and a little bit of snob value in a three-star hotel, they will flock to you.

The people who like to drop the word 'seven-star' will be mobbed by the proles taking selfies outside the front door. The word on the street will be that seven-star is bollox. The Dubai Travelodge is just as good. Lenny Henry has just cut the ribbon for the new Premier Inn. So it must be good.

And slowly the seven-star snobs will become ripe for being hooked by a nine-star creation in some place they didn't know existed until they googled it yesterday. By then Dubai will no longer be a statement vacation. Cheaper hotels. Cheaper flights. Ah, we used to love Dubai, but . . .

Dubai will realize that the rich have no friends. Only interests.

I've reached the point where I'll have to either win the lottery or sell my shares before I enjoy another stay in Dubai. Obviously I feel monstrously sorry for myself, but it's the locals I really pity. By the time I get back to Dubai, it's all going to have turned into a nightmare for them.

One of the funniest things I have seen in Dubai was the evening when Mrs TSF was taking a picture of a Bugatti Veyron that had pulled up outside a splendid hotel. The female passenger got out of the car and walked towards the hotel. She walked straight at Mrs TSF with an aggression I usually associate with sharks and the music from *Jaws*. She looked like trouble. I was standing next to Mrs TSF, waiting for a taxi with our kids. As the woman got closer she said to Mrs TSF, 'Out the way, you immigrant.'

We were stunned.

First, we Brits can never be immigrants. We are always expats. So the joke was on her.

Second, as I mentioned, Mrs TSF went to a really bad finishing school. She can cut up rough when needed. She waited for the woman to walk past and then stamped on the back of her burqa. Bang. The woman came down just like Madonna when she took her tumble at the Brit Awards. She looked like she'd been hooked backwards by a giant invisible fisherman and his giant invisible rod.

The bellhops all came running to pick her up, but her fella, seeing this, didn't want it known that he was with her. They don't do being embarrassed very well at all out there. It's an experience they pay handsomely to avoid. It's all about the entrance, the flounce, the statement. So he glanced up, saw the mess on the pavement, then nobly took his phone out of his pocket as if it were ringing. He 'answered' it and walked behind the car and through a side entrance into the hotel.

Unbelievable.

Meanwhile Mrs TSF and I lit up a pair of stogies, doffed our cloth caps and walked off into the sunset laughing like scamps.

A few days later, myself, Matty and Caney (not footballers; they live in Downton Abbey, I swear) saw the same geezer in the same hotel club. All on his own but sitting at a huge table, with a huge ice bucket loaded with Ace of Spades champagne and vodka and crap like that.

I asked the waiter who he was.

'Oh he's very important man, thank you sir.'

'Well, what does he do? Who does he play for?'

'His family invested moneys into building Dubai since many years.'

'Oh right. Why is he sitting on his own then?'

'Sir, he is looking for a new wife.'

'And he'll find one in here, will he?'

'Sir, he will find many of his wives in here.'

Sure enough, later that evening his table became crowded with local women who were basically interviewed by him. It was the Dubai equivalent of Simon Cowell walking into a nightclub in Newcastle. Much enthusiasm for the auditions.

I watched him and realized that we did the same for years in the hope of achieving the same thing. Well, a simple shag anyway, but always with this pretence we weren't looking for anything. I watched his moves, and he was an upmarket version of what we used to be. And, sadly for him, an upmarket version of what he will eventually be. I brought this city to the top, he will say, and now it's a bloody League One destination?

I looked at him and wondered what became of the woman who got out of his Veyron earlier in the week. What was her fate for embarrassing him?

The novelty wears off everything. The older you get, the quicker the process.

Epilogue

'And that's the hardest part. Today everything is different; there's no action . . . have to wait around like everyone else. Can't even get decent food – right after I got here, I ordered some spaghetti with marinara sauce, and I got egg noodles and ketchup. I'm an average nobody . . . get to live the rest of my life like a schnook.'

Henry Hill, *Goodfellas*

Hey, Henry Hill, that's how I feel, mate. My career went up a few leagues and so did the income. All the things we were able to piss our money away on back in the day? I've forgotten half of them.

I'm almost glad my career didn't start in the Premier League and that Dubai wasn't the first destination on our hit list. I'd be sat here today even more broke than I actually am.

I miss it, Henry, mate. We've got to find a way to be happy being schnooks again. I know that, but fuck it, I want the private planes and I want the cash to be able to go where I want.

I'm a travel snob. I've learned that much about myself. For you, Henry, it's spaghetti in marinara sauce. For me, it's first class to some place I can boast about later. Same thing though, Henry. I'm not putting you down.

But these days cash is tighter than my control of a ball used to be at the peak of my career.

(You see what I've done in that sentence? I've admitted to a little financial embarrassment but reminded you that I had the first touch of a magician. Subtle.)

How do I feel about the wantonly wasteful side of professional football? All that expensive oneupmanship? What's my view now that I'm retired and all grown up? Well, it's a bit like when you burn your tongue on scalding soup. You know you did it, and you try to forget the fact that you were so stupid, but every time you try to cleanse your mouth with a drink of water, you feel that burning sensation again. You can lay all the blame on a learning disorder if you like but, well, stupidity would be a learning disorder too, wouldn't it?

The blunt truth is that it all happened. It all fucking happened. My tongue was flicking into the hot broth along with everybody else's. Yeah, I tried to play the casual observer, the smart, quiet, sensitive, detached one. I sat at the back, seemingly uninterested in the debauchery in front of me. I read my books. But there were times when I was interested. Incredibly so. To the point that I would insist on being involved. Give me some of that soup. Pour it over me, bitches.

It can be a delicious thing to be a footballer sometimes, because playing to the footballer stereotype can help you avoid an awful lot of pointless small talk. You point at what you want. Yes or no? Usually yes.

Would I be happier if we had shut all that out? Stayed living in a small place, done the same things I always did, went to the same places I'd always gone to and just let the money pile up in the bank? I don't know. Neither do you. Every life has choices in it, and unlike video games, you don't get to go back and play the scene again. So just get on with it. Live the life you have now.

That's the real problem. Some players love that action so much. The more of it the better. I can sermonize about living the life you have now but often that feels as hard as cold turkey or detox. And if you're like me and not always looking for trouble and high living then, looking back, there are moments of guilt and self-loathing that can't be ducked.

Am I proud of everything I've done in my career, and how I behaved in my leisure time as a professional footballer? No, not overly. Then again, if I'd just sat back and watched, this would be a fucking short book and the last fifteen years would have been a dull journey.

Anyway, hindsight is best served blurry. It always annoys me when footballers say that they have no regrets. Trust me, we all have regrets. If you don't have regrets, you haven't grown and you haven't lived. I have hundreds of regrets, to the point where I sometimes wish I could do it all over again properly.

But it all happened, and I can't change it. You have regrets? Then learn from them. That's enough.

I'm not offering excuses. If you are just joining the queue waiting for an apology, take a ticket and get to the back of the line. It's going to take a while.

For large parts of my football career I was a twenty-something with more money than I needed and fewer smarts than I thought I had. No help from anybody. No pathways illuminated or wise counsel given.

I was still thinking of nothing but football when I realized there were leeches, rodents and parasites trying to climb into my pockets. Soon enough, footballers and close family were the only people I could trust.

I didn't like much of what footballers did, or how they acted, or even how they dressed. But it was all I had. Of course I was going to get involved. It was either that or wither and die. And I was one of the smart ones, so they told me.

Now my old smart suits hang better, because there is no bulging wallet to spoil the lines. That's how smart I am.

The last time we were in Dubai, Mrs TSF and I experienced a revelation which I will call the Hobnob Moment.

We were having a sit-down and a simple cup of tea and a couple of biscuits after a meal in a fancy restaurant. I dunked my biscuit into my tea (fact: you can't take the council estate out of the kid) and the biscuit broke off. (I won't go into the physics of it all.) So myself and Mrs TSF looked into this cup and just started laughing. Amid all this poshness, a pure Peter Kay moment just seemed hilarious and weirdly welcome. We laughed our heads off.

Within about five seconds our table had been descended on by the emergency services – about five waiters and a maître d', all thinking there was something wrong with the tea. There was a sense of 'Here's our chance to sacrifice somebody, lads.

Rajiv left the tea bag in the cup. Let's have him flogged and deported.' It felt really, really uncomfortable. They were torn between getting a defibrillator to revive the biscuit or a cop to arrest Rajiv.

I explained that it was just my biscuit. Everybody needed to calm down. In Britain we lived through the Blitz. Soggy biscuits are nothing to us. They insisted on replacing the whole thing. It was over the top and annoying and left a bad taste.

I just said to Mrs TSF, 'Fuck this, come on, let's go.'

We yearned for a bit of Costa del Sol at that moment. Imagine telling a waiter over there that there was a bit of broken biscuit in your tea. 'So? What do you want, fucking jam on it as well?'

Maybe it was high time to get back to the real world.

We've got to the end of the beach. We've had all their weird cocktails, and forgotten our £500 sunglasses, and scattered a trail of wasted cash behind us. Now we aren't goodfellas any more. We're the same as all the others around us now. We feel a bit empty. What separated us from the others has now gone.

For a while as a retired player you still have everything, and it's set against this backdrop of opulence and luxury. Really, though, you're an empty man and you need to find something to do. And fast.

Hierarchy of human needs? Fulfilment is higher than seven-star hotels.

Bankers can go back to their jobs, even the mafia guy can return to crime after prison, but a footballer can't ever go back.

And when you first have that thought, it hits you like a truck. You know that if you don't make your way back to the

343

real world soon, they're going to come looking for you. They're going to kick the door down and come in swinging a baseball bat.

Hey! Careful of our thousand-buck glass replica of the Burj. It's lovely, you know. Ooooh, that hurt. You're from the Bureau, aren't you . . .